D0906978

SHAKESPEARE'S CROSS-CULTURAL ENCOUNTERS

Also by Geraldo U. de Sousa

SHAKESPEARE: A Study and Research Guide, 3rd edition
(*with David M. Bergeron*)

Shakespeare's Cross-Cultural Encounters

Geraldo U. de Sousa
Associate Professor of English
Xavier University
Cincinnati, Ohio

First published in Great Britain 1999 by
MACMILLAN PRESS LTD
Houndmills, Basingstoke, Hampshire RG21 6XS and London
Companies and representatives throughout the world

A catalogue record for this book is available from the British Library.

ISBN 0–333–74016–5

First published in the United States of America 1999 by
ST. MARTIN'S PRESS, INC.,
Scholarly and Reference Division,
175 Fifth Avenue, New York, N.Y. 10010

ISBN 0–312–21721–8

Library of Congress Cataloging-in-Publication Data
Sousa, Geraldo U. de, 1952– .
Shakespeare's cross-cultural encounters / Geraldo U. de Sousa.
p.   cm.
Includes bibliographical references and index.
ISBN 0–312–21721–8 (alk. paper)
1. Shakespeare, William, 1564–1616—Knowledge—Europe.
2. Shakespeare, William, 1564–1616—Political and social views.
3. Shakespeare, William, 1564–1616—Characters—Europeans.
4. Culture conflict—England—History—16th century.   5. Culture
conflict—England—History—17th century.   6. English drama–
–European influences.   7. Culture conflict in literature.
8. Europeans in literature.   9. Europe—In literature.   10. Aliens
in literature.   I. Title.
PR3069.E87S68   1998
822.3'3—dc21   98–34140
                                                                    CIP

© Geraldo U. de Sousa 1999

This book is printed on paper suitable for recycling and made from fully managed and sustained forest sources.

10   9   8   7   6   5   4   3   2   1
08   07   06   05   04   03   02   01   00   99

Printed and bound in Great Britain by
Antony Rowe Ltd, Chippenham, Wiltshire

To Rejânia and David
and
the memory of my parents

Contents

List of Plates

ix

Acknowledgements

Hardy, deliberate mules always found the way to our house. As usual, my father would give the shy muleteers permission to disburden the pack animals and put the mules and horses to pasture. For a day or two, the muleteers would camp out under our trees, and then, following an old trail, head for the *sertão*, the mysterious, stark and yet beautiful hinterland of Minas Gerais, a region of Brazil whose geography, culture, and metaphysics João Guimarães Rosa faithfully captured in his novel *Grande Sertão: Veredas* (1956). The caravans transported merchandise to remote destinations. On the borders of the *sertão*, I as a child caught glimpses of a former way of life, the magic of an oral culture, the enduring Messianism of rural Brazil, and, thanks to my father's hospitality, the packers' home remedies, incantatory story-telling, and spirituality.

Curiously, forgotten or neglected childhood memories, bearing the tell-tale signs of the magical *sertão*, came back to my mind during my first visit to Lisbon several years ago. Of all my recollections, none seemed more vivid or puzzling than a story, which I assumed my mother had told me, about a Brazilian washerwoman. To the day she died, my mother always denied any knowledge of this story, however, and she probably assumed that the tale was the product of my fertile imagination or that of a mule-driver. The story may be summarized as follows: the washerwoman is doing her laundry and staring into the horizon. Seemingly out of nowhere, a Portuguese caravel (a small Renaissance ship) comes into view, slowly gliding towards the shore, and finally setting anchor. A captain comes ashore and invites her to trade her harsh life in the New World for the comforts of the Old. She bids farewell to her children, promising never to forget them. Puzzled by a story whose moral I could not understand, I remember asking: 'Where did she go?' My mother pointed her finger and said that the captain first took her to Africa. 'Then to Lisbon,' my mother added, moving her hand as if to indicate beyond. Henceforth, I assumed that one could not reach Lisbon without passing through Africa. Years later in Lisbon, so far away from the mule-drivers' route, I retraced the washerwoman's steps, although something was missing: I had reached Lisbon but not by way of Africa. From her story, however, may stem my own interest in the cross-cultural experience.

That oral culture from the borders of the *sertão* still enriches my life. In unspoken ways, it may also have inspired me to undertake this project and to venture into the intertwined paths, the *veredas*, of Shakespeare's own expedition into the borderlands of his world.

In researching and writing this book, I have incurred debts of gratitude on three continents over several years. I have compiled a cross-cultural list of institutions and persons, whose support, assistance, and encouragement made this book possible. First, I would like to express my gratitude to my home institution, Xavier University, for granting me a sabbatical leave and therefore permitting me to undertake a long-term research project of this nature. I especially thank Norman Finkelstein, Carol Rankin, John Getz, Ernest Fontana, Max Keck, Leo Klein, Robert Rethy, Robin Ikegami, Rhoda Cairns, and Tyrone Williams for their support. I am grateful to Christy Rhode, who worked as my research assistant and checked my quotations. For me, scholarship and teaching inform and support each other; therefore, I thank all of my students at Xavier University, who have inspired me with their intelligence, kindness, and interest.

I also thank the following institutions, libraries, museums, art galleries, and foundations for supplying illustrations and for generously granting permission to reproduce them: The Library of the Marquess of Salisbury, Hatfield House; Fundación Casa Ducal de Medinaceli, Seville, Spain; the British Library; the Folger Shakespeare Library; the Huntington Library; Washington University Libraries and the department of Special Collections, Washington University, St Louis, Missouri; Hebrew Union College–Jewish Institute of Religion, Cincinnati, Ohio; Courtauld Institute of Art; the Nelson-Atkins Museum of Art, Kansas City, Missouri; the Kimbell Art Museum, Fort Worth, Texas; and Cornell University Press.

Chapter 6 is a refocused and revised version of my essay, '*The Tempest*, Comedy and the Space of the Other,' which was first published in a collection of essays, *Acting Funny: Comedy Theory and Practice in Shakespeare's Plays*, edited by Frances Teague, published by Fairleigh Dickinson University Press, and Associated University Presses (1994). I am grateful to Associated University Presses for permission to reprint it here.

The staffs of the following libraries, where I conducted much of my research, deserve my gratitude: McDonald Library, Xavier

University; the Folger Shakespeare Library; the British Library; the University of Kansas Libraries and Spencer Research Library; the Guildhall Library, London; and the USIS Library, Casa Thomas Jefferson, Brasilia, Brazil. Brad Sabin Hill, Head of the Hebrew Section of the Oriental and India Office Collections, the British Library, was particularly helpful when I was researching English representations of Jewish life in Renaissance Europe.

In Britain, I thank the staff of Macmillan, with whom it has been a pleasure to work, and the anonymous reader who read my manuscript for Macmillan for wonderful insights and suggestions. In Brazil, I thank Marco Antônio da Rocha and the Fulbright Commission, Brasilia, for their support; and Rosa Maria Barboza de Araújo, Fundação Casa de Rui Barbosa, Rio de Janeiro, for her assistance. Ednei Giovenazzi, celebrated and talented actor of the Brazilian stage and television, has also been a good friend. I have gained invaluable insights about Shakespeare from Giovenazzi's performance of Shylock on the Brazilian stage, from our conversations, and from our correspondence.

Several friends and scholars have nurtured me. I would like to thank Coppélia Kahn, Fran Teague, Bruce Smith, Gail Kern Paster, Jeanne Addison Roberts, Richard F. Hardin, Jack Oruch, and James Yoch. I especially remember Jeanne Roberts' enthusiasm for and faith in this project and Coppélia Kahn's words of encouragement at a crucial moment in the composition of this book. Daryl Palmer has been an exemplary friend and colleague. He read an early version of this book, heard multiple versions of my chapters, offered wonderful insights, and displayed extraordinary generosity in helping and encouraging me. Mary Davidson read the entire manuscript, advised on illustrations, and supported me in innumerable ways. I also thank Beulah Moore Bergeron, John B. Timmer, Sister Mary V. Maronick of the Sisters of Charity, Charmian Hearne, Anne Rafique, and Ângela and Josafá do Couto.

Finally, my thoughts go to my parents; to Rejânia Aparecida dos Reis Soares Araújo, my sister and god-daughter; and to David M. Bergeron, fellow scholar, mentor, faithful friend. To them, I offer this book.

Lawrence, Kansas, and Cincinnati, Ohio   June 1998

Introduction

Things alien fascinate Shakespeare and reveal an interest in a multicultural and cosmopolitan environment of foreign commercial transactions and cross-cultural interactions. References to distant lands on world maps, foreign commodities, strange artifacts, and exotic cultures and customs abound in his plays. Through metaphor and allusion, a picture of the world emerges from his drama. Maria, in *Twelfth Night*, compares Malvolio's grinning face to a map: 'He does smile his face into more lines than is in the new map with the augmentation of the Indies' (III.ii.70–1).[1] She alludes to the first map engraved in England based upon Mercator Projection, included in the second edition of Hakluyt's *The Principal Navigations Voyages Traffiques & Discoveries of the English Nation* (1598).[2] Sir John Falstaff, in *Merry Wives of Windsor*, does not distinguish colonial from sexual conquest. He views Mistress Page as 'a region in Guiana, all gold and bounty' (I.iii.63); he expresses his desire for Mistress Ford and Mistress Page in the language of commerce: 'They shall be my East and West Indies, and I will trade to them both' (I.iii.64–6). Benedick of *Much Ado About Nothing* offers to accomplish the most preposterous quest he can think of: to travel to Africa to measure the length of Prester John's foot or to do 'any embassage to the Pygmies,' or to go to Asia to 'fetch a hair off the great Cham's [Khan's] beard' (II.i.236–46). In *Lear*, we find a reference to a 'pygmy's straw' and in *The Winter's Tale* to an 'Ethiopian's tooth' (IV.iv.357). Macbeth speaks of the exquisite 'perfumes of Arabia' (V.i.47–8) and Othello of the 'Arabian trees' from which the Arabians extract a 'med'cinable gum' (V.ii.350–1). Antipholus of Syracuse, in *The Comedy of Errors*, fears 'Lapland sorcerers' (IV.iii.11), and Bassanio, in *The Merchant of Venice*, shuns 'the beauteous scarf / Veiling an Indian beauty' (III.ii.98–9). A survey of such references reveals a veritable cabinet of wonders, fragments of early anthropological perspectives, cross-cultural attitudes, and archeological curiosities.

Although one could argue that ethnographical representation always entails a fragmentary, distorted quality, I am not, however, primarily interested in brief allusions or metaphors, but rather in sustained, extended explorations of cross-cultural encounters: how different cultures meet, interact, and view one another. As a point of definition and departure, I take Brabantio's hospitality. As Brabantio's dinner guest, Othello stages the story of his life for the entertainment of his hosts, whom he regales with a narrative of battles, sieges, 'disastrous chances,' 'hairbreadth scapes,' slavery and manumission, cannibals and headless men – stories that Desdemona and her father greedily devour. Othello reports her instruction to him, 'If I had a friend that loved her,/I should but teach him how to tell my story,/And that would woo her' (I.iii.164–6). In Brabantio's house, representatives from two very different worlds meet: the 'erring barbarian' and the 'supersubtle Venetian.' I would therefore like to define the cross-cultural encounter as the locus where a foreigner – a Moor, an Amazon, an Egyptian, a Jew – and a European interact, where the domestic and the alien meet. Cross-cultural encounters may take the form of seduction or confrontation, discovery or recovery, desire or loathing, wonder or disillusionment, peace or war.

At this site of cultural interaction, one can distinguish what the anthropologist James Clifford defines as 'an ethnographic perspective,' which 'values fragments, curious collections, unexpected juxtapositions – that works to provoke the manifestations of extraordinary realities drawn from the domains of the erotic, the exotic, and the unconscious.'[3] As another anthropologist, James A. Boon, remarks, cultures continually fabricate caricatures of each other and of themselves, and 'every culture appears, *vis-à-vis* every other, exaggerated.'[4] He adds that 'ethnographic writing about other cultures consists, like cultures themselves, in an exaggeration of differences.'[5]

I will argue that Shakespeare recovers fragments of alien worlds through which he explores the distortions and caricatures that cultures create of one another. Repeatedly, Shakespeare represents cultures which define themselves as ideological opposites that are engaged in a dynamic yet unstable process of negotiation and confrontation. In fact, writing about *Henry V*, Erich Auerbach best captures the instability of the Shakespearean world, when he remarks: 'the very ground on which men move and actions take their course is more unsteady and seems shaken by inner disturbances. There is no stable world as background, but a world which is perpetually reengendering itself out of the most varied sources.'[6] In the drama of Shakespeare, cultures meet on an even more unstable ground: a problematic space, always culturally, politically, and psychologically charged. At the dark frontiers of cross-cultural interaction, we find distortion, caricature, exaggeration, and a profound sense of accentuated cultural difference.

I offer here a cultural study, an approach which explores how cultural practice – such as rituals, human sexuality, religious belief, politics and power, hospitality, property rights, and class structure – impinges upon literature and the theater. My method, although predominantly historical, draws extensively on literary theory and analysis, feminist and gender studies, and anthropology, through which I place Shakespeare at the center of a cultural debate about Europe's encounters with and colonial domination of foreign lands and alien peoples; but, unlike other studies, this book explores the dynamic interplay of three concepts – gender, text, and habitat – as metaphors for moments of cultural definition. First and foremost, the cross-cultural encounter becomes a clash of gender systems. Gender becomes the foundation for an oppositional view of culture. One gender system confronts and is threatened by another, which is perceived as alien and forbidden. In some of the plays, text functions as the archival repository of a culture's values, beliefs, prejudices, and practices, affirming traditions and according privileges. When cultures meet, cultures contest textual representation, as they do gender systems. Foreigners attempt to generate, modify, decipher, or interpret texts. Members of European cultures resist alien attempts to assert ethnic, racial, or religious difference. The word 'habitat' evokes the complex ecological relationships of humans and all living things to their surroundings. In the cross-cultural encounters in Shakespeare's plays, the environment becomes allegorical, functioning as a place of projections for the culture's fears, prejudices, desires, and textual and sexual fantasies. This is the landscape of the mind, a space where – to paraphrase Angus Fletcher – we fight repressed versions of ourselves, forge alliances with splintered aspects of ourselves, and travel in a world simultaneously familiar and utterly alien.[7] When taken together, the three concepts – gender, text, habitat – define the extent to which Shakespeare radically reinterprets, refashions, and reinscribes the traditional aliens of the European imagination, such as Jews, Moors, Amazons, and gypsies.

I have selected ten plays to illustrate the range of Shakespeare's cross-cultural representation. The first part of the book focuses on such topics as symbolic inversion, same-sex partnerships, and the gender instability that arises from the partial recovery of alien gender systems in *A Midsummer Night's Dream*, *The Two Noble Kinsmen*, and the *Henry VI* trilogy. In these plays, we see that the cross-cultural encounter becomes a form of gender instability threatening not only acceptable gender roles but also national and cultural identity. I have juxtaposed comedy, romance, and history in order to underscore the extent to which Shakespeare guides gender issues to the frontiers of culture and links historical events and a fictional narrative. The cross-cultural encounter reveals the gender exchanges which subvert cultural identity.

The central section, focusing on *The Merchant of Venice*, *Titus Andronicus*, and *Othello*, also explores the dynamic interaction between fiction and history and highlights the centrality of the written word to the Shakespearean cross-cultural encounters. As a repository of cultural values in these dramas, writing advances and protects the interests and power of dominant European cultures, but it also unveils a deep racial rift. A textual war with clear gender implications emerges. Portia becomes the champion of Venetian traditions and exclusionary beliefs, waging a war through textual interpretation. Staging the rape of Lavinia, Aaron finds an identity not in his own past but in the violent racial and sexual fantasies of Roman texts. Although Othello generates written records and thus participates in Venice's historiographical enterprise, his racial difference and cultural past invite speculation about and reconstruction of an alien culture and gender system.

The last two chapters move from history to romance, tracing the dynamic and mutual relations of character to habitat, of culture to the environment, of gender to cultural difference. I am particularly interested in how Shakespeare reinterprets and refashions Cleopatra's racial and cultural identity, which seems to depend on the unique nature of Egyptian ecology. In reconstructing Egypt's ecology and refashioning the cultural differences between Egyptians and Romans, Shakespeare lays bare a profound sense of gender and ideological instability through which exchanges of cultural identity occur. Finally, *The Tempest* brings together the interaction of the three concepts examined in this book. The cross-cultural encounter hinges on texts, gender exchanges, and cultural and environmental dislocation. In this play, Shakespeare explores a double process of estrangement and eventual cultural reintegration.

I attempt to place Shakespeare's plays in the historical and anthropological context of Europe's colonial encounters and the large body of early modern ethnographic materials on alien cultural practices and on racial and gender difference. Europe's colonial encounters cover a wide spectrum of experiences. Stephen Greenblatt refers to the 'wonder' which characterized some initial responses to the New World. He writes: 'Columbus's voyage initiated a century of intense wonder. European culture experienced something like the startle reflex' one can observe in infants: eyes widened, arms outstretched, breathing stilled, the whole body momentarily convulsed.'[8] But European responses to alien worlds seem much more ambivalent, as wonder gives way to overt and covert warfare and destruction.

Portuguese explorations of Africa and the beginning of the African slave trade, for example, already anticipate and perhaps offer a rehearsal for later European colonial conquests. In 1453, the Portuguese chronicler Azurara records in the pages of history the experience of Africans who were taken to Portugal. He depicts a wrenching scene of the Africans being rounded up and enslaved:

> But what heart could be so hard as not to be pierced with piteous feeling to see that company? For some kept their heads low and their faces bathed in tears, looking one upon another; others stood groaning very dolorously, looking up to the height of heaven, fixing their eyes upon it, crying out loudly, as if asking help of the Father of Nature; others struck their faces with the palms of their hands, throwing themselves at full length upon the ground; others made the lamentations in the manner of a dirge, after the custom of their country. And though we could not understand the words of their language, the sound of it right well accorded with the measure of their sadness.[9]

Azurara records that families were torn asunder, sons from their fathers, husbands from wives, brothers from brothers: 'No respect was shown either to friends or relations, but each fell where his lot took him' (82). Those who resisted were beaten; all were shackled.

As if to justify the cruelty of the slave holders, Azurara speaks of the seductive nature of European life. He adds that after the slaves came to Portugal, 'they never more tried to fly, but rather in time forgot all about their own country, as soon as they began to taste the good things of this one.'[10] Azurara voiced the Eurocentric belief that Europe entices, seduces, makes aliens forget their cultural past. Azurara's Eurocentric perspective leads him to conclude that material goods and comfort can help sever one's cultural and affective roots. He therefore attempts to justify an ideology of domination and exploitation, which, he assumes, is a precondition for material progress and economic prosperity. He belongs to what Lisa Jardine refers to as an age of 'conspicuous consumption' and 'unashamed enthusiasm for belongings.'[11] Early modern Europeans, according to Jardine, celebrated ownership: they prized and accumulated material wealth from ostentatious oriental tapestries to exotic birds and foreign human specimens.

Europe's interest in things alien may be characterized, as Steven Mullaney, for example, does, not only as a program of material but also of ideological and cultural appropriation: 'Learning strange tongues or collecting strange things, rehearsing the words and ways of marginal or alien cultures, upholding idleness for a while – these are the activities of a culture in the process of extending its boundaries and reformulating itself.'[12] Likewise, Wlad Godzich compares the Renaissance explorer to the medieval knight in order to explain European expansionism: 'the adventurous knight leaves Arthur's court – the realm of the known – to encounter some form of otherness, a domain in which the courtly values of the Arthurian world do not prevail. The quest is brought to an end when this alien domain is brought within the hegemonic sway of the Arthurian world: the other has been reduced to (more of) the same.'[13] Tzvetan Todorov argues that early modern Europeans seem particularly well-equipped to 'assimilate the other, to do away with an exterior alterity' in part because of their 'remarkable qualities of flexibility and improvisation which permit them all the better to impose their own way of life.'[14] Economically, alien worlds become a source from which to extract material goods and, culturally, a *tabula rasa* upon which Europe inscribes its languages and its cultural values.

Quite often the search for commodities cannot, however, be altogether separated from what might be judged as a genuine desire to understand the diversity of the world's races, cultures, and habitats. This ambivalence becomes apparent in artistic representation. A theatrical entertainment, for example, staged France's Henri II's entry into Rouen in 1550, offered a Brazilian habitat, complete with trees, birds, and animals, and a battle between two rival Brazilian tribes.[15] Frobisher's expeditions to the

Meta Incognita also generated a re-creation of an Eskimo culture and habitat. On his first voyage, Frobisher seized a native: 'when he founde himself in captivitie, for very choller and disdain, he bit his tong in twayne within his mouth: notwithstanding, he died not thereof, but lived untill he came in Englande, and then he died of colde which he had taken at sea.'[16] In England, an artist drew the Indian's picture 'with boate and other furniture, both as he was in his own, & also in English apparel.'[17] A hand-colored woodcut in Gerrit de Veer's *Warhafftige Relation der dreyen newen unherhörten seltzamen Schiffart* (Nuremberg, 1598) depicts an extraordinary scene in which the Eskimo paddles his kayak on the river Avon and kills two ducks.[18] Such representations serve in part to educate Europe about the diversity of the world's cultures and scenes, while surveying the range and potential of the world's resources.

Another example illustrates how the theater appropriates the foreign for domestic artistic consumption. On his return voyage from Brazil in 1532, Captain William Hawkins transported to England a Brazilian cacique (Indian chief), whom he presented to King Henry VIII at Whitehall:

> ... at the sight of whom the King and all the Nobilitie did not a litle marvaile, and not without cause: for in his cheekes were holes made according to their savage maner, and therein small bones were planted, standing an inch out from the said holes, which in his owne Countrey was reputed for a great braverie. He had also another hole in his nether lip, wherein was set a precious stone about the bignes of a pease: All his apparel, behaviour, and gesture, were very strange to the beholders.[19]

Decades later, Shakespeare evokes this event as an allusion and a joke in his play *Henry VIII*, when the Porter complains: 'Or have we some strange Indian with the great tool come to court, the women so besiege us' (V.iv.30–3).[20] Shakespeare reminds the audience of the emissary from the New World, although only the most sensational and prurient element survives in the Porter's imagination.

European perception of alien worlds is profoundly ambivalent, ranging from fascination to overt xenophobia. In *History of Trauayle* (1577), Richard Eden expresses his fascination when he marvels at the colors that 'God useth in the composition of man': 'whiche doubtlesse can not be considered without great admiration in beholdying one to be whyte, and an other blacke, beyng colours utterly contrary: some lykewyse to be yealowe, whiche is betweene blacke and white: and other of other colours, as it were of divers liveries.'[21] But exploration leads to exploitation, discovery to domination, wonder to loathing. Utter rejection of things alien is apparent in Queen Elizabeth's xenophobic order of 1601: 'whereas the Queen's Majesty is discontented at the great number of negars and blackamoores' which are crept into the realm since the troubles between her Highness and the King of Spain, and are fostered here to the annoyance of her own people.'[22] The queen appointed Casper Van Senden to gather these aliens and to transport them out of the country. Eden's admiration and the Queen's order represent opposite but often intertwined impulses. In fact, Shakespeare's unique contribution comes from an ability to reaffirm individual human dignity at moments of intense cultural conflict and racial and ethnic prejudice. In his drama, the cross-cultural encounter involves cultural definition, introspection, identity exchange. Some scholars, however, have argued for Shakespeare's Eurocentric views and interests, rather than a multi-cultural perspective. J. D. Rogers writes: 'Europe is Shakespeare's centre, and although things outside intrude now and then, like spectres from another world, his plots, themes and scenes are almost exclusively European.'[23] This view strikes me as reductive because it dismisses the richness of what Shakespeare has written. Indeed, Shakespeare, I believe, repeatedly grapples with the profound significance of cross-cultural interaction for both his characters and his culture.

Shakespeare seems to recognize the mutual dependency of cultures, and he challenges Eurocentric isolationism and feelings of ideological superiority.[24] Analogous to this, a modern anthropological approach views cultures as 'equally significant, integrated systems of differences.'[25] Yet, paradoxically, Boon argues, cultures hold the mirror up to each other: 'A ''culture'' can materialize only in counterdistinction to another culture.'[26] I contend in part that Shakespeare's drama shows that English culture could not understand itself except in juxtaposition to others.

Shakespeare wrote in an age of unprecedented intercultural exchanges. Thomas Heywood argues that London, being a world metropolis like ancient Rome, should provide for the entertainment of the most varied foreign visitors. The city should proudly exhibit its gorgeous theaters and sumptuous spectacles: 'Rome was a metropolis, a place whither all the nations knowne under the sunne resorted: so is London, and being to receive all estates, all princes, all nations, therefore to affoord them all choyce of pas-times, sports, and recreations.'[27] Naturally, London could boast of a relatively large number of foreign visitors and residents, including ambassadors, tradesmen, and artisans. Dutch and Italian merchants in London were responsible, for example, for two of the triumphal arches in James's 1604 royal entry. In Heywood's view, the English stage should fulfill the expectations of and should mirror the poten-tial audience for which it was intended.[28]

Heywood's dream of a multicultural, multiracial theater could only be fulfilled much later, when Shakespeare's drama had been translated and staged, not just in Western Europe but also around the world. Two extraordinary examples illustrate the point. The highlight of the 1979 Edinburgh International Festival was the appearance of the Rustaveli Company of the former Soviet Repub-lic of Georgia in a production of *Richard III*, which was performed in the Georgian language without simultaneous English transla-tion.[29] In 1986, China held its first National Shakespeare Festival of twenty-five performances of *A Midsummer Night's Dream, King Lear, Richard III, Merry Wives of Windsor, The Merchant of Venice*, and *Timon of Athens*, and of an operatic adaptation of *Othello*. The festival opened on 10 April with a production of *A Midsummer Night's Dream*: 'China's coal miners' troupe dressed up as Athenian lovers, mesmerising fairies and comical Artisans to weave a web of tangled relationships in *A Midsummer Night's Dream* proving, as the capital's art critics wrote, that "All the world's a stage." '[30] Another critic wrote that 'The Chinese love Shakespeare so much that in few years time, they will say the bard was Chinese.'[31]

Other examples of Shakespeare's appeal to contemporary multi-national audiences abound; but I do not intend to explore staging problems and issues, to trace stage history, or even to gauge audi-ence response to Shakespeare's plays either in the Renaissance or in subsequent periods. Rather, I propose to situate Shakespeare's texts in the historical and cultural context of a large body of early mod-ern anthropological and ethnographic literature about race, ethni-city, gender, and environmental influences on cultural practice and to study Europe's Others, who, like Othello and the Africans of Azurara's chronicle, find themselves at the interstices of European life. Indeed, Shakespeare's plays offer a wealth of material on the Renaissance concepts of ethnic, racial, and cultural diversity.

1

'The Uttermost Parts of Their Maps': Frontiers of Gender

The things of this world can be truly perceived only by looking at them backwards.

Balthasar Gracian, Society of Jesus, *El Criticon* (1651).

According to Plutarch, some historiographers of his time dismissed 'the uttermost parts of their maps,' saying that these remote foreign regions were 'unnavigable, rude, full of venomous beasts, Scythian ice, and frozen seas' and therefore unworthy of scholarly attention; but by doing so, adds Plutarch, the historiographers were merely trying to hide either the limits of their knowledge or their utter ignorance.[1] Plutarch believed that it is preferable to rely on doubtful and spurious material than to ignore it altogether.[2] Therefore, mythology provides information for his biographies because such material sheds light on the Greek and Roman character. Likewise, I propose that Amazons provide a worthwhile point of departure for a study of cross-cultural encounters in Shakespeare. Through these figures, Shakespeare takes us to the frontiers of culture and gender and introduces cultural difference as a form of gender difference.

The encounters between Amazons and Athenians in Shakespeare's drama permit us to investigate gender and power inversion and a less known dimension of the Amazon legend: namely, how an all-female society generates a same-sex partnership and dual queenship.[3] In short, I contend, Shakespeare participates in and alters a tradition involving the representation of the Amazons: the Amazons themselves generate a gender double consisting of a partnership between a female warrior and her 'wife.' This gender double is patterned after yet subverts relationships between men and women in Greek society. In both *A Midsummer Night's Dream* and *Two Noble Kinsmen*, written in collaboration with John Fletcher,

Shakespeare revisits, refashions, and reinterprets the Amazon myth.[4] The presence of Amazons in these plays unleashes a series of symbolic inversions, whereby alien gender systems are partially concealed and partially revealed.

My discussion of gender in Shakespeare's plays will center first on gender inversion, in part because Amazons subvert expected early modern notions of womanhood. As Balthasar Gracian of the Society of Jesus argues in *El Criticon* (1651), 'The things of this world can be truly perceived only by looking at them backwards.'[5] An upside-down perspective permits writers like Gracian to imagine the world in fascinating ways. A few examples will serve to illustrate the point. An anonymous Venetian woodcut (Plate 1), entitled *Il Mondo alla Riversa* (*c.* 1560s), and a late sixteenth-century Dutch one, published by Ewout Muller, depict such popular images of reversals as a cart going before a horse, women going to war while the men stay home and spin, ships travelling on land, and a client telling the fortune of a gypsy.[6] In a similar fashion, two adjoining misericords at Westminster Abbey portray women thrashing men.[7] Images of the world turned upside down, where nothing is as it seems, present an oppositional view of culture, invert and subvert power relations, and permit the artist to reconfigure the imaginary cultural map. Everything has its opposite. Therefore, 'symbolic inversion' may be defined as 'any act of expressive behavior which inverts, contradicts, abrogates, or in some fashion presents an alternative to commonly held cultural codes, values, and norms be they linguistic, literary or artistic, religious, or social and political.'[8] As a form of symbolic inversion, Amazons, as I argue below, function as a cultural double, which marks both the difference female/female, male/female, and European/non- European.

Extraordinary gender inversions may also occur as accidents of nature. These Amazon-like figures proved to be a source of wonder and amusement in the Renaissance. Of these, the painting (Plate 2), *Magdalena Ventura with Her Husband and Son* (Museo Fundación Duque de Lerma, Palácio Tavera, Toledo, 1631), by Jusepe de Ribera is one of the most striking examples. The canvas bears the Latin inscription, '*En magnv[m] naturae miracvlvm*,' announcing the 'great wonder of nature' depicted therein. Indeed, from the shadows emerge three figures: a bearded middle-aged woman with a large exposed breast holding a swaddled infant in her arms, and an older man. The child's lips are on the verge of touching the woman's breast, while Magdalena's husband stands in the shadowy background. The inscription reveals that, born in Abruzzi, Naples, Magdalena was 52 years old when this canvas was painted and 37 when ' "she began to become hairy and grew a beard so long and thick that it seems more like that of any bearded gentlemen than of a woman who had borne three sons by her husband, Felici de Amici, whom you see here." '[9] A nonpictorial example as striking as Ribera's painting comes from *Fugger Newsletters*. One night, while getting ready for bed, Daniel Burghammer, a soldier of the Madrucci Regiment in Piadena, Italy, 'complained to his wife, to whom he had been married by the Church seven years ago, that he had great pains in his belly and felt something stirring therein. An hour thereafter he gave birth to a child, a girl.'[10] During examination, he confessed that he was 'half man and half woman' and that he had slept with a Spaniard and thus became pregnant. The report adds that 'The aforesaid soldier is able to suckle the child with his right breast only and not at all on the left side, where he is a man.' Considered a wondrous event, the birth of this girl caused a sensation among the nobility and the soldiers, who celebrated the child's christening with many ceremonies.[11]

The figure of the Amazon combines notions of symbolic inversion and gender aberration and marks the frontier between European and alien. Ancient writers, such as Herodotus, Plutarch, Diodorus of Sicily, Statius, Strabo, Quintus Smyrnaeus, and their followers provide the basis for subsequent representations of the Amazons in the West, including those in *A Midsummer Night's Dream* and *Two Noble Kinsmen*.[12] The Amazon myth, as it came down to Shakespeare, consists of a cluster of contradicting elements. Amazons conjure up images of spectacular female defiance, subversion, or 'aggressive, self-determining desire.'[13] As Gail Paster contends, the Amazons with their self-mutilated bodies, 'half maternal and half martial,' differ from the Renaissance ideals of womanhood in their 'complete uninterest in an erotic appeal governed by male desire' and in their 'emotional distance from or refusal to become absorbed into the personal and maternal gratifications, the social rewards, of nurture.'[14] To substantiate this view, one needs only to turn to Herodotus, who gives the following account of the bloodthirsty nature of the Amazons:

> In the war between the Greeks and the Amazons, the Greeks, after their victory at the river Thermodon, sailed off in three ships with as many Amazons on board as they had succeeded

in taking alive. (The Scythians call the Amazons *Oeorpata*, the equivalent of *mankillers*, *oeor* being the Scythian word for 'man', and *pata* for kill'.) Once at sea, the women murdered their captors....[15]

Unskillful at the art of navigation, the Amazons drifted at sea until they arrived at the land of the Scythians. After a certain period, Scythian youths mated with the Amazons, who persuaded them to abandon their homeland inasmuch as their cultural differences were irreconcilable:

'We and the women of your nation could never live together; our ways are too much at variance. We are riders; our business is with the bow and the spear, and we know nothing of women's work; but in your country no woman has anything to do with such things – your women stay at home in their wagons occupied with feminine tasks, and never go out to hunt or for any other purpose. We could not possibly agree. If, however, you wish to keep us for your wives and to behave as honourable men, go and get from your parents the share of property which is due to you, and then let us go off and live by ourselves'.[16]

The Amazons and their mates left Scythia and settled down on the other side of the Tanais River. The Scythian ephebes thus agreed to live in a subservient position in a society controlled by women.

Following in the footsteps of Herodotus and others, Renaissance writers situate the Amazon kingdom in Asia, although some begin to associate the Amazons with Africa and the New World.[17] Many of these writers regard the Amazons as monsters, although others view them positively. According to myth, the African Amazons inhabited the Mountains of the Moon, as Duarte Barbosa, writing in 1518, describes them: 'This king always takes with him into the field a captain, whom they call Sono, with a great band of warriors, and five or six thousand women, who also bear arms and fight.'[18] Likewise, Samuel Purchas gives a detailed account of a legion of women who serve an African chief who must wage 'continuall warre, for the maintenance of his estate': 'And among all the rest of his Souldiers, the most valourous in name, are his Legions of Women, whom he esteemeth very highly and accounteth them as the very sinewes and strength of his militarie forces.'[19]

European explorers also believed that the Amazons inhabited the American continent. In a letter describing his first voyage, Columbus writes of a land where there are no males, where the 'women engage in no feminine occupation,' but use bows and arrows of cane, like those already mentioned, and they arm and protect themselves with plates of copper, of which they have much.'[20] Sir Walter Raleigh was told by a South American cacique that a tribe of women warriors lived 'on the South side of the river in the provinces of Topago.'[21] The ubiquitous nature of the Amazon myth does not escape Raleigh.[22] He writes that the land of the Amazons was rich with gold and 'a kinde of greene stones,' but also very dangerous. These women not only excelled in arms but formed a sisterhood that shunned the company of men, except during the mating season, which was apparently governed by the moon:

> [The Amazons] doe accompany with men but once in a yere, and for the time of one moneth, which I gather by their relation, to be in April: and that time all kings of the borders assemble, and queenes of the Amazones; and after the queenes have chosen, the rest cast lots for their Valentines. This one moneth, they feast, dance, and drinke of their wines in abundance; and the Moone being done, they all depart to their owne provinces.[23]

Their primary concern was 'to increase their owne sex and kind'; and even when they took prisoners, they first mated with them and then killed them because, as Raleigh explains, they were 'very cruell and bloodthirsty.' In essence, Raleigh believes that this society was devoid of affection and that the women could not become emotionally attached to their mates.

In the same vein, John Bulwer surveys different tribes of Amazons presumably spread throughout the world, vehemently attacking their way of life. Bulwer disapproves of Amazon subversion of male authority. He writes, for example, that unlike the ancient Amazons who seared off their right breasts, the African Amazons sear off their left breasts (see Plate 3): 'The chiefe of the Guard of the King of *Congo* are left-handed *Amazons*, who seare off their left Paps with a hot Iron, because it should be no hinderance to them in their shooting.'[24] He strongly condemns them: '*But these Amazons discarding the tendernesse of their Sex, and desiring to improve themselves Viragoes, abreviate Natures provision for an unnaturall conveniency*'

(324). He suggests that the Amazons have a dangerous political agenda:

> It is true, that they had an intent withal in that feminine Com-
> mon-wealth of theirs, to avoid the Domination of men, to lame
> them thus in their infancy, both in their Arms and Legs, and
> other limbs, that might anyway advantage their strength over
> them, and made only that use of them, that we in our world
> make of women.[25]

Bulwer condemns this political agenda, which threatens to subvert the prevailing gender hierarchy of his own society.

Renaissance writers endow the Amazons with an ethnographical and historical character and with a strong theatrical and literary presence, in part because femininity was often cast as 'the specta-cular gender,' the Amazons, being superwomen, were even more spectacular.[26] Through these representations, Europeans can observe hypothetical or mythological upside-down worlds, where females hold sway over males. Two types of Amazons appear in the Renaissance: 'bad' Amazons hate, emasculate, maim and subject men, whereas 'good' ones epitomize virtue, chastity, and bravery. At Christmas, 1551, a masque of 'Ammazons women of warre' was performed at court.[27] In 1578, 'A Maske of Amasones' was performed for Queen Elizabeth and the French Ambassador. In the masque, Amazons appeared in full armor, richly decorated in gold and silver; they carried shields 'with a devise painted thereon and Iavelinges in their handes one with a speach to the Queenes majestie delivering a Table with writinges unto her highnes comying in with musitions playing on Cornettes apparrelled in longe white taffeta.'[28] The mas-que dissolved into a dance of the Amazons and the lords, similar to the masque of Cupid and the Amazons in *Timon of Athens*.[29] At the baptism of Prince Henry of Scotland in 1594, a curious masque was staged as part of the festivities:

> Last of all came in three Amazones in women's attire, very
> sumptuously clad; and these were the Lord of Lendores, the
> Lord of Barclewch, and the Abbot of Holy-roote-house: so all
> these persons being present, and at their entrie making their
> reverence to the Queene's Majestie, Ambassadours and Ladies,
> having their pages ryding upon their led horse, and on their left
> armes bearing their masters' impresse or device. [30]

The cross-dressed courtiers and their pages offered a morally meaningful spectacle mapping the landscape with the virtues of the court, at the head of which was the king's 'lyon's head with open eyes,' signifying 'Fortitude and Vigilancie.' Likewise, a noble Amazon, Penthesilea, appears in the company of other famous warrior queens in Jonson's *Masque of Queens*.[31] Like the personifications of Fortitude, Justice, or Hope, the Amazons could also epitomize virtue and military prowess.

The literature of the period also depicts the Amazons as aberrations of nature. In Book V of *The Faerie Queene*, Spenser brings together two opposite viragos, the virtuous Britomart and the evil Radigund, queen of the Amazons, who face each other in battle.[32] Seeking revenge for Bellodant's rejection of her love, Radigund challenges Artegall to single combat and defeats him. He must wear women's clothes and do humiliating ordinary housework: 'To spin, to card, to sew, to wash, to wring' (Bk 5.4.31).[33] Radigund's hatred of one man turns into hatred of all men. Not without irony must Britomart, a female cross-dresser, do battle with Radigund to rescue the cross-dressed Artegall. After the defeat of Radigund and the deliverance of the captive knights, Britomart reigns over the kingdom of the Amazons, repealing 'the liberty of women' and restoring women to 'mens subiection' (Bk 5.7.42). A symbol of androgynous perfection, she is both an Amazon and *not* an Amazon: she rejects Radigund's political agenda and accepts women's subservience to men as part of Artegall's justice system. Spenser intimates that we must measure the Amazons not only in relation to patriarchal societies but against each other. In a country such as England, ruled by a female monarch, Spenser and other writers recover and rehabilitate the Amazon myth to suit their political or ideological purposes, without upsetting patriarchal values. Amazons live in 'a strangely "double," hybrid culture,' made up of creatures who are simultaneously feminine and masculine.[34] As a cultural fantasy, the myth fascinates and frightens.

Another dimension of the Amazon myth remains to be discussed, namely that the Amazons evolved from submissive wives in order to form an all-female community of warriors and to institute a two-queen system of government. Surprisingly, modern scholars have ignored this dimension. I will argue that this version of the myth informs Shakespeare's representations of the encounters between Amazons and Greeks. According to this version, the tribesmen were defeated in battle and killed. Seeking redress, their wives took up arms themselves and slaughtered the killers of their husbands (see Plate 4). Once they got a taste of power, the wives refused to submit themselves again to any males and rejected all marriage proposals from neighboring tribes. This version actually inverts the usual sequence of the myth: the women imitate their deceased husbands in their tactics and form of government.[35] From the experience, a dual-queen system emerges, whereby one queen stays at home while the other plunders and conquers abroad.

In *The Palace of Pleasure* (1566; 1575), William Painter opens his second volume of novellas with a detailed account of a 'Woman's Commonwealth': 'it is no wonder to the skilfull that a whole Monarche, and kingdome should be intierly peopled with that Sexe: so to the not well trained in Histories, this may seeme miraculous.'[36] Here Painter introduces the two-queen system of Amazon government. He writes that, having emerged victorious from warfare, the Amazons

> fortified themselves in those places, and wan other countreys adjoyninge, choosinge amonge them two Queenes, the one named Martesia, and the other Lampedo. These two lovingely devided the army and men of Warre in two partes, eyther of them defendinge (with great hardinesse) the Landes which they had conquered.[37]

According to Painter, the two-queen form of government proved to be quite successful, as the Amazons expanded their conquests into other neighboring tribes, edifying a number of cities, among which Ephesus was the most famous.

This version of the myth establishes a division of labor between what I will refer to as 'female husband'[38] or 'warrior,' the Amazons' traditional occupation, and her 'wife,' the function traditionally reserved for conquered or enslaved males. The two-queen system served the Amazons well until the time of the expedition of Hercules and Theseus. At that time, the queens were Oritia and Antiopa: 'one of the two Queenes was goinge out of the countery with the greatest part of her women, to make Warre, and conquer new Countreyes, in so mutch that he [Hercules] found Antiopa, which doubted nothinge, ne yet knewe of his comminge.'[39] Caught unprepared, many Amazons were slain; and others, including Menalipe and Hippolyta, sisters of the queen, were made prisoners. Antiopa, by giving her armor to Hercules, obtained the release of Menalipe;

but Theseus refused to release Hippolyta, with whom he had fallen in love. When the warrior queen Oritia heard of the news, she enlisted the help of the Scythians, who later failed to deliver the reinforcements promised. As a result, the Amazons, weakened and betrayed, lost the war and eventually their kingdom was wiped out.

A number of writers corroborate Painter's discussion of the two queens. Sir Walter Raleigh, for example, confirms that the Amazons had not one but two queens, giving their names as 'Lampedo & Mathesia.'[40] In *Batman vppon Bartholome, His Booke De Proprietatibus Rerum* (1582), Stephen Batman further proves the Renaissance belief in the Amazons' dual queenship. He describes a tribe in a 'Country, parte in Asia, and parte in Europe,' near Albania. After the Goths had cruelly slain their husbands, 'their wives tooke their husbands armour and weapon,' and avenged their husbands' murder. They also killed 'all the young males and olde men and children, and saved the females, and departed . . . . and purposed to live ever after without companye of males.'[41] The system of government, based upon their deceased husbands' regime, rests upon a form of marriage or a same-sex partnership:

> And by ensample of ther husbandes that had always two kings over them, these women ordeyned them two Queenes, that one was called Marsephia, and that other Lampeta, that one should travaile with an hoast and fight against ennimyes, and that other should in the meane time governe and rule the communalties.[42]

One queen rules at home, while the other wages war and earns a living for the tribe. The two-queen form of government rests upon a division of labor between 'warrior' and Amazon 'wife'; it reflects the Amazons' dual nature – defiance and submission – and replicates in a same-sex partnership the male–female gender relations.

Shakespeare was undoubtedly familiar with William Painter's translations of tales from Italian and Latin authors. Materials from *Palace of Pleasure* provide sources for *All's Well That End's Well*, *Romeo and Juliet*, *Timon of Athens*, and *The Rape of Lucrece*. I postulate that in *A Midsummer Night's Dream* Shakespeare, in part through Painter's account, comes to an understanding of the relationship of the Amazon myth to a cultural center, its reversible effects, and the unique dual-queen system. The center becomes a generating matrix, much like other male-dominated societies, which use the myth to justify patriarchal control. In choosing to set the play at a time shortly after the war of the Amazons, Shakespeare also creates the sense that the challenges to Athenian patriarchy still exist. The action of the play moves into a world turned upside down and into the realm of symbolic inversion. Further, the dual queenship of the Amazons manifests itself in a curious way. Hippolyta is, of course, the only true Amazon to appear in the play, but she does not behave like a warrior queen; curiously, she does not protest against Theseus' destruction of her people and her new role as his bride. Instead, Titania emerges as a substitute Amazon. Through such displacements and symbolic inversion, Shakespeare intertwines the Amazon Hippolyta and her double, Titania.

That Athens of *A Midsummer Night's Dream* consists of a patriarchy is quite obvious. Accepting the foundation of Athenian myth, Shakespeare establishes Theseus as the center of that system, with Egeus and Oberon functioning as ancillary corresponding patriarchs. Thus the play opens when Theseus is at the peak of his power. In fact, Plutarch underscores that Theseus's victory 'was not a matter of small moment.' The Amazons, according to Plutarch, posed a fundamental threat to Athens, having 'first conquered or subdued all the country thereabouts.'[43] When the Amazons staged their assault on Athens, the Athenians were at first driven back but were able to kill scores of Amazons. 'Afterwards,' he writes, 'at the end of four months, peace was taken between them by means of one of the women called Hippolyta.'[44] Shakespeare's Theseus, like Plutarch's, portrays himself as an admirer of his kinsman Heracles. M. Bowra suggests that Heracles was 'almost the ideal embodiment of the Greek settler, who destroyed aboriginal monsters and gave peace to the regions he traversed.'[45] Thus, according to Page duBois, Heracles' 'violent history served as a model of colonization, mythically recounting his adventures as he moved from the western to the eastern boundaries of the world, exterminating creatures who stood in the way of the civilizing presence of the Greeks.'[46] Theseus, she adds, 'was a man of the *polis*, a beautiful, graceful youth'; but by association some of the myths involving Heracles were transferred to him.[47] Thus mythology associates the two heroes as destroyers of what the Greeks considered unacceptable others.[48] By defeating the Amazons, Theseus establishes himself as the quintessential defender of Athenian patriarchy; in fact, Plutarch and others credit him with the supremacy and hegemony of 'the noble and famous city of Athens.'[49]

In the Athens of Shakespeare's comedy, Theseus defends a patriarchal center, which emerges in counterdistinction to the inverted world of the Amazons. The play's perspective thus oscillates between the patriarchal world of the Athenians and the fragmentary images of the Amazon world. A tension arises from the suppression and erasure of Hippolyta's memory as an Amazon and the momentary transgressions embodied in the recovery of an Amazonian perspective.

Echoing the focus of its sources in the stories of Pyramus and Thisby in Ovid's *Metamorphoses* and Chaucer's *Legend of Good Women*, Shakespeare's play reaffirms patriarchal values, and ideologically links Theseus, Egeus, and Oberon. Theseus 'woos' with his sword, as he reminds his Amazonian bride: 'Hippolyta, I wooed thee with my sword,/And won thy love doing thee injuries' (I.i.16–17). Not surprisingly, then, Theseus sides with Egeus and affirms the centrality of the father to this system, as he explains to Hermia:

> To you your father should be as a god,
> One that composed your beauties; yea, and one
> To whom you are but as a form in wax,
> By him imprinted, and within his power
> To leave the figure, or disfigure it.

(I.i.47–51)

In this patriarchal ideology, Hermia becomes the wax seal which Egeus can mould at will. Theseus enforces laws that advance the interests of this patriarchy. Egeus asserts his prerogative as a father, insisting that Hermia belongs to him: 'And she is mine, and all my right of her/I do estate unto Demetrius' (I.i.97–8). When he reappears in Act IV, Egeus still demands enforcement of the law, even urging Demetrius to affirm male prerogative. As James Calderwood notes, Egeus is a 'man whose identity is totally absorbed by paternity.'[50] Although for unexplained reasons Theseus overrules Egeus at this point, the two men seem inextricably connected on another level. Curiously, as Calderwood points out, the father of the Theseus of mythology was named Aegeus/Egeus.[51]

Likewise, another patriarch, Oberon, engages in a dispute with his wife Titania about how to dispose of Titania's surrogate child, the Indian boy. Shakespeare clearly envisions Oberon as Theseus's counterpart, under whose guidance and control the wood outside of Athens remains. Like Theseus and Egeus, Oberon confronts Titania's challenge to his patriarchal authority. Much of the play's action consists of various characters' effort to challenge, reverse, and invert these patriarchies and to move into an upside-down symbolic realm.

Symbolic inversion projects alternatives to the patriarchal center. Through images of inversion, Shakespeare depicts a world that seems uncertain about its boundaries, where the focus of cultural and gender relations oscillates between the cultural center, represented by Theseus's patriarchal authority, and a marginal world, embodied by upside-down images and situations. The play offers shifts of perspective, as if vibrations from the Amazon challenge still threatened the Athenian world. In her pursuit of Demetrius, Helena defines the inverted world that struggles to assert itself:

> The story shall be changed:
> Apollo flies and Daphne holds the chase,
> The dove pursues the griffon, the mild hind
> Makes speed to catch the tiger – bootless speed,
> When cowardice pursues, and valor flies.

> (II.i.230–4)

In *A Midsummer Night's Dream*, symbolic inversion offers momentary alternative perspectives that challenge or escape patriarchal surveillance and control.

As Jeanne Roberts argues, Amazons are quintessential creatures of the Wilds; thus, several symbolic inversions occur in the Wilds, presumably a realm figuratively bordering on the regions from which Hippolyta came. Desire, of course, precipitates the inversions in Hermia's defiance of her father and the lovers' escape to the woods. In a land where women have few rights, Hermia speaks her mind: 'I know not by what power I am made bold,/Nor how it may concern my modesty/In such a presence here to plead my thoughts' (I.i.59–61). Defiantly, she expresses her will to die, rather than marry Demetrius, 'whose unwishèd yoke/My soul consents not to give sovereignty' (81–2). Considering Theseus's earlier comments about the dowager who withers out 'a young man's revenue,' it is ironic that another dowager, Lysander's aunt, would offer shelter from the harsh laws of Athens. Similarly, Helena relies on the power of love to transform the most unpleasant experience into something wonderful: 'Things base and vile, holding no quantity, / Love can transpose to form and dignity' (232–3).

Likewise, desire and madness intertwine and create unpredictable reversals and inversions, as Hermia and Helena observe:

> HERMIA: I frown upon him; yet he loves me still.
> HELENA: O that your frowns would teach my smiles such skill!
> HERMIA: I give him curses; yet he gives me love.
> HELENA: O that my prayers could such affection move!
> HERMIA: The more I hate, the more he follows me.
> HELENA: The more I love, the more he hateth me.

> (I.i.194–9)

According to Hermia, love has such power that it can turn 'a heaven unto a hell' (207) or vice versa. Love or desire motivates some of the principal inversions in the play: Hippolyta's 'subjection,' the young lovers' escape to the woods, and even Titania's momentary desire for Bottom.

In the woods, the realm of symbolic inversion, anything is possible, and nothing is as it seems. When he first enters the woods, Lysander loves Hermia; after Puck mistakenly anoints his eyes, he wakes up and falls in love with Helena, as he says: 'Not Hermia, but Helena I love. / Who will not change a raven for a dove?' (II.ii.113–14). When he falls asleep in III.ii, Puck again anoints his eyes, so that when he wakes up in Act IV, he loves Hermia once more. When Demetrius enters the woods, he loves Hermia, but, after Oberon anoints his eyes (III.ii.102–9), he wakes up to find himself in love with Helena. These sudden reversals become so confusing that Helena thinks that both men are mocking her: 'You both are rivals, and love Hermia; / And now both rivals to mock Helena' (III.ii.155–7). Even Hermia's and Helena's friendship seems to disintegrate into rivalry, as they exchange insults (III.ii). No less startling is the final reversal when the lovers wake up in Act IV. Although Egeus sounds harsh, Theseus reverses himself, allowing Hermia and Lysander to be together. Lysander summarizes his reaction, finding all reconciled: 'My lord, I shall reply amazedly, / Half sleep, half waking; but as yet, I swear, / I cannot truly say how I came here' (IV.i.145–7). Demetrius's love for Hermia has 'melted as the snow,' his love for Helena rekindled. Hermia seems equally amazed: 'Methinks I see these things with parted eye, / When everything seems double'

(IV.i.188–9). Demetrius wonders, 'Are you sure / That we are awake?' (IV.i.192–3). The play thus toys with the inversions and reversals that love and human desire can bring about, reinforcing Theseus's remark about the power of the imagination. The chaotic and seemingly unpredictable inversions provide propitious conditions for the happy ending, whereby the young lovers end up together and thus invert the tragic ending of the story of Pyramus and Thisby. The mechanicals' staging of the play-within-the-play in Act V reinforces and underscores this inversion, turning a tragedy into a comedy (farce).

In these symbolic inversions Shakespeare grounds the most striking inversion of all: Hippolyta's transformation into a bride. Obviously, from Athenian perspective this is no inversion at all, but rather the way things are supposed to be. Of her original upside-down world, little is left, except her perspective, her memory, and her body presumably mutilated according to the Amazon custom. In fact, a tension arises between her physical presence in an oppressive patriarchal world, which apparently requires suppression of her memory, and moments that underscore her past life. Although in Act I, scene i, Theseus speaks of the war of the Amazons, Hippolyta seems reticent, apparently unable or afraid to discuss the subject herself. Egeus, Theseus's patriarchal avatar, interrupts the conversation with a complaint against his daughter Hermia. The interruption deflects the tension from the discussion about the 'injuries' Theseus has inflicted on the Amazons. Only in Act IV, when the noises of Theseus's hounds remind her of the past, does Hippolyta specifically allude to her life as an Amazon:

> I was with Hercules and Cadmus once,
> When in a wood of Crete they bayed the bear
> With hounds of Sparta. Never did I hear
> Such gallant chiding; for, besides the groves,
> The skies, the fountains, every region near
> Seemed all one mutual cry. I never heard
> So musical a discord, such sweet thunder.

> (IV.i.111–17)

Theseus remarks that his hounds are 'bred out of the Spartan kind,' perhaps fearing that she misses her former existence. She never mentions the war, although earlier Theseus himself felt free to bring up the subject. Whether Hippolyta remembers the war, she does not say, although her memory takes her and us briefly to a moment prior to the war. Her interaction with Theseus apparently presumes erasure of her former identity and of most of her memories.

That Hippolyta no longer behaves or acts like an Amazon also underscores the suppression of her memory. One cannot detect in her a sense of bitterness or even resentment, although Shakespeare's other warrior queens, Margaret and Tamora, become very bitter and vow revenge after defeat. The reference to the war and subjugation of the Amazons suggests irreconcilable differences. Contrary to what we might expect, the play presents only slight signs of disagreement between Hippolyta and Theseus in their different perceptions of time and the moon, understanding of the nature of love, and response to 'Pyramus and Thisby.' Theseus, burning with desire, believes that time moves slowly and the moon, an old woman, keeps a young man from enjoying what is rightly his: 'but O, methinks, how slow/This old moon wanes! She lingers my desires,/Like to a stepdame or a dowager,/Long withering out a young man's revenue' (I.i.1–6). The old woman becomes an obstacle that he wishes he could remove. Hippolyta, however, comforting him, observes that four days will pass away quickly, 'then the moon, like to a silver bow/New-bent in heaven, shall behold the night/Of our solemnities' (I.i.7–11). For her, the moon becomes a dynamic, martial silver bow ready to shoot its arrow across the sky. The metaphor momentarily recovers a memory of the bow and arrow, with which the Amazons used to fight and which, according to the legend, required that they sear off their breasts, the very emblem of their identity.

Hippolyta's perspective again differs, however slightly, from Theseus in how she responds to the account, which was given offstage, of what befell Hermia, Lysander, Helena, and Demetrius in the woods. Theseus dismisses the events as being 'More strange than true,' arguing that the 'seething brains' and the 'shaping fantasies' of lovers, like the imagination of lunatics and poets, 'apprehend/More than cool reason ever comprehends' (V.i.2–6). Favoring reason over emotion, Theseus says that the imagination can play tricks on the mind. For a fearful mind, he adds, 'How easy is a bush supposed a bear' (V.i.22). Even if that is true, contends Hippolyta, the experience has a constructive outcome:

> But all the story of the night told over,
> And all their minds transfigured so together,
> More witnesseth than fancy's images
> And grows to something of great constancy;
> But howsoever, strange and admirable.

(V.i.23–7)

Quite taken with the strangeness of the events, she believes that the narrative and the night spent in the woods can generate a reality that excites wonder and binds the lovers together.

Finally, Theseus and Hippolyta also respond to 'Pyramus and Thisby' differently. Whereas Theseus seems tolerant, Hippolyta offers some of the sharpest criticism of the performance, as she says, 'This is the silliest stuff that ever I heard' (V.i.208). Theseus defends the mechanicals' effort, 'The best in this kind are but shadows; and the worst are no worse, if imagination amend them' (V.i.209–10); Hippolyta, however, does not back down: 'It must be your imagination then, and not theirs' (211–12). Having shown sympathy for the Athenian lovers, Hippolyta grows impatient with the parody into which the mechanicals' play actually unfolds. In her last statement in the play, she is amused at Thisby's excessive display of passion, apparently because Pyramus does not seem to deserve it: 'Methinks she should not use a long one [passion] for such a Pyramus. I hope she will be brief' (V.i.309–10). Despite these differences, nowhere can one find a serious conflict in Theseus and Hippolyta's relationship. The play suggests that love can effect the most outrageous or unexpected transformations. Thus, while seemingly on the verge of remembering and maintaining a perspective of her own, Hippolyta has been silenced, absorbed, and acclimated into a patriarchy, whose values oppose those of the Amazon matriarchy.

Hippolyta's memory alone proves unable to recover any substantial dimension of her identity as an Amazon. Yet to recover essential components of that identity, Shakespeare creates a substitute Amazon in Titania, without raising all the issues that led to the war between Athenians and Amazons. Through Titania, Shakespeare partially recovers what Athenian society has violently repressed, namely the same-sex partnership that some Renaissance writers found in the dual queenship of the Amazons.

When Titania and Oberon appear, Shakespeare immediately links them with Theseus and Hippolyta. As usual in this play, he does this through inversion: Titania, though aligning herself with Theseus, defies Oberon; Oberon, though siding with Hippolyta, attempts to control and subjugate his wife. The quarrel between Titania and Oberon focuses first on mutual accusations of sexual involvement with Theseus and Hippolyta. Titania accuses Oberon of having had an affair with Hippolyta, 'the bouncing Amazon,/Your buskined mistress and your warrior love' (II.i.70–1). This gives Oberon an opportunity to remind the audience of Theseus's troubled past and perhaps Titania's role in it:

> How canst thou thus, for shame, Titania,
> Glance at my credit with Hippolyta,
> Knowing I know thy love to Theseus?
> Didst not thou lead him through the glimmering night
> From Perigenia, whom he ravishèd?
> And make him with fair Aegles break his faith,
> With Ariadne, and Antiopa?

> (II.i.74–80)

Titania denies these charges as the 'forgeries of jealousy,' but these are reminders of Theseus's double identity as a ravisher and a cruel lover. This passage also recovers the identity of another Amazon, Antiopa, giving the play two Amazons: Theseus's current bride and a former lover, whom he forsook.[52] Momentarily, the play recovers fragments of both Theseus's and Hippolyta's identity that appear nowhere else in the text, as if Amazons should always come in pairs. If, as Painter, Batman, and Raleigh suggest, Amazons formed same-sex partnerships, one queen staying at home while the other waged war, where is the other queen, Hippolyta's partner, the belligerent one who battled the Athenians? Whether Antiopa or Menalipe was that partner the play does not say; if Hippolyta herself was her own double, her warlike side seems conspicuously absent, utterly repressed.

Soon, however, Titania partially takes on the role of Hippolyta's absent double. Modern productions frequently underscore the doubling by having the same actress play both parts, as it is clearly possible from the text itself; and by having the same actor play Theseus and Oberon. In his celebrated 1970 production, Peter

Brook employed doubling to connect the worlds of the fairies and of the mortals. The effect was electrifying as Clive Barnes writes in his review: 'At once the play takes on a new and personal dimension. The fairies take on a new humanity, and these human princelings, once so uninteresting, are now endowed with a different mystery.'[53] The text supports the connection. Indeed, an 'Amazon' ideology emerges from Titania's conflict with Oberon: aggression, a battle of the sexes, a community of women. Ostensibly, as Puck indicates, the marital disagreement involves the custody of an Indian boy, but he also suggests an underlying cultural conflict:

> For Oberon is passing fell and wrath,
> Because that she, as her attendant, hath
> A lovely boy, stolen from an Indian king;
> She never had so sweet a changeling.
> And jealous Oberon would have the child
> Knight of his train, to trace the forests wild.
> But she perforce withholds the lovèd boy,
> Crowns him with flowers, and makes him all her joy.

> (II.i.20–7)

The Amazon custom was to raise daughters but to return boys to the fathers or kill them. According to the myth, whenever the Amazons decided to retain a boy in their community, he was forced to cross-dress and do ordinary women's work. Oberon assumes that it is his prerogative to raise the boy and turn him into a knight 'to trace the forests wild,' while Titania wants, on the contrary, to crown the child with flowers and make him join her female retinue.

Titania treats Bottom in a similar way. Having acquired an ass's head, Bottom elicits the desire of the fairy queen, who exclaims at his sight: 'What angel wakes me from my flow'ry bed?' (III.i.116) and 'Thou art as wise as thou art beautiful' (134). Titania immediately attempts to take control over him, 'Thou shalt remain here, whether thou wilt or no' (III.i.138), and orders her attendants to fetch him jewels and sing 'while thou on pressèd flowers dost sleep' (144). She also envisions purging him of his 'mortal grossness' and transforming him into 'an airy spirit.' Later, Bottom appears in Titania's bower, as she directs him to sit down on her 'flow'ry bed' (IV.i.1). Like the

Amazons, Titania defies masculine rule and in her own way wants
to bring males under her control.

Titania describes herself as leader of an Amazonian sisterhood,
modeled upon Diana's, which includes female mortals. She
describes the Indian boy's mother:

> His mother was a vot'ress of my order,
> And in the spicèd Indian air, by night,
> Full often hath she gossiped by my side,
> And sat with me on Neptune's yellow sands,
> Marking th'embarkèd traders on the flood;
> When we have laughed to see the sails conceive
> And grow big-bellied with the wanton wind;
> Which she, with pretty and with swimming gait
> Following (her womb then rich with my young squire),
> Would imitate, and sail upon the land
> To fetch me trifles, and return again,
> As from a voyage, rich with merchandise.
> But she, being mortal, of that boy did die,
> And for her sake do I rear up her boy;
> And for her sake I will not part with him.

                                              (II.i.123–37)

Titania mentions only the boy's mother, not his father. Whether the
mother was an Amazon, Titania does not say, but this Indian
woman, considering the absence or anonymity of the boy's father,
presumably followed the Amazon custom of having an annual sexual tryst with neighboring tribesmen; hence the lack of involvement
of the father in the boy's life. The language of this speech also
evokes the same-sex partnership of the Amazons. The two women
sat side by side and gossiped on an Indian beach, observing acts of
conception. Like a ship, its sails impregnated by the wanton wind
and grown big-bellied, the votaress, also pregnant, would embark
upon voyages to fetch trifles for Titania. Through these images,
Titania aligns herself with a world that resembles that of the
Amazons.

A Midsummer Night's Dream splits the role of the Amazon into
parts that never interact with each other: the momentarily defiant
Titania and the submissive Hippolyta. Not surprisingly, both Titania
and Hippolyta eventually have to submit themselves to males: one

tricked by a patriarch; the other, overpowered by one. By transfer-
ring the belligerent Amazon to the Fairyland, Shakespeare suggests
that Theseus has thoroughly suppressed the Amazon identity and
has appropriated the female husband's double for the role of the
Greek 'wife.' Shakespeare thus adds another twist to the Amazon
myth: the cross-cultural interaction between Athenians and Amazons depends not only on the repression of part of the Amazon
nature but also on the reaffirmation of the Amazon double, which
the myth itself contains. In the process, however, the most repres-
sive gesture occurs: the suppression of the Amazons' same-sex partnership and form of government. However, Shakespeare may
have been dissatisfied with the suppression of the Amazons' same-
sex partnership in *A Midsummer Night's Dream*. Two decades
later, he and Fletcher revisit the myth to make this point more
explicit.

Instead of one Amazon, *Two Noble Kinsmen* has two, Hippolyta
and her sister Emilia, through whom the play recovers the contradictory, irreconcilable doubleness of Amazon identity. Hippolyta
and Emilia have not yet severed their cultural or emotional ties to
their culture, and the play recovers substantial elements of the
Amazon world. In *A Midsummer Night's Dream*, Hippolyta has
accepted her position as Theseus's wife, but in *Two Noble Kinsmen*,
Emilia questions Athenian gender boundaries. Deferral of her deci-
sion to choose between Palamon and Arcite opens a locus for the
representation of the Amazons' same-sex partnership and of Greek
male homoerotic bonding.

The configurations of desire in *Two Noble Kinsmen* have invited a
range of interpretation represented by Richard Hillman and Richard
Abrams.[54] Hillman argues that 'only by a highly selective and literal-
minded use of the evidence can Emilia be painted as a frank and
self-conscious lesbian.'[55] Abrams argues that 'in *Two Noble Kinsmen*,
however, strict differentiation of sexual kind breaks down, becoming as fluid as in King James's openly homosexual court.'[56] Both
critics, however, ignore the spectrum that human sexuality covers.
Eve Sedgwick has proposed the term 'homosocial desire' to describe
a continuum of 'social bonds between persons of the same sex.'[57]
She writes:

> At this particular historical moment, an intelligible continuum of
> aims, emotions, and valuations links lesbianism with the other
> forms of women's attention to women: the bond of mother and

daughter, for instance, the bond of sister and sister, women's friendship, 'networking,' and the active struggles of feminism.[58]

She adds that 'The continuum is crisscrossed with deep discontinuities – with much homophobia, with conflicts of race and class – but its intelligibility seems now a matter of simple common sense.'[59] Using Sedgwick's model, Winfried Schleiner examines the homosocial bonds between women in *Amadis de Gaul*, demonstrating that 'the continuum of female bonds, expressed in a language derived from the Neoplatonic conventions of the period, is broad and continuous and includes the unambiguously erotic.'[60] In *Two Noble Kinsmen*, Shakespeare and Fletcher address the homosocial dimension of Amazon society, something that Shakespeare only indirectly hinted at in *A Midsummer Night's Dream*.

In *Two Noble Kinsmen*, the Prologue indicates that 'Chaucer, of all admired, the story gives,' which serves as the foundation for Fletcher and Shakespeare's play. Although the play follows the source in its basic plot, it differs from *The Knight's Tale* in significant ways. Nowhere does Chaucer's Knight discuss the Amazon way of life, although he refers in passing to Theseus's victory over the 'regne of Femenye' (l. 866).[61] He also indicates that 'if it nere to long to heere,' he would tell 'How wonnen was the regne of Femenye/By Theseus and by his chivalrye,' 'And of the grete bataille for the nones/Bitwixen Athenes and Amazones' (ll. 875–80). With this apology, the Knight gets the past out of the way, so that he can discuss Palamon and Arcite's pursuit of Emilie. References to either Ypolita's or Emilie's life as an Amazon are conspicuously absent, whereas Shakespeare and Fletcher emphasize them. Thus, when a 'compaignye of ladyes,' dressed in black, interrupts Theseus's progress, they do not appeal to Ypolita or Emilie to intercede in their behalf; rather, like Hermia in *A Midsummer Night's Dream*, they ignore the Amazons and address Theseus directly. Having been thrown in jail, Palamon and Arcite lament their fates, but not in the language of sexual inversion that, as we will see, their counterparts in *The Two Noble Kinsmen* use. The Knight seems aware of the lifelong friendship between Perotheus and Theseus; but as he indicates, this is not the place to discuss it:

> For in this world he [Perotheus] loved no man so,
> And he loved hym als tendrely agayn.
> So wel they lovede, as olde bookes sayn,

That whan that oon was deed, soothly to telle,
His felawe wente and soughte hym doun in helle, –
But of that storie list me nat to write.

(ll. 1196–201)

The Knight makes no mention of Emilie's friend Flavina; nor do Ypolita and Emilie, unlike Fletcher and Shakespeare's characters, discuss the Amazons' same-sex partnerships.

In a striking departure from Chaucer and *A Midsummer Night's Dream*, *Two Noble Kinsmen* almost immediately attempts to reconstruct the Amazon world in both its pseudo-historical and affective dimensions, raising questions of whether the two Amazons are still warriors or whether they have abandoned their way of life. The three widowed queens, interrupting the wedding procession of Theseus and Hippolyta, remind everyone of the former power of the Amazons. The three queens ask Theseus, Hippolyta, and Emilia to intervene and avenge their husbands' death. Unlike Hermia, the queens recognize Hippolyta's military reputation and emotional hold over Theseus. The Second Queen addresses and describes Hippolyta:

> Honoured Hippolyta,
> Most dreaded Amazonian, that hast slain
> The scythe-tusked boar; that with thy arm, as strong
> As it is white, was near to make the male
> To thy sex captive, but that this thy lord,
> Born to uphold creation in that honour
> First nature styled it in, shrunk thee into
> The bound thou wast o'erflowing, at once subduing
> Thy force and thy affection.

(I.i. 77–85)[62]

The Second Queen refers to Hippolyta as a 'soldieress' and mentions two of her principal accomplishments: she killed the scythe-tusked boar and almost enslaved all males. The queen also suggests that Hippolyta now has more power over Theseus than ever before: he will obey her word. On the one hand, the queen accepts the submissive position of women; after all Theseus, as she indicates, was born to uphold the natural order. On the other, she knows that Hippolyta has exceeded all women in her bravery and strength. Likewise, the Third Queen finds a sympathetic response from Emilia. Emilia considers herself a champion of women's causes, 'What woman I may stead [help] that is distressed/Does bind me to her' (I.i.36–7). Emilia, feeling a special bond to all women, refers to the Third Queen as 'a natural sister of our sex' (I.i.125).

Neither Hippolyta nor Emilia can take up arms to defend these women's causes; instead, they must fall on their knees and entreat Theseus to act. Hippolyta offers to abstain from the nuptial bed, asking Theseus to postpone the completion of the ceremony and consummation of their marriage in order to undertake the three queens' cause: 'Prorogue this business we are going about, and hang/Your shield afore your heart, about that neck/Which is my fee, and which I freely lend/To do these poor queens service' (I.i.196–9). Emilia threatens not to take a husband, unless Theseus acts (I.i.200–6). Their pleas have the intended effect on Theseus, who instructs Pirithous to 'Lead on the bride' and proceed with the wedding celebrations while he goes to war (I.i.207–9). Although their reputation as warriors still lives, Hippolyta and Emilia have, however, completely renounced their military careers and subjected themselves to the power of Theseus.

Further, the appearance of the three queens asking for help triggers a recollection of Hippolyta and Emilia's Amazon past, something that neither Chaucer in *Knight's Tale* nor Shakespeare in the earlier comedy permits. Hippolyta and Emilia remember the same-sex solidarity necessary for successful military exploits. Hippolyta points out to Emilia:

> We have been soldiers, and we cannot weep
> When our friends don their helms, or put to sea,
> Or tell of babes broached on the lance, or women
> That have sod their infants in – and after ate them –
> The brine they wept at killing 'em.
>
> (I.iii.18–22)

They cannot weep when their friends go to war or when women repress their maternal instincts and commit the atrocities of war, mutilating, killing, and eating their children. Emilia remembers her own special relationship with her friend Flavina: 'I was acquainted/Once with a time when I enjoyed a playfellow;/ You were at wars'

(I.iii.49–51). She and Flavina have experienced 'things innocent,' a strong bond of love and desire:

> But I
> And she I sigh and spoke of were things innocent,
> Loved for we did, and like the elements
> That know not what nor why, yet do effect
> Rare issues by their operance, our souls
> Did so to one another; what she liked
> Was then of me approved, what not, condemned.

(I.iii.59–65)

Emilia concludes that 'the true love 'tween maid and maid' may be stronger than the love for the opposite sex ('sex dividual') (I.iii.81–2). Thus, Shakespeare and Fletcher endow Emilia and Hippolyta with memory in order not only to recover a warrior past but also the comradeship and same-sex partnership of a warrior society.

Further, Emilia and Hippolyta become commentators on Greek society, seeing in Pirithous and Theseus an affirmation of same-sex bonds. Eager to understand, accept, and encourage such bonds, they momentarily project their now repressed same-sex comradeship on the relationship between Pirithous and Theseus. Observing Pirithous languish in the absence of Theseus, Emilia and Hippolyta discuss the significance of their friendship, reminding themselves of what they felt for their fellow warriors. Emilia points out: 'How his longing/Follows his friend' (I.iii.26–7). Hippolyta adds a comment on the special friendship between Pirithous and Theseus: 'Their knot of love,/ Tied, weaved, entangled, with so true, so long,/And with a finger of so deep a cunning,/May be outworn, never undone' (I.iii.41–4). Through these positive comments, the Amazons thus reveal that before the conquest their society depended on homosocial bonds.

Hippolyta, having perhaps a more pragmatic viewpoint, suggests that Emilia should abandon personal and cultural beliefs: 'You're out of breath,/And this high-speeded pace is but to say/That you shall never – like the maid Flavina – /Love any that's called man' (I.iii.82–5). When Emilia reaffirms her determination to remain single, 'I am sure I shall not [marry]' (I.iii.86), Hippolyta again insists marriage must prevail over same-sex friendship, 'I will now in and kneel, with great assurance/That we, more than his Pirithous, possess/The high throne in his heart' (I.iii.95–7). But Emilia refuses to give in, 'I am not/Against your faith, yet I continue mine' (I.iii.98–100). Hippolyta seems eager to believe that marriage bonds will supersede same-sex relationships, but Emilia remains unconvinced, perhaps realizing that nothing can replace her love for Flavina.

Retaining an independent perspective, Emilia defers choosing between the two kinsmen. Here deferral becomes a metaphor for her own sexual indeterminacy and rejection of marriage. She remains the outsider, puzzled by a culture that turns her into a trophy in a deadly chivalric exercise. When talking to a woman in the garden outside the prison where Palamon and Arcite are being held, she concludes that 'Men are mad things' (II.ii.125). In Act III, scene vi, Emilia, like Hippolyta, takes pity on the two kinsmen, and asks Theseus to banish them (215); but Theseus does not accept this resolution: 'Can these two live,/And have the agony of love about 'em,/And not kill one another?' (219–21). Emilia still does not understand, 'Shall anything that loves me perish for me?' (III.vi.242), a veiled reference to the dead Flavina.

Deferral acquires further homoerotic association in Act IV, which centers on Emilia's dilemma and ultimate refusal to choose one of two knights. Her words reveal that she is thinking of homoerotic bonds, rather than marriage, which one of the lovers is demanding: 'Just such another wanton Ganymede/Set Jove afire with, and enforced the god/Snatch up the goodly boy and set him by him,/A shining constellation' (IV.ii.15–18). She is here concerned about how the lovers' weeping mothers will react (IV.ii.4; 63). Emilia's reference to Diana in IV.ii.58 and her prayer at Diana's altar in Act V, scene i suggest that she would gladly remain Diana's votarist (V.i.148–54). Emilia is reluctant to leave her worship and convictions. In Act V, scene iii, away from the scene of the combat, she imagines – to her horror – that the two friends are mutilating each other's body for her sake; but she concludes: 'It is much better/I am not there – O, better never born/Than minister to such harm' (V.iii.64–6). To the end of the play, Emilia only reluctantly participates in the rivalry between Palamon and Arcite. She believes that they love each other much more than they could possibly love her.

Metaphors of sexual inversion and references to same-sex partnerships provide a sounding board for Emilia's reluctance in entering marriage. In fact, even the Thebans Palamon and Arcite, trapped in their roles as knights who must defend the tyrant Creon with whose policies they do not agree, speak a language of same-sex partnership. When Theseus defeats and captures them, Arcite and Palamon see the prison as a means of seclusion from the temptations of life, where they will remain 'unmarried' (II.ii.29): 'We shall know nothing here but one another' (II.ii.41). The prison will be their 'holy sanctuary' (II.ii.71). They envision, as Arcite proposes, a marriage between the two of them: 'We are one another's wife, ever begetting/New births of love' (II.ii.80–1). In his edition of the play, Eugene Waith assumes that these words are merely metaphorical and that the relationship described is Platonic (pp. 50–6). Likewise, as Lois Potter reports, the 1988 Reitaku University production of *The Two Noble Kinsmen* made 'no suggestion of same-sex love, either between Palamon and Arcite or in connection with Emilia (the lines that might have supported it having in any case been cut),' although the producers brought Chaucer, Shakespeare, and Fletcher on stage to comment on the play.[63] As Potter indicates, 'when Shakespeare and Fletcher discussed the role of Pirithous, Shakespeare did comment (in the Japanese text), 'I think he's *almost* in love with Theseus. But he's a very loyal friend ... like you.'[64] On the other hand, the all-male production by the Cherub Company at the 1979 Edinburgh International Festival underscored the homoerotic nature of various relationships in the play.[65]

Whether or not modern editors and producers deny this homoerotic dimension, the language of the vows of affection exchanged between Palamon and Arcite in fact resembles King James's own private correspondence with his favorite the Duke of Buckingham a few years later:

> My only sweet and dear child,
> ... And yet I cannot content myself without sending you this present, praying God that I may have a joyful and comfortable meeting with you and that we may make at this Christmas a new marriage ever to be kept hereafter; for, God so love me, as I desire only to live in this world for your sake, and that I had rather live banished in any part of the earth with you than live a sorrowful widow's life without you. And so God bless you, my sweet child and wife, and grant that ye may ever be a comfort to your dear dad and husband.[66]

As David M. Bergeron observes, 'Marital terms pervade the letter, implying certainly that James saw his relationship to Buckingham as a marriage; at the same time, he looked upon the favorite as a son, his only "sweet and dear child".'[67] Bergeron adds, 'Buckingham had become James's family, and everything that remained dear to him.'[68] Unlike Palamon and Arcite, James and Buckingham are not, of course, fighting over the same woman, but the language of their correspondence employs the bonds of marriage as a metaphor for same-sex desire.

So do Palamon and Arcite. If they were at liberty, adds Arcite, 'A wife might part us lawfully, or business;/Quarrels consume us' (II.ii.89–90). And Palamon agrees, 'Is there record of any two that loved/Better than we do, Arcite' (II.ii.112–13). But, of course, they cannot remain isolated from their social obligations, as King James and Buckingham could not; and before long they are engaged in deadly combat for the hand of Emilia, challenging each other about who first took 'possession' of her. In their roles as males, they must be both soldiers and husbands.

Paralleling Emilia's deferral, Palamon and Arcite seem reluctant to fight each other for the same woman and, therefore, jeopardize friendship and family relations. Although they cannot altogether trust each other in matters of love, they briefly agree to a truce: 'By all the honesty and honour in you,/No mention of this woman; 'twill disturb us' (III.iii.14–15). Throughout the play, the two friends constantly find excuses to postpone the ultimate and decisive battle for the hand of Emilia. Arcite nurses Palamon back to health after Palamon escapes from prison: 'Your person I am friends with,/And I could wish I had not said I loved her,/Though I had died; but loving such a lady,/And justifying my love, I must not fly from't' (III.vi.38–42). Their identities seem to be defined as soldiers first, knights who must fight for the love of a lady. They are uncomfortable yet cannot avoid fighting each other. Both find more excuses not to fight, exchanging courtesies, offering weapons to each other; and finally when they run out of excuses for the delay, 'Is there aught else to say?' asks Arcite (III.vi.93).

When the combat takes place in Act V, Arcite summarizes the dilemma that he is experiencing, once again using the language of sexual inversion with which the play abounds:

> I am in labour
> To push your name, your ancient love, our kindred,
> Out of my memory, and i'th' selfsame place
> To seat something I would confound.
>
> (V.i.25–8)

When Arcite wins the combat by injuring Palamon, he seems confused about his gains and losses, 'Emily,/To buy you I have lost what's dearest to me/Save what is bought, and yet I purchase cheaply,/As I do rate your value' (V.iii.111–14). Theseus praises Palamon, saying that the gods would have the knight die a bachelor, 'lest his race/Should show i'th' world too godlike' (V.iii.117–18). Emilia herself questions the outcome of events:

> Is this winning?
> O all you heavenly powers, where is your mercy?
> But that your wills have said it must be so,
> And charge me live to comfort this unfriended,
> This miserable prince, that cuts away
> A life more worthy from him than all women,
> I should and would die too.
>
> (V.iv.138–44)

Shortly thereafter, Pirithous makes the absurdity of the resolution apparent when he reports that Arcite was thrown off his horse and killed but that Palamon, though wounded, has survived the combat and will have Emilia by default.

Other metaphors of sexual inversion abound, combining Amazonian inversion and Greek homoeroticism. Palamon, for example, imagines himself as a female and Emilia as a male who would ravish him: 'Were I at liberty, I would do things/Of such a virtuous greatness that this lady,/This blushing virgin, should take manhood to her/And seek to ravish me' (II.ii.258–61). Theseus fantasizes about switching places with a woman, transforming Arcite from servant to master of his heart, as he instructs Emilia: 'Sister, beshrew my heart, you have a servant/ That, if I were a woman, would be master' (II.v.62–3). In a most amusing report, the Messenger compares the biceps of the freckle-faced knight to the rising belly of a pregnant woman:

> His arms are brawny,
> Lined with strong sinews – to the shoulder-piece
> Gently they swell, like women new-conceived,
> Which speaks him prone to labour, never fainting
> Under the weight of arms.
>
> (IV.ii.126–30)

These examples reinforce a pattern of using homoerotic desire to define marital bonds.

Both the Greek and Amazonian societies wrestle with a conflict that transcends the individuals involved. The play presents desire as a force beyond one's control that pulls the individual toward marital union. Arcite wins the battle but loses his life; Palamon loses the battle but gains the hand of Emilia. Palamon, the ultimate victor in the struggle with his cousin Arcite for the hand of the Amazon Emilia, summarizes the paradox of desire, something that ultimately cannot fulfill them: 'O cousin,/That we should things desire which do cost us/The loss of our desire' (V.iv.108–11). In gaining Emilia, Palamon has lost the dearest thing in his life.

At first glance, the marriage of Theseus and Hippolyta might suggest that the Greeks have finally absorbed the Amazons into their culture, including the Amazons' acceptance of male supremacy. The consummation of the marriage is, however, deferred as three queens appeal to Theseus to rescue the dead bodies of their husbands from the tyrant Creon of Thebes, who refuses to grant permission to bury them. Instead of playing husband to Hippolyta, Theseus must be the soldier. Instead of playing the wife to Theseus, Hippolyta interacts with Emilia in a debate about female sexuality. Deferral becomes a metaphor for the characters' sexual indeterminacy and true desire.

Even the absurd nature of the Jailor's Daughter's love for Palamon underscores that the characters end up with a substitute, rather than what they truly desire.[69] The Jailor's Daughter loves Palamon but her social status makes the relationship impossible: 'To marry him is hopeless,/To be his whore is witless' (II.iv.4–5). She recognizes how absurd her love is: 'Then I loved him,/Extremely loved him, infinitely loved him,/And yet he had a cousin, fair as he too' (II.iv.14–16). She has every reason to love Arcite just as well but does not. Later she helps Palamon escape, hoping that he will 'use' her, or she will proclaim him 'no man' to his face (II.vi.31). She tries to nurse him to life and provides him with files to remove his shackles; but Arcite usurps her place: in Act III, scene iii, he appears with 'food and files' (2) before she does. Once again the two friends seal a self-sufficient bond that excludes the Jailor's Daughter. But the absurdity of her desire becomes even more apparent when the doctor prescribes the cure for her madness: the Wooer must impersonate Palamon. He will sing for her, embrace her, and even go to bed with her. Like the other characters, the Jailor's Daughter thus ends up with a substitute for Palamon, not what she truly desires.

In both plays marriage can lead to irrational behavior and suffering. In *A Midsummer Night's Dream*, Hippolyta's nonperformative presence subsumes a radical cultural difference that is suppressed by other characters' performance: the lovers' intense pursuits of one another; Hermia's defiance of her father; Titania's subversion of Oberon's authority; Theseus's patriarchal role; and even the mechanicals' mock performance of a romantic tragedy. In *Two Noble Kinsmen*, both Hippolyta and Emilia also offer a nonperformative presence, but their Amazonian cultural values are not altogether suppressed, although Theseus's military prowess and Greek homosocial bonding compete and attempt to replace the Amazons' same-sex partnerships. The knights' reluctance to fight for her and reaffirmation of same-sex bonding draw attention to Emilia's own reluctance and her remembrance of the Amazon past. Emilia remembers, demurs, defers: in doing so, she resists assimilation into Athenian society. The vocal but reluctant rivalry between Palamon and Arcite and Emilia's questioning of Athenian cultural practices permit the recovery of an inverted culture. As Bruce Smith points out, 'On the issue of male bonding versus marriage Shakespeare finished his career, not with one of the reconciliations that are the common theme of his other later plays, but with a fresh recognition of the impasse between the two.'[70] In doing so, Shakespeare transforms the tradition of dramatic representation by recovering the same-sex bonding that some of his sources associated with the Amazons' dual queenship system.

2

Joan of Arc, Margaret of Anjou, and the Instability of Gender

You should be women,
And yet your beards forbid me to interpret
That you are so.

Banquo (*Macbeth*, I.iii.45–7)

Saint Paul writes to the Galatians of a world where all difference has been erased: 'For as many of you as have been baptized into Christ have put on Christ. There is neither Jew nor Greek, there is neither bond nor free, there is neither male nor female: for ye are all one in Christ Jesus' (Gal. 3.27–8). As we will see below, Paul provides the theological justification for the transvestism of such religious figures as Joan of Arc. But if religion or some force erases all differences, what happens to the distinctions that cultures typically make? In the *Henry VI* trilogy, Shakespeare confronts this troubling question in his exploration of the clash between English and French medieval societies. As in *A Midsummer Night's Dream* and *The Two Noble Kinsmen*, Shakespeare again focuses on the violation of gender boundaries between male and female as a metaphor for cross-cultural differentiation, but in the history plays French gender instability becomes an urgent threat to English national and cultural identity.

This chapter focuses on the gender instability that two French female warriors, Joan of Arc and Margaret of Anjou, bring about. A question emerges about how Shakespeare distinguishes French from English characters in the *Henry VI* plays. In these plays, he does not, for example, underscore the specific Frenchness of their language as he does in part for the purposes of humor in *Henry V*. This later play depicts Pistol's amusing attempt in Act IV, scene iv, to talk to a French soldier who speaks no English; Katherine's French lesson in Act III, scene iv; and her effort to communicate in broken English with Henry V in Act V, scene ii. When she confesses, 'I cannot speak your England,' her future husband reassures her: 'O fair Katherine, if you will love me soundly with your French heart, I will be glad to hear you confess it brokenly with your English tongue' (V.ii.104–7). The French King, Charles VI, however, speaks fluent English throughout; whereas the boastful, cowardly Dauphin mixes English with French phrases and expletives such as 'O Dieu vivant!' (III.v.5) and 'Ça, ha!' (III.vii.12). In the *Henry VI* plays, Shakespeare does not emphasize such linguistic differences; rather, he connects the Frenchness of Joan of Arc, the French courtiers, and Margaret to a specific gender anomaly: the French female characters usurp what the Englishmen interpret as proper masculine gender roles, and thus create a profound sense of gender instability that poses a threat to the English themselves.

Both Joan and Margaret emerge from a cultural matrix similar to that of the Amazons, but unlike Hippolyta and Emilia, they offer strong performative presences and threaten to deploy by military means an alien cultural system.[1] In the *Henry VI* trilogy, English culture confronts a culture from which it should differ and yet to which it seems intimately connected and upon which it depends. French culture, no less alien and fantastical than the Amazon kingdom, emanates from the two women warriors, Joan of Arc and Margaret of Anjou. Unstable and fraught with inner disturbances, this fantastical world, where gender exchanges are deployed, subverts English ideological certainty.

To demonstrate how these women provide the foundation for the cross-cultural contrast and become conduits to guide the action to the frontiers of culture, I will discuss first Joan of Arc and then Margaret of Anjou both as historical figures and then as characters in Shakespeare's drama. However, I should underscore that Shakespeare does not altogether observe this distinction between history and fiction. Perhaps, like Edmund Spenser, Shakespeare realized that the method of the 'poet historical' must perforce differ from that of the historiographer:

For an Historiographer discourseth of affayres orderly as they were donne, accounting as well the times as the actions, but a Poet thrusteth into the middest, even where it most concerneth him, and there recoursing to the thinges forepaste, and divining of things to come, maketh a pleasing Analysis of all.[2]

Shakespeare stages the collapse of the real and the imaginary, what Michel de Certeau calls 'practice' and 'text.'[3] As Graham Holderness describes the phenomenon, Shakespeare's English chronicle plays, only in a most limited sense, can be accepted as '*historical evidence*': 'as the record of an Elizabethan intellectual's view of his own society, mediated through fictional reconstructions of that society's past.'[4] The plays become 'a loose and confused mixture of historically authenticated facts and imaginatively-invented fictions.'[5] But I believe that that is precisely Shakespeare's point.

To create this effect, Shakespeare suggests that the cross-cultural encounter in the *Henry VI* plays relies upon the erasure of the difference between what Sidney called 'reporting' and 'representing'; as a result, it subverts the cultural map not only of France but also of England. In *1 Henry VI*, the English characters often seem disoriented: the ground upon which they stand constantly shifts, wiping out customary markers and erecting unrecognizable ones. Through cross-cultural representation, the other two plays, grounding Margaret of Anjou in a similarly fantastical world, reconstruct alien gender systems.

The historic Joan of Arc belongs to a long tradition, dating back to the early Christians, of transvestite female saints of the *Golden Legend*.[6] The cults of female transvestism arose from a monastic culture, and were based on the passage from Galatians already cited.[7] John Anson suggests that the phrase, 'putting on Christ,' was construed as a justification for female saints to take on the male or androgynous form of Jesus.[8] Early Christian groups, such as the Naassenes, rejected heterosexual intercourse; sought 'imperishable pleasure,' which had a homosexual dimension; and practiced baptismal rites to recover 'the journey of the soul to the bliss of bisexual completeness' and 'the original perfection of the Male.'[9] The Naassenes found the authority for a bisexual union in the words of Jesus in the apocryphal *Gospel of Thomas*: 'See, I will draw her [Mary Magdalene] so as to make her male so that she also may become a living spirit like you males. For every woman who has become male will enter the Kingdom of heaven' (118).[10] Another early sect, the Valentinians, believed in a bisexual Adam as a type of Christ, 'with whom the male seed remained to produce the angels while the female was withdrawn to form Eve and the race of the elect'; the Valentinians thought that the Savior would unite 'the female chosen who made up the Church with the male angels from whom they had originally emanated. "Therefore," explains

Clement [of Alexandria], "the woman is said to be changed into a man, and the church here on earth into angels." [11] These bisexual and androgynous cosmogonies apparently believed that the 'transvestite disguise is assumed as a kind of impenetrable panoply for preserving inviolate an immaculate virginity for Christ.' [12]

Famous transvestite saints include Thecla, Pelagia, Marina, Athanasia of Antioch, and the bearded female saints, Uncumber, Galla, and Paula of Avila. [13] St Pelagia, after a long pilgrimage, lived as a man known as Pelagius on Mount Olivet; another St Margarita-Pelagius escaped from the altar in male attire and joined a monastery as Pelagius; Marina lived as a monk by the name of Marinus, who was accused of seducing and impregnating a girl but 'true to the code of the transvestite saints, suffered ostracism from the monastery rather than admit to her true sex'; Athanasia-Athanasius of Antioch lived for many years as a transvestite monk. [14] The bearded female saints offer a fascinating example of transvestism. St Uncumber or Wilgefortis decided to remain a virgin and devote herself to Christianity, but her non-Christian father and ruler of Portugal decided otherwise. When ordered to marry, she protested to no avail: 'her prayer was answered by the sudden growth of a long drooping mustache and a silky curling beard.' [15] Her father ordered her to cover her face with a veil and proceed with the wedding plans. When the bridegroom lifted her veil, however, he refused to marry her and the ruler of Portugal had her crucified. Vern L. Bullough notes that 'in England Uncumber became the patron saint of married women who wanted to rid themselves of their husbands.' [16] The abundance of transvestite female saints contrasts with the scarcity of male transvestite saints, suggesting perhaps that, according to early beliefs, 'Female cross-dressers were tolerated and even encouraged, since they were striving to become more malelike and therefore better persons.' [17] Obviously, in Shakespeare's representation of Joan of Arc, no such thing occurs.

Some scholars argue that Joan's adamant desire to cross-dress in obedience to the voices that spoke to her may suggest a popular survival of gnostic cults and heresies in France. [18] The ecclesiastical authorities certainly found her male attire most disturbing. Her judges questioned her repeatedly in order to discover why she had received the sacraments in her masculine attire. Transcripts of the trial document the judges' obsession with her male disguise: 'wholly forgetful of womanly honesty, and having thrown off the bonds of shame, careless of all the modesty of womankind, she wore with an astonishing and monstrous brazenness, immodest garments belonging to the male sex.'[19] Under cross examination, Joan revealed that her father, anticipating Joan's career as a cross-dressed warrior, often had a dream about her going off with men-at-arms. Her father obviously did not approve of this. According to Joan's mother, he often wished his daughter were dead.

Joan revealed also that voices told her to go to Robert, captain of Vaucouleurs, whom she required 'to have a male costume made for her, with arms to match; which he did, reluctantly, and with great repugnance, finally consenting to her demand.'[20] The report continues:

> When these garments and these arms were made, fitted and completed, the said Jeanne put off and entirely abandoned woman's clothes; with her hair cropped short and round like a young fop's, she wore shirt, breeches, doublet, with hose joined together and fastened to the said doublet by 20 points, long leggings laced on the outside, a short mantle reaching to the knees, or thereabouts, a close-cut cap, tight-fitting boots and buskins, long spurs, sword, dagger, breastplate, lance and other arms in the style of a man-at-arms, with which she performed actions of war and affirmed that she was fulfilling the commands of God as they had been revealed to her.[21]

Accompanied by a knight, a squire, and four servants, she left Vaucouleurs and began her martial career. Furthermore, the court argued, Joan disobeyed ecclesiastical decrees by wearing 'short, tight, and dissolute male habits,' including 'rich and sumptuous habits, precious stuffs and cloth of gold and furs,' 'short tunics,' 'tabards and garments open at the sides,' and when she was captured, 'she was wearing a loose cloak of cloth of gold, a cap on her head and her hair cropped round in man's style.'[22] She took communion, wearing male attire; later, when admonished by her judges to put on women's dress and take communion, 'She would not agree, and preferred not to take Communion and the holy offices, rather than abandon this dress.'[23]

Article LIII of accusations underscores the political dimension of Joan's transvestism:

> The said Jeanne, against the bidding of God and His Saints, proudly and presumptuously assumed domination over men;

she appointed herself leader and captain of an army which rose at times to the number of 16,000 men, in which there were princes, barons, and other nobles, all of whom she made fight under herself as principal captain.[24]

The next article suggests that she refused 'to have the company or care of womenfolk,' always preferring the company of men. The judges, supported by the leading theological and ecclesiastical authorities, concluded that Joan was 'schismatic,' 'apostate,' and deviant from the faith. After her abjuration, which included violation of the dress code for women of her rank and bearing of arms, Joan was sentenced to perpetual imprisonment. She was told 'to put off her male costume and take woman's dress,' which she did, and her hair, 'which had hitherto been cut short round the ears,' was 'shaved off and removed.'[25] Four days later, the judges summoned her once more for having resumed 'a man's dress, a short mantle, a hood, a doublet and other garments used by men.'[26] This time her explanation was startling: 'she answered that she had taken it [men's attire] of her own will, under no compulsion, as she preferred man's to woman's dress.'[27] She argued that it was 'more lawful and convenient' to wear men's dress 'since she was among men.'[28] The unforgiving judges deemed her unrepentant and turned her over to the secular authorities to be burnt at the stake.

King Henry VI, in a letter written two years after Joan's execution, refers to her tumultuous career as a warrior and to her transvestism as 'a thing abominable to God.'[29] The judges, he adds, found her 'superstitious, a witch, idolatrous, a caller up of demons, blasphemous towards God and His saints, schismatic and greatly erring in the faith of Jesus Christ.'[30] Like King Henry VI, the English chronicle writers that Shakespeare consulted seem very much aware of Joan of Arc's transvestism and martial career. Edward Hall, in *The Union of the Two Noble and Illustre Famelies of Lancastre and Yorke* (1548), suggests, however, that Joan suffered from gender confusion. Hall writes that a female of twenty years of age came to the Dauphin.[31] She was dressed 'in mans apparell,' and so bold 'that she would course horses and ride them to water, and do thynges, that other yong maidens, bothe abhorred & wer ashamed to do.'[32] Later he refers to her as 'This wytch or manly woman,' equating witch and mannish woman as Shakespeare does in *Macbeth*, where Banquo describes the Weird Sisters in comparable terms: 'You should be women,/ And yet your beards forbid me to interpret/ That you are so' (I.iii.45–7).[33]

Joan's cross-dressing gave rise to other assumptions about her character. Holinshed writes that, after her capture, Joan debased herself 'to confesse hir selfe a strumpet, and (unmaried as she was) to be with child.'[34] She had 'conversation with wicked spirits' and the Dauphin also profaned his 'sacred estate, as dealing in divelish practises with misbeleevers and witches.' The chronicle writers discredit Joan's claim that she was an emissary from God. Edward Hall writes that the French glorified Joan of Arc as 'the maide of GOD,' and that they believed that 'by her Orleaunce was vitailed: by her, kyng Charles was sacred at Reynes, and that by her, the Englishmen wer often tymes put backe and overthrowen'; he concludes, however, that she was not sent by God but rather she was 'an enchanteresse, an orgayne of the devill, sent from Sathan, to blind the people and bryng them in unbelife.'[35] Neither Hall nor Holinshed could understand why the French would allow a woman to deceive them, let alone one who seemed to be a strumpet, an enchantress, and an agent of the devil.

From the English perspective, Joan defied patriarchal expectations in attire, choice of career, and behavior. Hall notes that such victories brought shame and disgrace to the French nation:

> What blotte is this to the Frenche nacion: What more rebuke can be imputed to a renoumed region, then to affirme, write & confesse, that all notable victories, and honorable conquestes, which neither the kyng with his power, nor the nobilitie with their valiauntnesse, nor the counsaill with their wit, not the commonaltie with their strenght, could compasse or obtain, were gotten and achived by a shepherdes daughter, a chamberlein in an hostrie, and a beggers brat: whiche blindying the wittes of the French nacion, by revelacions, dreames & phantasticall visions, made them beleve thynges not to be supposed, and to geve faithe to thynges impossible.[36]

Hall suggests that Joan's career transformed and came to represent French culture. This assessment clearly affected Shakespeare's perception of Joan and French culture. As Richard F. Hardin points out, 'Like many characters of historical fiction, Joan of Arc in Shakespeare's *First Part of Henry the Sixth* is largely a creation of other texts, and some would have the dramatist (perhaps in his late twenties) powerless to consolidate her amid the passions and contradictions that beset these texts.'[37] By the time Shakespeare decided to write a play focusing on Joan of Arc, her image had already been filtered through several layers of representation. In the historic phenomenon of Joan's transvestism and military career, Shakespeare found a gender reconfiguration and a cultural remapping that epitomized the English–French cultural confrontation and dynastic disputes.

Shakespeare's Joan of Arc appears in a play, *1 Henry VI*, which from a gender perspective stands out for the conspicuous absence of English women. No English woman appears in *1 Henry VI*. Of the six scenes set in England, one could logically expect to find English women in at least three: Act I, scene i, and Act V, scenes i and v. The first scene, set at Westminster Abbey, opens with the funeral procession of Henry V. Unlike *Richard III*, a play that opens with Lady Anne leading the funeral of her father-in-law Henry VI, *1 Henry VI* makes no mention of a woman in the cortege, although we might expect to find at least Henry's widow, Catherine of Valois, among the mourners. Even more puzzling, as the noblemen lament the death of Henry V, Bedford suggests that mourning is the duty of women; the masculine ideal requires that men die in combat, and 'none but women [be] left to wail the dead' (I.i.51). If women are so central to the mourning and funeral practices of the English, where are they? Instead of women, we find English males gathered around the coffin, taking the place of wailing widows, mothers, and daughters in their duty as mourners. Likewise, the two scenes set in the royal palace in London, Act V, scenes i and v, present no English women. No other play, except perhaps for *Timon of Athens*, where women appear in two scenes and only briefly, shows a society so devoid of females.[38]

The case of the missing English women corresponds to Phyllis Rackin's compelling argument about Shakespeare's chronicle plays. Rackin contends that these plays focus on males and that women play roles that are incidental to a historical – hence, predominantly masculine – agenda or project: 'Aliens in the masculine world of history, women can threaten or validate the men's historical projects, but they can never take the center of history's stage or become the subjects of its stories.'[39] Furthermore, she adds, 'The women who do appear are typically defined as opponents and subverters of the historical and historiographic enterprise, in short, as antihistorians.'[40] Yet I do not believe that this accounts for the complete absence of English women in *1 Henry VI* and the presence of English women in the other two parts of *Henry VI* and, of course, in all other chronicle plays. Instead, I contend that this becomes only the first sign of a strange redrawing of the gender map.

The process of reconfiguration and realignment of the cultural coordinates begins with the staging of Henry V's funeral in *1 Henry VI*. Gestures of displacement and replacement intertwine with acts of substitution and representation. The funeral procession displaces Henry V's role to the realm of memory and signals numerous substitutions. On the English side, ambitious and bickering factions assume control in the name of Henry VI, the child-king; on the French side, Joan takes charge, effecting an almost symmetrical, though inverted, substitution of Henry V's power: her heroic exploits replace the deeds of Henry V and offer the French an opportunity to counter Henry V's own assault upon France and to shake off the English yoke. Joan expresses an opportunistic, perhaps cynical, view of temporal accomplishments: 'Glory is like a circle in the water,/ Which never ceaseth to enlarge itself/Till by broad spreading it disperse to naught' (I.ii.133–5). She concludes, 'With Henry's death the English circle ends' (135) and the French one begins. Indeed, she seems to be right: the French crown a new king in Rheims, and one by one regain control over their cities.

A series of symbolic substitutions follows, seemingly underscoring the absence of human causality. If, as Gloucester states, Henry V, brandishing his sword, made history by spreading his arms 'wider than a dragon's wings' (I.i.11), his funeral signals the death of history because no one can truly take his place. Exeter believes that only with the help of supernatural forces and 'magic verses' could 'subtile-witted French/ Conjurers and sorcerers' 'have contrived his end' (I.i.25–7). Human agents operating as representatives of unknown forces brought about the young king's death. Likewise, the French pronounce the death of history. Joan of Arc, who leads them to victory, claims to be an agent of a divine force: 'God's mother deignèd to appear to me/ And in a vision full of majesty/ Willed me to leave my base vocation/ And free my country from calamity' (I.ii.78–81). Joan, transformed and refashioned by the vision, rises from her lowly social status: 'And whereas I was black and swart before,/ With those clear rays which she infused on me/ That beauty am I blessed with, which you may see' (I.ii.84–6). Empowered by her dream, Joan breaks the fetters of her class and humble origins and of her status as a woman. She is and she is *not* herself: referentiality replaces subjective autonomy.

In *1 Henry VI*, the possibility of divine intervention disorients the French and makes them ideologically uncertain as if they realized that, though presumably divinely sanctioned, such an inversion irrevocably casts them in roles that they cannot control, thrusts them into narratives that have a will of their own. In whatever fashion they can, the French attempt to come to terms with this representational phenomenon. They argue that, if Joan indeed represents Christ's Mother, she must, after she has completed her tasks in this world, join the communion of saints. The Dauphin promptly promises to canonize her and thus remove her from the earthly realm:

> In memory of her, when she is dead,
> Her ashes, in an urn more precious
> Than the rich-jewelled coffer of Darius,
> Transported shall be at high festivals
> Before the kings and queens of France.
> No longer on Saint Denis will we cry,
> But Joan de Pucelle shall be France's saint.

(I.vi.23–9)

Even before she has proven herself on the battlefield, the Dauphin wants to displace the national saint in order to enshrine a new one. Later, when the English troops take over Rouen, the Frenchmen once again turn to Joan, offering, as the Bastard of Orleans puts it, to 'make thee famous through the world' (III.iii.13); and Alençon adds: 'We'll set thy statue in some holy place/ And have thee reverenced like a blessèd saint' (15–16). Either naively or cunningly, these saint-makers believe that they have the power to control how the world perceives or represents her. At any event, they believe that, if she is God's representative, she must be turned into the statue of a saint and find her rightful place in French culture.

Alternately, the French suppose that, if not a statue of a saint, then she must be a woman – full of sexual desire. Joan herself seeks the Dauphin's acceptance of her as his 'warlike mate' (I.ii.92), challenging him to single combat, defeating him, and earning the accolades of an 'Amazon' who fights with 'the sword of Deborah' (104–5); he offers her, instead, a sexual partnership: 'Impatiently I burn with thy desire;/ My heart and hands thou hast at once subdued' (I.ii.108–9).[41] Joan temporarily wards off his sexual advances, 'I must not yield to any rites of love,/ For my profession's sacred from above' (I.ii.113–14), although she promises to 'think upon a recompense' (116). After she succeeds in breaking the siege on Orleans, the Dauphin thinks of her promise as 'like Adonis' garden' (I.vi.6), a bower of sexual bliss. Later, when the English catch the French '*half ready and half unready*' (II.i.38, stage direction), after a day 'caroused and banqueted' (II.i.12), there is a strong suggestion that she and the Dauphin may have had a sexual encounter. Either as a saint or as a sinner, Joan could find a niche in French culture without redrawing the cultural and ideological configuration of a woman's power.

But on the heels of Joan's military exploits, that configuration of gender roles cannot be sustained. When Alençon, who earlier remarked that 'women are shrewd tempters with their tongues' (I.ii.123), wants to take credit for the victory of the French forces, 'All France will be replete with mirth and joy/ When they shall hear how we have played the men' (I.vi.15–16), the Dauphin corrects him: ' 'Tis Joan, not we, by whom the day is won' (I.vi.17). Alençon's desire for the Frenchmen to 'play the men' and the Dauphin's rebuke suggest that in fact they cannot. A fundamental exchange of gender roles has indeed already occurred. As a representative of the divine will, Joan authorizes the forbidden: the poor daughter of a shepherd fights and speaks for and represents the French nation.

Joan's violation of gender roles, manifested as an exchange, disturbs the English characters' sense of cultural stability.[42] Talbot, Bedford, and Burgundy engage in an anxious conversation about Joan of Arc, none of them quite sure about how to view her:

> TALBOT: A maid, they say.
> BEDFORD: A maid? and be so martial?
> BURGUNDY: Pray God she prove not masculine ere long,
> If underneath the standard of the French
> She carry armor as she hath begun.
>
>   (II.i.21–4).

If, as Burgundy suggests, Joan may prove 'masculine,' she would turn out to be a man pretending to be a woman dressed as a man.[43] The customary boundaries do not hold: the flower of English chivalry must do battle with and be defeated by a woman.

More than the French, the English seem completely disoriented. Take, for example, Act I, scene v, which re-presents Act I, scene ii in which Joan defeats the Dauphin in single combat. In Joan's presence, Talbot feels lost and emasculated: 'Where is my strength, my valor, and my force?/ Our English troops retire, I cannot stay them;/ A woman clad in armor chaseth them' (I.v.1–3). When he fights Joan and is defeated by her, she spares his life but not his honor or ideological certainty. By fighting her and being defeated by her, Talbot implicitly acknowledges the legitimacy of the Other. Quite shaken, he discovers something utterly alien: 'My thoughts are whirlèd like a potter's wheel;/ I know not where I am nor what I do' (I.v.19–20). Unlike his father and the Dauphin, the young John Talbot, however, declined Joan's challenge, as Joan points out:

> Once I encount'red him and thus I said,
> 'Thou maiden youth, be vanquished by a maid.'
> But with a proud majestical high scorn,
> He answered thus, 'Young Talbot was not born
> To be the pillage of a giglot wench.'
> So, rushing in the bowels of the French,
> He left me proudly, as unworthy fight.

> (IV.vii.37–43)

He succeeds where his father fails, although eventually both fall to the French. By refusing to fight a woman, he does not acknowledge her worth as a warrior, and he avoids compromising his reputation. For the young Talbot's father, however, ideological markers of masculinity and culture disappear. After his defeat, Talbot defines Joan in terms that his culture understands. Unlike the French, who want to turn her into a saint or a sinner, Talbot wishes to reduce her to an agent of the devil. This he accomplishes by means of name calling. If she becomes a witch, he can easily explain her victory.

Talbot and others recognize the power of name calling; they attach to Joan all the labels associated with witchcraft. Talbot starts the process by demonizing the enemy: 'Pucelle or pussel, Dolphin or dogfish,/ Your hearts I'll stamp out with my horse's heels/ And make a quagmire of your mingled brains' (I.iv.107–9). When the two first encounter, he refers to her as 'devil,' 'devil's dam,' and 'witch' (I.v.5–6); and in the same breath as a 'high-minded strumpet' (I.v.12). Later he again speaks of her deceitful nature and of the cowardly French who 'join with witches and the help of hell' (II.i.18). Talbot, Bedford, and Burgundy call her names, referring to her as 'that witch, that damnèd sorceress' and 'vile fiend and shameless courtesan' (III.ii.38; 45). When Joan taunts Bedford, who had been 'brought in sick in a chair,' Talbot reinforces the image the English are trying to forge for her:

> Foul fiend of France and hag of all despite,
> Encompassed with thy lustful paramours,
> Becomes it thee to taunt his valiant age
> And twit with cowardice a man half dead?

(III.ii.52–5)

Such statements are intended to shape public opinion, of the audience inside the play and of the larger theater audience, and to determine the outcome of the debate about Joan's place in history. Yet later he again attaches a label to her, 'railing Hecate' (III.ii.64), and makes a reference to her 'old familiar' (i.e. servant devil) (122). Burgundy accuses her of bewitching him (III.iii.58). Name calling replaces the Dauphin's desire to sleep with her, although both processes spring from the same matrix: the desire to dominate and define a woman who escapes definition. The rejection and contempt, the name calling and the insults have the desired ideological and psychological effects. The English define themselves as the ones who do fight without the help of a witch. Joan's transformation can also be explained by the English perception of witchcraft beliefs. Reginald Scot explains: 'The witch . . . seeing things sometimes come to passe according to hir wishes, . . . being called before a Justice, . . . confesseth that she hath brought such things to passe. Wherein, not onelie she, but the accuser, and also the Justice are fowlie deceived and abused.'[44]

Joan's gender exchange and her seeming successes transform the surroundings into something tumultuous and unstable. By blurring the distinction between historiography and fictional narrative production, Shakespeare expresses this instability. To put it differently, he deploys fantasy as historical truth. In Act V, scene iii, the stage, whose boundaries had already dilated to produce apparently supernatural thunder and lightning in Act I, scene i, momentarily creates the illusion of bringing together sign and referent. Joan, defeated and desperate, seemingly generates or projects around her representations of the powers that control her. History and story meet: fictional narrative intrudes upon and becomes a part of a historical moment. Here we encounter the most remote and disorienting space of all: in an area secluded from the battlefield – away from where history is being recorded – Joan wanders off:

> The regent conquers and the Frenchmen fly.
> Now help, ye charming spells and periapts,
> And ye choice spirits that admonish me,
> And give me signs of future accidents. *Thunder.*
> You speedy helpers that are substitutes
> Under the lordly monarch of the north,
> Appear and aid me in this enterprise!

(V.iii.1–7)

Alone, she names them her 'familiar spirits' and admits to their previous help and to her payment for such help, 'I was wont to feed you with my blood' (14); but she finds herself abandoned by them:

> See, they forsake me! Now the time is come
> That France must vail her lofty-plumèd crest
> And let her head fall into England's lap.
> My ancient incantations are too weak,
> And hell too strong for me to buckle with.
> Now, France, thy glory droopeth to the dust.

(V.iii.24–9)

As a witch, Joan finds a niche in the dominant culture's web of significance and at the margins of history. In fact, York acknowledges this fact, when he surrounds her and points out her transformation: 'See, how the ugly witch doth bend her brows/ As if, with Circe, she would change my shape' (V.iii.34–5).

As the end of the play nears, however, ideological markers become more recognizable, especially in the scene in which Joan denies her father's paternity. She and her father are brought out by guards; they have obviously been talking. She refuses to acknowledge him, although he observes that he has been looking for her:

> Ah, Joan, this kills thy father's heart outright.
> Have I sought every country far and near,

> And, now it is my chance to find thee out,
> Must I behold thy timeless cruel death?
> Ah, Joan, sweet daughter Joan, I'll die with thee!
>
> (V.iv.2–6)

If this scene were an impartial report, the last sentence might explain her reasons for rejecting her father: to save his life. But no such disinterested probing occurs; the English, accepting the rejection at face value, use her words to justify the death penalty that they are about to impose. Joan has denied, rejected, and insulted her own father.

This refusal, however, signals to the English her ultimate rebellion against patriarchal rule, and it gives them the assurance that her execution is deserved. But she has an even more disturbing effect on both the English and French males: she emasculates them. The Dauphin cannot win in single combat. Burgundy loses his resolve to support the English forces. The Dauphin instructs her to 'enchant him with thy words' (III.iii.40). She eloquently persuades him to defend his country and 'wash away thy country's stainèd spots' (III.iii.57). Moved by her words, Burgundy changes sides, as if by magic: 'Either she hath bewitched me with her words,/ Or nature makes me suddenly relent' (III.iii.58–9). A 'union' with Joan signifies impotence and gender instability.

Like Joan of Arc, Margaret of Anjou was known for her military prowess. Twentieth-century historians characterize her as 'inexorable, arrogant, and passionately revengeful.'[45] Pope Pius II saw a connection between her and Joan: 'All marveled at such boldness in a woman, at a man's courage in a woman's breast, and at her reasonable arguments. They said that the spirit of the Maid, who had raised Charles to the throne, was renewed in the Queen.'[46] Tudor historiographers describe Margaret in a similar way. Edward Hall writes that Margaret of Anjou, like Joan of Arc, was a mannish woman: 'This woman excelled all other, as well in beautie and favor, as in wit and pollicie, and was of stomack and corage, more like to a man, then a woman.'[47] Queen Margaret, he adds, was a woman 'whose breath ruled, and whose worde was obeyed above the kyng and his counsail' (125).

The policy makers in Henry VI's court may have tried to distance Margaret from Joan by fashioning an idealized image of the new queen. Margaret made her entrance into the city of London in 1445, where pageants were staged in her honor. History and fiction coalesced to shape a mythological, religious, and political context that would fit the newly-fashioned image of the queen. These civic entertainments made theatrical history: 'the devisers of the 1445 triumph provided their actors for the first time with a complete series of mimed speeches.'[48] As Gordon Kipling notes, the pageants draw from the themes of the Advent of Christ to judge man's soul after death.[49] Margaret, the 'bearer of Grace,' unites England and France and brings peace to the warring nations.[50] Other pageants present her advent 'allegorically as a reflection of the Grace wrought by Christ through Mary at the Incarnation.'[51] The Expositor drives the point home, as he asks the Queen of Heaven to ' "Praie for oure Queene that Crist will here governe/ Longe here on lyve in hire noble astate,/ Aftirward crowne here in blisse eterne" ' (ll.153–5).[52] As Kipling notes, 'Throughout the show, the pageantry has insistently characterized Margaret as a type of Mary: royal Virgin, Daughter of Jerusalem, bearer of Grace.'[53]

The pageant did little, however, to imprint this idealized image in history or in drama. Like the Pope and the Tudor chroniclers, Shakespeare grounds both Joan and Margaret in the same cultural matrix. Margaret's entrance into the world of the *Henry VI* trilogy coincides with Joan's exit, as if to suggest that the two French women simply switch places. If Joan was the mysterious, distant Other that the English feared and attempted to discredit and eventually succeeded in destroying, Margaret will engage their imagination in their own immediate space. Joan, as we recall, was introduced by the Bastard of Orleans; Margaret, by Suffolk, an unsavory character who after capturing her immediately starts scheming how to become her lover: 'She's beautiful, and therefore to be wooed;/ She is a woman, therefore to be won' (V.iii.78–9). He reminds himself that he has a wife, 'Then how can Margaret be thy paramour?' (V.iii.82). After considering an annulment of his marriage, he comes to the solution as if in an afterthought: 'I'll win this Lady Margaret. For whom?/ Why, for my king' (V.iii.88–9). Displaying the same eagerness with which the Dauphin wanted to turn Joan into a lover or a saint, Suffolk offers Margaret the English crown, negotiating a marriage contract with her without the prior authorization of Henry VI. Instead of demanding ransom for her liberty, Suffolk offers to return Maine and Anjou to Reignier. Before the scene is over, he demands a 'loving token,' a kiss, for Henry. When Suffolk kisses her, she boldly corrects him: 'That for thyself. I will not so presume/ To send such peevish tokens to a king' (V.iii.181; 185–6). In her presence, roles reverse: the captive becomes captor; instead of being wooed, she becomes the wooer; instead of demanding ransom for her, the English offer payment. By some unknown force, Margaret seems to effect a reversal of the customary structures of power.

Margaret affects King Henry VI in a similar way. In the last scene of *1 Henry VI*, Suffolk convinces King Henry to marry her. Henry, as if by magic, desires her: 'Your wondrous rare description, noble earl,/ Of beauteous Margaret hath astonished me' (V.v.1–2). Suffolk was ready to break his marriage vows; likewise, Henry forgets his previous commitment to marry the Earl of Armagnac's daughter. When the lords raise the question of Margaret's impoverished state, Suffolk argues:

> A dow'r, my lords? Disgrace not so your king
> That he should be so abject, base, and poor
> To choose for wealth and not for perfect love.
> Henry is able to enrich his queen,
> And not to seek a queen to make him rich.
>
> (V.v.48–52)

He also adds that Margaret's courage and military skills make her an ideal consort to the son of a conqueror:

> Her valiant courage and undaunted spirit
> (More than in women commonly is seen)
> Will answer our hope in issue of a king.
> For Henry, son unto a conqueror
> Is likely to beget more conquerors,
> If with a lady of so high resolve
> As is fair Margaret he be linked in love.
>
> (V.v.70–6)

Before the play is over, Suffolk is planning to create an adulterous love triangle, seeing himself as Paris, Margaret as Helen of Troy, and Henry as Menelaus (104–6); and thus, he adds, he 'will rule both her, the king, and realm' (108). As Joan exits the national scene, another Frenchwoman has already taken her place. Little does Suffolk know that in fact Margaret, not he, will be in charge.

In *Henry VI Parts 2 and 3*, Shakespeare uses Margaret to present the civil war as a conflict grounded in cross-cultural difference. Joan of Arc threatened to emasculate men; Margaret, on the other hand, isolated from her cultural context, threatens to deploy an otherness that displaces and replaces the English ideological center. Like Joan, Margaret brings about a profound sense of gender instability, as she offers a strong performative presence backed up by her own military skills.[54] She unleashes a cross-cultural conflict and a power struggle in the attempts to decode, reconstruct, and construct her cultural and gender identity. The conflict intertwines two cultural systems, representing radically different ways of encoding experience. Through her actions, Margaret intrudes upon the dominant cultural field and alters the rules by which anything can signify.

Margaret displays a most unusual power over males. In *2 Henry VI*, Suffolk, now in England, introduces Margaret to Henry, who feels 'ravished' by her sight and her gracious speech. Cultural rules, however, have to be suspended to make room for Margaret. Though small and perhaps inconsequential at first, the cultural breach widens as Margaret sets foot on English soil. The marriage contract negotiated by Suffolk violates cultural practice and erases history, as Gloucester points out:

> O peers of England, shameful is this league.
> Fatal this marriage, cancelling your fame,
> Blotting your names from books of memory.
> Rasing the characters of your renown,
> Defacing monuments of conquered France,
> Undoing all as all had never been!

> (I.i.96–101)

Likewise, York vehemently adds, 'I never read but England's kings have had/ Large sums of gold and dowries with their wives' (I.i.126–7). The English expect a dowry from royal brides; yet Margaret brings none. Margaret becomes the means through which something alien threatens to replace English customs.

Margaret, even at the height of her military power, appears as an alien and an outsider, whose presence proves as disorienting as Joan's. She has the seeming ability to transform the space around herself and to change the rules of representation. In *2 Henry VI*

Margaret sees herself as an outsider in the English court, a French-woman trying to understand startling cultural differences:

> My Lord of Suffolk, say, is this the guise,
> Is this the fashions in the court of England?
> Is this the government of Britain's isle,
> And this the royalty of Albion's king?
> What, shall King Henry be a pupil still,
> Under the surly Gloucester's governance?
> Am I a queen in title and in style
> And must be made a subject to a duke?
>
> (I.iii.40–7)

She first questions the oddity of English customs: a king governs under the tutelage of a duke; a queen has the title but no power. This indeed resembles an upside-down world. Implied in this is her desire to have more power, which she immediately sets out to seek. She also reveals contempt for the way the English apparently conduct themselves. Later, upon Suffolk's announcement of Gloucester's death, Margaret boasts of her feats of bravery when she reminds King Henry that she abandoned her homeland and risked her life to be with him:

> Was I for this nigh wracked upon the sea
> And twice by awkward wind from England's bank
> Drove back again unto my native clime?
>
> (III.ii.82–4)

She then describes an offering she made to the sea gods:

> I stood upon the hatches in the storm,
> And when the dusky sky began to rob
> My earnest-gaping sight of thy land's view,
> I took a costly jewel from my neck,
> A heart it was, bound in with diamonds,
> And threw it toward thy land.
>
> (III.ii.103–7)

The gods accept her sacrifice, and she safely lands in England. She braves the rough English Channel to reach her bridegroom; whereas Henry awaits comfortably at home. She intimates that the English do things the contrary way, underscoring a gender reversal.

If queens are supposed to be rich, Margaret's perceived poverty further suggests an upside-down custom. For the English, her poverty signals her difference and puts her in direct conflict with the ostentatious Duchess of Gloucester. The Duke of Gloucester remarks about Margaret, 'She should have stayed in France, and starved in France' (I.i.133–4). Margaret expects riches with queenship and, therefore, resents the fact that the Duchess 'scorns our poverty' and brags that 'The very train of her worst wearing gown/ Was better worth than all my father's lands/ Till Suffolk gave two dukedoms for his daughter' (I.iii.79; 83–5). When Margaret drops her fan and the Duchess refuses to pick it up, Margaret *gives the Duchess a box on the ear* (I.iii.136, stage direction). Eleanor calls her 'proud Frenchwoman' and swears revenge (I.iii.138). The scene pits the ambitious duchess, who has royal aspirations, against the arrogant foreigner, who seeks to assert her position. From Margaret's perspective, then, nowhere else but in England could a mere duchess have more power than a queen. She thus sets out to rectify this apparent inversion.

The scenes involving the Duchess of Gloucester serve to define gender boundaries and provide the means to gauge Margaret's own performative presence later in the play. Eleanor makes it clear to the Duke of Gloucester that she aspires to the royal crown, wondering why he seems so pensive:

> What seest thou there? King Henry's diadem,
> Enchased with all the honors of the world?
> If so, gaze on and grovel on thy face
> Until thy head be circled with the same.
> Put forth thy hand, reach at the glorious gold.

(I.ii.7–11)

If his hand is too short, she will 'lengthen' it with hers. When he relates the dream of the broken staff upon which are placed the heads of Somerset and Suffolk, she sees it as a sign of power to punish those who defy Gloucester's authority; and she relates her own dream:

Methought I sat in seat of majesty
In the cathedral church of Westminster;
And in that chair where kings and queens were crowned,
Where Henry and Dame Margaret kneeled to me
And on my head did set the diadem –

(I.ii.36–40)

Gloucester chastises her for her ambition. She, however, expresses her discontent with the cultural constraints placed upon her gender: 'Were I a man, a duke, and next of blood,/ I would remove these tedious stumbling blocks/ And smooth my way upon their headless necks' (I.ii.63–5). This scene is particularly important because it clearly defines what is permissible in the English culture of the play, and it serves to define the parameters that both Eleanor and Margaret violate. Eleanor's pursuit of power goes outside the methods employed by men: to remove the heads of opponents as if they were stumbling blocks. Instead, she turns to witchcraft. Her consultation is arranged by John Hume, a priest; but it is the incident of the fan that drives her to the margins of her culture, as Buckingham points out: 'She's tickled now; her fume needs no spurs,/ She'll gallop far enough to her destruction' (I.iii.148–9).

Shakespeare dramatizes the conspiracy of 1441 of Eleanor Cobham, Duchess of Gloucester, with Roger Bolingbroke, a conjuror; Thomas Southwell, a priest; and Margery Jourdain, a witch. Edward Hall discusses the fall of the Duchess, who 'was accused of treason, for that she, by sorcery and enchauntment, entended to destroy the kyng, to thentent to advaunce and to promote her husbande to the croune.'[55] She was examined, judged and convicted and had to 'do open penaunce, in. iij. open places, within the citie of London' and later was banished to the Isle of Man.[56] Testimony revealed that her accomplices played an important part: 'thei, at the request of the duchesse, had devised an image of waxe, representyng the kynge, whiche by their sorcery, a litle and litle consumed, entendying therby in conclusion to waist, and destroy the kynges person, and so to bryng hym death. . . .'[57] Shakespeare omits references to wax effigies; instead, he introduces the compilation of written records to incriminate the duchess.[58] Though an eyewitness to the consultation, Southwell, who is in York's employ, realizes that his verbal account apparently does not suffice and a written report must be produced. With paper and pen in hand, he writes down the Duchess's subversive questions (posed by Bolingbroke) and the spirit's answer. He writes very fast indeed, for when the Duke of York appears shortly after the consultation has ended, the written report is ready for perusal. The Duke of York reads the report aloud: "The duke yet lives that Henry shall depose;/ But him outlive, and die a violent death..." (I.iv.58–9). With this writing in hand, York has Eleanor, Margery Jourdain, and Bolingbroke tried and sentenced. The stage direction explains the Duchess's punishment: '*Enter Duchess of Gloucester barefoot, and a white sheet about her, with a wax candle in her hand, and verses written on her back and pinned on*' (II.iv. 17 ff.). The power of writing becomes apparent, as she observes:

> Methinks I should not thus be led along,
> Mailed up in shame, with papers on my back,
> And followed with a rabble that rejoice
> To see my tears and hear my deep-fet groans.

> (II.iv.30–3)

Even the largely illiterate crowd could hardly miss the meaning of the inscription. The Duchess of Gloucester's consultation, a temporal, ephemeral event, generates permanent written records. Her actions and fate foreshadow Margaret's own pursuit of power and eventual punishment.

Margaret, like the Duchess of Gloucester, seeks to represent her husband; but Margaret succeeds, whereas the Duchess fails. Margaret becomes the warrior that the Duchess presumably aspired to be. As a result, Henry and Margaret exchange genders. In *2 Henry VI*, Margaret seeks to acquire and consolidate power; in *3 Henry VI*, she reaches the pinnacle of political and military power. The ostentatious power of the Duke and the Duchess of Gloucester leads her to a recognition of Henry's weakness: 'all his mind is bent to holiness,/ To number Ave-Maries on his beads' (*2 Henry VI*, I.iii.53–4). She asserts herself cautiously, at first anchoring her decisions in Henry's kingship. When Salisbury questions her appointment of Somerset to the Regency of France, she retorts, 'Because the king forsooth will have it so' (*2 Henry VI*, I.iii.113); Gloucester, however, challenges her, 'Madam, the king is old enough himself/ To give his censure. These are no women's matters' (*2 Henry VI*, I.iii.118–19). She outwits Gloucester and forces him to give up his 'staff': 'If he [Henry] be old enough, what needs your grace/ To be Protector of his excellence?' (*2 Henry VI*, I.iii.116–17). From the Duchess's experience, Margaret eventually learns that English society does not, in actuality, accord English women much power; to exercise power women must figuratively become men.

By Act III, scene ii, Margaret has already brought about a symbolic gender switch with her husband.[59] When Suffolk quietly accepts banishment for his involvement in the murder of Gloucester, Margaret taunts him: 'Fie, coward woman and soft-hearted wretch./ Hast thou not spirit to curse thine enemy?' (III.ii.307–8). Later, she also lectures her husband on manhood: 'What are you made of? You'll nor fight nor fly./ Now is it manhood, wisdom, and defense/ To give the enemy way, and to secure us/ By what we can, which can no more but fly' (*2 Henry VI*, V.ii.74–7). *3 Henry VI* further confirms the attempted gender switch. Margaret calls Henry a 'timorous wretch' (*3 Henry VI*, I.i.231). Like the Duchess of Gloucester, she wishes she were a man, condemning Henry for making York heir to the throne: 'Had I been there, which am a silly woman,/ The soldiers should have tossed me on their pikes/ Before I would have granted to that act' (*3 Henry VI*, I.i.243–5). But she goes far beyond the Duchess, when she also announces her intention to divorce him: 'I here divorce myself/ Both from thy table, Henry, and thy bed/ Until that act of parliament be repealed/ Whereby my son is disinherited' (I.i.247–9). She holds her own parliament (I.i.35) and becomes the commander-in-chief of the army. Clifford, recognizing the queen's power, orders Henry out of the battlefield, for 'The Queen hath best success when you are absent' (*3 Henry VI*, II.ii.74). Henry's displacement is so absolute that he envisions becoming a shepherd (II.v). Margaret seeks to become her husband, to rule in his behalf, and to wield his power on the battlefield.

Like Joan of Arc, Margaret dons armor and becomes a military leader. As we have seen, the gender exchange for Joan, disorienting though it is, has clear witchcraft associations. I think that in a more subtle way it has the same effect on Margaret. By cross-dressing, both women violate cultural boundaries and seem to appropriate in a fetishist way the male body, through which they deploy an alien field of signification. A widespread form of witchcraft was known as *Invultuacio* or image magic, an ancient practice that uses representation for magical purposes. The witch usurps power through impersonation and representation: through wax figures and magical drawings that configure the world within her sphere of influence.

By means of incantations, she imitates the rituals of power and claims control over the domain of representation:

> An effigy of wax, clay, wood, metal, or almost any substance, is pierced with nails, pins, or thorns, and burned or slowly roasted. The victim suffers corresponding torments, pines away as the puppet melts or crumbles, and dies when it is stabbed to the heart. Sometimes the image is buried or drowned instead of being consumed by fire....[60]

Reginald Scot attests to the prevalence of popular belief in *invultuacio*: 'But concerning these images, it is certeine that they are much feared among the people, and much used among cousening witches....'[61] *Invultuacio* suggests a belief that the referent and the sign remain inextricably connected: an injury suffered by the representation affects the represented.

The witch possesses the ability to produce representations. The case of Elizabeth Stile of Windsor (1578/9) brought to light claims that a Mother Dutten killed her victims by making a red wax picture of them; she pierced each image with hawthorne pricks.[62] Elizabeth Sowthernes, a witch in Lancashire, confessed that 'the quickest way to kill a person by witchcraft was to make a 'clay picture' in the shape of the victim, dry it thoroughly, and prick it with a pin. Burning a part of the picture would consume the corresponding part of the victim's body. In order to kill the person immediately, it was only necessary to burn the entire picture' (145). Often illiterate, the witch yet can claim powers to represent, and through representation, control.

In *1 Henry VI*, there is an attempt to use *invultuacio*. The scene in which the Countess of Auvergne tries to trap and destroy Talbot foreshadows Joan's own private scene when she conjures up her familiar spirits. Away from the battle front, the Countess attempts to subdue and destroy the English through witchcraft means. Although she suggests that she wants to imitate Tomyris, the Scythian queen who slew Cyrus the Great in battle, she is no warrior like Joan of Arc. The English have magnified Talbot's fame to the point that they use his name, along with St George, as their battle cry, as for example during their attack on Orleans (II.i). The Countess realizes that there is a discrepancy between the man and the representation or 'rare reports' (II.iii.10). When Talbot pays her a visit, she finds him not to be a Hercules or a second Hector, as she had expected; instead, she finds 'a child, a silly dwarf,' a 'weak and writhled shrimp' (*1 Henry VI*, II.iii.22–3). She reveals that she has his portrait hanging in her gallery:

> Long time thy shadow hath been thrall to me,
> For in my gallery thy picture hangs;
> But now the substance shall endure the like,
> And I will chain these legs and arms of thine
> That hast by tyranny these many years
> Wasted our country, slain our citizens,
> And sent our sons and husbands captivate.

(1 Henry VI, II.iii.36–42)

She desires to control the man by capturing his shadow or representation; now she hopes to seize the real thing, the 'substance.' To defeat her, Talbot says that he is but a 'shadow' of himself (*1 Henry VI*, II.iii.50) and brings the English troops to demonstrate his 'real' power. He blows his horn, and immediately his followers come to his rescue, as he asks her, 'Are you now persuaded/ That Talbot is but a shadow of himself?' (*1 Henry VI*, II.iii.61–2). She agrees that he is more than 'may be gathered by thy shape' (69), as she offers to feast him and his soldiers. She accepts the futility of her endeavor.

In contrast, the Duchess of Gloucester in *2 Henry VI* consults a conjuror and a witch; but although the Duchess of history employed *invultuacio*, Shakespeare's does not. Instead of wax figures being recovered, Southwell, as we have seen, presents a written report to York. One wonders whether Shakespeare implies a distinction between domestic and foreign types of witchcraft. Instead, Margaret and Henry are the ones interested in images. Margaret realizes that her husband loves to worship 'brazen images of canonized saints' (*2 Henry VI*, I.iii.58–9). When Henry is lamenting the death of Gloucester, Margaret taunts him: 'Erect his statue and worship it,/ And make my image but an alehouse sign' (*2 Henry VI*, III.ii.80–1). In Act IV, scene iv, as the stage direction indicates, '*Enter the King, with a supplication, and the Queen with Suffolk's head*'. She cradles the head in her arms: 'Here may his head lie on my throbbing breast,/ But where's the body that I should embrace?' (5–6). Margaret comes to associate images with power and dismembered bodies as representations of that power. In *3 Henry VI*, Warwick, in fact, describes Margaret's power in terms of *invultuacio*:

> The proud insulting queen,
> With Clifford and the haught Northumberland,
> And of their feather many moe proud birds,
> Have wrought the easy-melting king like wax.

(II.i.168–71)

Ironically, Henry VI becomes a wax effigy, not for the Duchess of Gloucester, as the historiographers report, but for Margaret.

In *3 Henry VI* Margaret's action echoes the practice of *invultuacio*, especially in the mock coronation and murder of the Duke of York. She turns him into a representation of what he would like to become; once he becomes that representation, she destroys him. She makes it clear that York had pursued an illusion:

> Come, make him stand upon this molehill here
> That raught at mountains with outstretchèd arms,
> Yet parted but the shadow with his hand.
> What, was it you that would be England's king?

(I.iv.67–70)

She points out to him that without his 'mess of sons,' he is but a sign, powerless and defenseless. She wants to turn him into a figure of madness: 'Stamp, rave, and fret, that I may sing and dance' (I.iv.91). As he stands mute, she sends for a paper crown, which she sets on his head:

> Ay, marry, sir, now looks he like a king.
> Ay, this is he that took King Henry's chair
> And this is he was his adopted heir.

(I.iv.96–8)

She gives the final order, 'Off with the crown, and with the crown his head' (I.iv.107). York insults her father and calls her 'She-wolf of France,' 'Amazonian trull,' 'tiger's heart,' 'opposite to every good/ As the Antipodes are unto us,' 'ruthless queen,' and of course a 'beggar' (I.iv.111–49). These resemble the tactics that the English used to undermine Joan of Arc's authority and military accomplishments. Perhaps Shakespeare is suggesting that English culture connects

Joan and Margaret as military leaders and as witches. In fact, in *Richard III*, when Richard wants to discredit Margaret, he calls her 'Foul wrinkled witch' (I.iii.163).

As Margaret brings about the destruction of York, she forgets that she herself is but a representation, an extension of her husband and her son. Once both of these are killed, she has no power on her own. Her complete displacement occurs at the end of *3 Henry VI*, as Clarence, Richard, and Edward stab her son Edward, Prince of Wales (V.v.). Yet *invultuacio* intertwines with gender violation, specifically with Margaret's desire to usurp the power of English men.

The *Henry VI* trilogy opens with an exclusion of English women. This signals not only that the world of these plays views feminine qualities as negative but also that we should expect a gender anomaly. When Winchester claims that 'the church's prayers made him [Henry V] so prosperous' (*1 Henry VI*, I.i.32), Gloucester rebuts:

> The church? Where is it? Had not churchmen prayed,
> His thread of life had not so soon decayed.
> None do you like but *an effeminate prince*,
> Whom like a schoolboy you may overawe.

> (I.i.33–6; italics mine)

Gloucester's statement, however, may be an attempt to compensate for the embarrassment that his strong-willed wife may be causing him, as Winchester quickly points out: 'Thy wife is proud. She holdeth thee in awe/ More than God or religious churchmen may' (I.i.39–40). A weak and effeminate prince will direct English affairs; French women will attempt to shape and control the direction of English history. The as yet absent Duchess of Gloucester already plots but eventually does not succeed in controlling her husband. Rather, two French women, Joan of Arc and Margaret of Anjou, succeed where the English duchess cannot. When French women assert power, men lose theirs. Margaret and Joan desire to be at or near the center of power; yet from the English characters' perspective, the closer they get to that center, the more culturally removed from it they seem.

The *Henry VI* plays present history as a cross-cultural story in which two French women deploy an alien reality that challenges English ideological certainty. The clash between English and French medieval societies becomes a conflict between French women and

English men. Joan and Margaret offer a dominant performative presence, guiding the action to the frontiers of culture. Through a gender exchange, they subvert a male-dominated world. Their actions, grounded in an alien field of signification, suggest an alternative culture that seems as cruel and as threatening as the Amazon world. The world of these history plays does not seem far removed from that of *A Midsummer Night's Dream* and *The Two Noble Kinsmen*.

3

Textual Encodings in
The Merchant of Venice

Here you may both see all manner of fashions of attire, and heare all the languages of Christendome, besides those that are spoken by the barbarous Ethnickes; the frequencie of people being so great.

Thomas Coryat, *Coryat's Crudities* (1611)

The presence and influence of the Amazons, Hippolyta and Emilia, and the assertive French female warriors, Joan and Margaret, generate a powerful sense of instability that endangers gender roles and threatens to erode national and cultural identity. The next two chapters will focus on Jews and Moors in order to explore the place of the written word in the cross-cultural experience. I will argue that in *The Merchant of Venice*, *Titus Andronicus*, and *Othello* the cross-cultural encounter, while retaining its gender foundation, becomes a textual negotiation.

One must not underestimate the power and the centrality of written records. As Michel de Certeau argues, 'Writing *produces history*,' hence efforts to regulate the production, preservation, dissemination, and control of records.[1] Two examples from history and fiction, respectively, illustrate how writing functions as a repository of culture. On 8 April 1605, Queen Anne gave birth to Mary, who, as Bergeron points out, 'had the distinction of being the first royal child born in England since Jane Seymour gave birth to the child who became Edward VI.'[2] The baptism occurred on 5 May, after 'much scurrying about and perusing of historical records in order to recall how a royal child should be baptized.'[3] The written record authorizes the resurrection and observance of a long-forgotten custom. Jack Cade, in *2 Henry VI*, astutely though misguidedly, recognizes the power of the written word: 'Away, burn all the records of the realm! My mouth shall be the parliament of England' (IV.vii.14–16). Archives constitute a record of customs, traditions, privileges, and titles of property and nobility, and therefore, perpetuate the injustices that Cade would like to eliminate.[4] To affirm his dignity and to gain rights, he feels that he must destroy literacy.

I contend that written documents govern life in the Venice and Belmont of *The Merchant of Venice*, as they do in other highly literate societies. These written records serve as the basis for legal, mercantile, and cultural transactions for the Italians. Through the written word, Italian culture intersects alien worlds. There is no illiterate Jack Cade here; rather Italians confront aliens in the reading and interpretation of texts. Through cultural encodings, these texts provide an ideological shield for the Italians and codify the premise of cultural superiority. Aliens who attempt to interpret the Italian texts generated in the play do so at their own peril.

When Portia, disguised as Balthasar, opens the proceedings in the Venetian court, she asks a now famous, though puzzling question, 'Which is the merchant here? and which the Jew?' (IV.i.172), as if she could not distinguish Jew from Venetian.[5] Similarly, when explaining the lottery, Portia suggests that no discrimination can be here made: 'I may neither choose who I would nor refuse who I dislike, so is the will of a living daughter curbed by the will of a dead father' (I.ii.21–4). These two passages serve as a fulcrum for a disjunction, of which Portia becomes an emblem and the center: the ostensible tolerance and the actual bitter ethnic and racial prejudice of everyday life. Venetians seek to establish fundamental and unresolvable distinctions – Christian/Jew, white/black, Venetian/non-Venetian – while in fact deceiving themselves that their country is a multicultural haven. A production of *The Merchant of Venice* which I saw in Brazil on 15 May 1993 helped me understand how.[6]

In this Brazilian production, the characters refused to confront the real issue of racial and religious prejudice and, instead, sought to explain racial and religious division as the result not of their own prejudices but of imbalanced humors, a pseudo-scientific, now discredited, theory which had prevailed for centuries in medicine, psychology, and even dramatic texts. This was done, in part, to situate the play in the context of Brazil's own sense of national identity. I will briefly discuss this production and its textual basis in order to show that this physiological, psychological approach shortchanges the rich cultural interpretation that centers primarily on texts.

The Brazilian producers consciously decided to downplay racial prejudice. Brazil has developed an image of racial and religious tolerance, where interracial marriages are not uncommon and where Afro-Brazilian religions and cults coexist with Roman Catholicism, the followers of one religion not hesitating to claim membership in another. The production stripped the text of overt racial references and sought to counter its anti-semitism. Shylock, played by the nationally renowned and beloved Brazilian actor Ednei Giovenazzi (Plate 5), elicited considerable sympathy from the audience. Morocco in this production did not apologize for his complexion as the text requires: 'Mislike me not for my complexion,/ The shadowed livery of the burnished sun,/ To whom I am a neighbor and near bred' (II.i.1–3). When he stated, 'Let's see once more this saying graved in gold' (II.vii.36), which the translator Bárbara Heliodora rendered as '*Ouçamos novamente a vóz do ouro*' [Let's listen again to the call of gold], and chose the wrong casket, Portia did not dismiss him with the racist comment: 'Let all of his complexion choose me so' (II.vii.77). Lorenzo did not accuse Launcelot of being responsible for the 'getting up of the Negro's belly' (III.v.34–5). The characters, however, not only seemingly became color blind, they also became more eccentric. Laughing like a lunatic, Morocco appeared in turban and Arabic white clothes and ridiculous red Turkish shoes. No distinction was made between Morocco and the other suitors: all of them seemed unacceptable because of personal eccentricities rather than ethnic or racial difference. The producers sought to transform the play into a comedy of humors to explain and justify the characters' prejudice.

To be sure, Shakespeare's text alludes to humors, and even the play's immediate dramatic context suggests a period of renewed interest in humors on the English stage. *The Merchant of Venice*, mentioned by Francis Meres in 1598, was entered in the Stationer's Register to James Roberts on 22 July 1598, and transferred to Thomas Heyes on 28 October 1600.[7] It is, therefore, contemporaneous with Jonson's *Every Man in His Humour* (1598) and *Every Man out of His Humour* (1599). But as I concluded from watching the Brazilian *Merchant of Venice*, the focus on humors oversimplifies the dynamics of racial and religious interaction in the play; it masks Portia's racism, Antonio's religious prejudice, and Shylock's resentment; consequently, it distracts from the real issues, which neither the characters in the play nor the Brazilian producers want to confront. I therefore propose to examine textual production and interpretation as the foundation for the deep-seated prejudices of Venetian life.

In *Shakespeare and the Geography of Difference*, John Gillies observes a pattern of 'intrusion' and 'exorbitance' in Shakespeare's Venetian plays. He suggests that to the Elizabethans Venice embodied a contradiction: 'between the idea of Venice as the constitutional heir of the ancient city-state . . . and the idea of Venice as an open or cosmopolitan city whose citizens mingled promiscuously with the peoples of the world.'[8] He cites, for example, Spenser's observation that Venice is the 'third Babel' and Thomas Coryat's description of St Mark's Square: ' "Here you may both see all manner of fashions of attire, and heare all the languages of Christendome, besides those that are spoken by the barbarous Ethnickes; the frequencie of people being so great." '[9] Gillies concludes that 'Self-consciously imperial and a "market place of the world", Shakespeare's Venice invites barbarous intrusion through the sheer "exorbitance" of its maritime trading empire.'[10] As an ancient city turned into a mercantile power, Venice interacts with aliens and thus, in the Elizabethan view, becomes contaminated by them. Contradictions abound in the play's repression and displacement of the 'myth of the voyager':

> The merchant adventurers of Shakespeare's Venice are at once triumphant and problematic. Shakespeare clearly has reservations about Antonio and the young Venetian 'Jasons' but is unable to express them fully.[11]

Shakespeare thus employs the myth to celebrate the 'merchant-adventuring ethic' of the Venetians while ignoring Medean 'anxieties about trade, intermixture and miscegenation' inherent in the ancient myth.[12]

I would like to suggest that Shakespeare does indeed underscore fundamental contradictions in the dynamics of interaction between Venetians and aliens. My argument, however, differs from Gillies' in a substantial way: Shakespeare demonstrates that Venice erects a protective barrier against dangerous contamination from its everyday interaction with alien worlds. He does so by emphasizing the written word: the cross-cultural encounter becomes a textual experience. He develops a two-pronged approach: appropriation and inversion of the Golden Fleece legend. In this he demonstrates the centrality of Portia to the preservation of Venetian traditions and values.

Both the caskets subplot and the Jessica–Lorenzo love story rely on the legend of Jason and the Golden Fleece, according to which ancient Greek adventurers sailed to distant and mysterious Colchis, today's Republic of Georgia, seeking the Golden Fleece. With the help of the enchantress Medea, the daughter of Aietes, the King of Colchis, Jason and the argonauts steal the golden fleece. Medea betrays her family and country. To delay her countrymen's pursuit of the argonauts, she kills her brother Apsyrtos and scatters the pieces of his body behind her, knowing that Aietes will stop to collect and bury his son's remains.[13]

The legend entered the English consciousness early. In *The Legend of Good Women* (c. 1380–6), Chaucer narrates Jason's quest of the 'fles of gold.'[14] In *The Hystorye/Sege and Dystruccyon of Troye* (London, 1513), John Lydgate offers an account of the Golden Fleece legend and an illustration of Jason killing a serpent.[15] Several pageants were staged for the coming of the Emperor Charles V into the City of London in June 1522, including the Golden Fleece, which here acquires an added signification:

> Also att the myddyll off London bryge dyd stande a pagiaunt of the story of Jason and medea wyth the dragon and ij bollys [bulls] beryng the goldyn flese, by cause the emperowr is lorde and gever of the tewson [*Toison d'Or*] and hedde & maker of all the kynghtys off the tewson, lyke as the kyng of englonde is of the ordyr of the kynghtys off the garter. And a childe in a goodly apparell salutyng the emprowr shewyng thatt his presens and comyng was lyke ioy to the cytee off london as the conqueryng off the golden fleese was wnto the people of Mynius.[16]

Robert Withington writes that the London Guild of the Drapers 'grasped the possibility of giving the Golden Fleece a trade-signification, for they used "our newe pageant of the *Goldyn Flees*" at midsummer.'[17] On 19 February 1547, a pageant of the Golden Fleece was staged for the royal entry of King Edward VI into London en route to his coronation at Westminster. Beside the throne, where a child representing King Edward VI sat, was, as Withington writes, 'the Golden Fleece, kept by two bulls and a serpent, their mouths flaming out fire, "according to the story of Jason." '[18] In the 1614 Lord Mayor's Show, *Himatia-Poleos*, written by Anthony Munday, we once again find the Golden Fleece; and a shepherd first apologizes for his presence and then sings the praises of the fleece: 'Why gaze yee so upon me? am I not a man, flesh, bloud, and bone, as you are? Or in these silken sattin Townes, are poore plaine meaning Sheepheards woondred at, like Comets or blazing Starres? Or is it this goodly beast by me, that fills your eyes with admiration?'[19] Anthony Munday contributed a water pageant, which he called *The Triumphs of the Golden Fleece*, to Thomas Middleton's 1623 Lord Mayor's Show, *The Triumphs of Integrity*, designed to honor Martin Lumley, Draper.[20] The Golden Fleece appeared on the heraldic arms of the Drapers, with whom it had an obvious association. The Golden Fleece was thus well known to Londoners.

Three references mark the importance of the legend to the action of *The Merchant of Venice*. Bassanio introduces it early in the play:

> Nor is the wide world ignorant of her worth,
> For the four winds blow in from every coast
> Renownèd suitors, and her sunny locks
> Hang on her temples like a golden fleece,
> Which makes her seat of Belmont Colchos' strond,
> And many Jasons come in quest of her.

(I.i.167–72)

Portia's blonde hair and her fortune represent the golden fleece; Belmont, Colchis; and the suitors, new Jasons. The second reference occurs after Bassanio has chosen the right casket when Gratiano reminds us of what he and Bassanio have accomplished: 'We are the Jasons, we have won the Fleece' (III.ii.241). These two allusions focus on the Golden Fleece, rather than on Medea's role in helping Jason. Finally, in the third allusion, Jessica reminds us of Medea and indirectly of the role that the Asiatic princess played in the quest for the Golden Fleece: 'In such a night/ Medea gathered the enchanted herbs/ That did renew old Aeson' (V.i.13–15). Medea, the sorceress, had the power to heal; Jessica does not mention, however, Medea's power to destroy.

Shakespeare splits the legend into two seemingly independent elements, the quest for the Golden Fleece and the story of Medea, and encodes them, separately, into the caskets and the Lorenzo-Jessica subplots. The story of the caskets associates Portia with the Golden Fleece but not with Medea. Portia seems to inherit Medea's resourcefulness but not her viciousness. At least one text recognized Medea's mastery over rather than submission to foreign princes. In Anthony Munday's part of the 1623 Lord Mayor's Show, Medea, the enchantress, held dominion over six Indian kings: 'Sixe Tributarie Indian Kings, holding their severall dominions of *Medea*, and living in vassalage to her, are commaunded by her to rowe the Argoe, all of them wearing their Tributarie Crownes, and Antickely attired in rich habiliments.'[21] From this, one supposes that, if Shakespeare associated Portia with Medea, she would rule over, rather than submit to, foreign princes, thus inverting the legend. Jason and the Argonauts ventured into non-European territory in order to conquer the much sought-after prize. But Portia is European, not an alien.

Unlike Medea, Portia has both European and non-European suitors. In *The Merchant of Venice*, the quest for Portia's 'Golden Fleece' is thus further split between European and non-European adventurers, who seek her heart and fortune, as Shakespeare delineates a sharp contrast between these two groups of suitors. In her conversation with Nerissa in Act I, scene ii, Portia dismisses as eccentric the European adventurers who desist without accepting the lottery's terms. The lottery also erects an adequate barrier that the Prince of Arragon, because of his self-conceit and arrogance, cannot overcome. When Morocco appears, the rhetoric of choice changes. When the Servingman announces the approach of the Prince of Morocco, Portia desires his failure, not so much because he may be an eccentric like the others but because he belongs to a non-European race. She intimates that she cannot accept him under any circumstances: 'If he have the condition of a saint and the complexion of a devil, I had rather he should shrive me than wive me' (I.ii.121–2). In this regard, Claribel of *The Tempest*, who was forced by her father Alonso to marry the North African King of Tunis, resembles Portia. As Bergeron points out, 'Alonso in this judgment has violated ordinary political expectations and custom by marrying his daughter out of the European political sphere.'[22] As Bergeron underscores, Sebastian refers to Claribel's reluctance:

> You [Alonso] were kneeled to and importuned otherwise
> By all of us; and the fair soul herself
> Weighed, between loathness and obedience, at
> Which end o'th' beam should bow.

> (II.i.124–7)

Portia indicates that she faces the same dilemma 'between loathness and obedience.' In this context, one wonders why Alonso inexplicably decided to marry his daughter to the African king. We recall that another Italian father, Brabantio, steadfastly refuses to accept his daughter Desdemona's marriage to a Moor.

All those who want to try their luck must decipher the scriptural engravings on the caskets of gold, silver, and lead, designed by Portia's father. Choice of the right casket depends not upon valor but rather upon interpretation of texts and culture. From the three different suitors who make their choices, we learn that inside each casket lie other forms of representation: additional inscriptions, a picture of Portia, a skull, and the picture of a blinking fool. Morocco, in fact, asks a perfectly logical question, 'How shall I know if I do choose the right?' (II.vii.10). Portia replies, 'The one of them contains my picture, Prince' (II.vii.11). In the 'magic' of the caskets, only the most astute of ethnographers or an insider can discover how the representation on and of the caskets leads to representations *inside* the caskets. The silver casket, containing the blinking fool, offers no real choice at all. Like a Renaissance looking-glass, made of plate glass coated with an amalgam of quicksilver or silver,[23] the silver casket holds the mirror up to arrogant and frivolous suitors like Arragon who are not seeking Portia herself but rather the ability to boast that they have accomplished something where others have failed. The other two caskets, however, seem to be intimately intertwined: one contains the likeness of a living Portia, and the other the likeness of a dead person, which I submit could be Portia herself. Devised by Portia's dying father, both caskets, however, link life and death.

Morocco, of course, chooses the gold casket. As he maps his way through the labyrinth of material culture and ethnographic interpretation, we discover that his interpretive skills are culturally bound. The stage direction in Act II makes clear that Morocco is 'a tawny Moor,' although he views himself as a sub-Saharan African. Unlike the other suitors, Morocco anticipates Portia's rejection and offers an apology for his racial difference:

> Mislike me not for my complexion,
> The shadowed livery of the burnished sun,
> To whom I am a neighbor and near bred.
> Bring me the fairest creature northward born
> Where Phoebus' fire scarce thaws the icicles,
> And let us make incision for your love
> To prove whose blood is reddest, his or mine.
> I tell thee, lady, this aspect of mine

> Hath feared the valiant. By my love I swear
> The best-regarded virgins of our clime
> Have loved it too. I would not change this hue,
> Except to steal your thoughts, my gentle queen.

(II.i.1–12)

Morocco wants to be judged according to his valor, not the color of his skin. He explains that skin shade depends upon accidents of geography. The South, because of its proximity to the sun, inevitably differs from the North. He argues that Portia – white, born in Europe – lives where the sun barely thaws the icicles; whereas he – dark-complexioned, born in the South – lives where the sun has burnished and turned his skin into a 'shadowy livery.' Elsewhere, he tells her, his dark skin is an asset, not a liability: it inspires respect and desire.

Morocco's apology anticipates Portia's thinly disguised loathing, which becomes clear when she says that if she were not barred from 'voluntary choosing,' Morocco 'then stood as fair / As any comer I have looked on yet / For my affection' (II.i.20–2). It also seems to have another subtext. Robert Bassett, in his *Curiosities or the Cabinet of Nature*, underscores the difference between North and South. He argues that Northern climates do not produce monsters because being 'sensible of cold, which is an enemy of nature, they [monsters] cannot subsist long, especially in cold clymates; and by how much the more they are imperfect, the shorter time they live.' He also argues that the opposite holds true, namely that Africa brings forth more monsters than other regions:

> The reason is, because it is extreamly hot, and waters very scarce, and a Countrey very spacious, vast, and sandy; so that all sorts of beasts assemble and flocke to the Fountaines to drinke, where they couple together, without any respect of Species or Kinde, and thence it comes to passe that so many Monsters are there bred: Moreover *Affricke* being a Country very hot, (as is said) and heate being a friend to nature, Monsters live longer there, than in any other part of the World of a colder temperature.[24]

Morocco, in emphasizing the differences between North and South, may be trying to fend off European expectations about the monstrous nature of Africa.

Obviously no Desdemona, Portia remains indifferent as Morocco, like Othello, tells portions of the story of his life:

> By this scimitar,
> That slew the Sophy and a Persian prince
> That won three fields of Sultan Solyman,
> I would o'erstare the sternest eyes that look,
> Outbrave the heart most daring on the earth,
> Pluck the young sucking cubs from the she-bear,
> Yea, mock the lion when 'a roars for prey,
> To win thee, lady.

> (II.i.24–31)

Portia does not devour his narrative of desire and valiant exploits; instead, she relies on her father's lottery for protection, reciting its rules and conditions. When Morocco insists on making his choice, she delays: 'First, forward to the temple; after dinner / Your hazard shall be made' (II.i.44–5). Because of the lottery, she can seem impartial to this suitor, although she clearly deems him unacceptable on racial grounds.

Morocco falsely assumes that the lottery levels the playing field. As he explains, others have equally been encouraged to pursue Portia's hand:

> All the world desires her;
> From the four corners of the earth they come
> To kiss this shrine, this mortal breathing saint.
> The Hyrcanian deserts and the vasty wilds
> Of wide Arabia are as thoroughfares now
> For princes to come view fair Portia.
> The watery kingdom, whose ambitious head
> Spits in the face of heaven, is no bar
> To stop the foreign spirits, but they come
> As o'er a brook to see fair Portia.

> (II.vii.38–47)

The image here clearly inverts the legend of the Golden Fleece. 'Fair Portia' is no alien Medea from far-away Colchis. 'Foreign spirits' threaten to seize a European prize and take it to alien territory.

Portia, however, sees these 'foreign spirits' as veritable monsters. In fact, she aligns herself with Hercules, the killer of monsters. Later, as Bassanio approaches in order to make his choice, she hopes that he will prove himself a new Hercules, who 'did redeem/ The virgin tribute paid by howling Troy/ To the sea monster' (III.ii.55–7). She sees herself as the virgin surrounded by the sea monster: 'I stand for sacrifice' (III.ii.57).

Although Portia and others emphasize the lottery as 'chance,' the solution to the puzzle consists of a culturally, ideologically encoded message. Most of the 'foreign spirits' seem incapable of deciphering the inscriptions correctly. Morocco, however, realizes that it may take more than a Hercules to free this virgin:

> If Hercules and Lichas play at dice
> Which is the better man, the greater throw
> May turn by fortune from the weaker hand.
> So is Alcides beaten by his rogue,
> And so may I, blind Fortune leading me,
> Miss that which one unworthier may attain,
> And die with grieving.

> (II.i.32–8)

Ironically, coming from regions that Portia considers barbarous, he could never be a Hercules and hence, unlike Bassanio, an acceptable husband for her. As we will discover, the choice depends upon a cultural insider's knowledge.

The answer that Morocco seeks depends on the analysis of cultural artifacts, representations and encodings, not simply on linguistic skills. The casket lies at the heart of his interpretation. We know, of course, that, as the *OED* indicates, the word casket meant 'A small box or chest for jewels, letters, or other things of value, itself often of valuable material and richly ornamented.'[25] On the other hand, the word coffin meant both 'a chest, case, casket, box' and 'the box or chest in which a corpse is enclosed for burial' (*OED*). In other words, a coffin was a casket, but a casket was not a coffin.[26] In his cultural imagination, however, Morocco connects these artifacts. I contend that for him the lead casket becomes an Elizabethan lead coffin. He associates the lead casket and death, bringing his knowledge, though partial and imperfect, of European cultures to bear upon his choice:

> One of these three contains her heavenly picture.
> Is't like that lead contains her? 'Twere damnation
> To think so base a thought; it were too gross
> To rib her cerecloth in the obscure grave.

> (II.vii.48–51)

Wealthy Europeans, he realizes, were buried in leaden coffins. The anthropoid coffins, writes Julian Litten, 'England's response in lead to the Egyptian mummy case, became fashionable in the fifteenth century and were still to be seen in some areas in the last decade of the seventeenth century. . . . .'[27] Henry VIII's sixth wife, Katherine Parr, for example, died at Sudeley Castle on 5 September 1548. A description of her funeral includes the following: 'Item, she was cearid and chestid in leade accordinglie, and so remaynid in her pryvie Chambre untill things were in a readyness.'[28] In 1868, Dean Stanley opened and examined Queen Elizabeth's vault in Westminster Abbey, wherein he found a body encased in a leaden coffin: 'The cereclothed corpse itself was enclosed within an anthropoid lead shell.'[29] However Morocco gained this knowledge, he associates lead with death; therefore, he expects to find a body cereclothed and encased in lead. Had he followed that logic, he would have found Portia's body placed in the lead casket by her dying father. Although his reasoning differs from Bassanio's, he comes close to decoding the representation devised by Portia's father.

Not wanting to find the representation of a dead Portia, he turns to the gold casket, the key to which he hopes to find from another European artifact, an English coin:

> They have in England
> A coin that bears the figure of an angel
> Stamped in gold – but that's insculped upon;
> But here an angel in a golden bed
> Lies all within.

> (II.vii.55–9)

He listens to the call of the gold casket, reaffirming the meaning of casket as a box inside of which something valuable is kept. Ironically, he finds not a representation of Portia but a dead body: 'A carrion Death, within whose empty eye/ There is a written scroll' (II.vii.

63–4). The inscription points out the obvious, 'All that glisters is not gold' (II.vii.65), a trite, well-known proverb. That he does not know it speaks more to his being an outsider than a greedy suitor. Another ironic reversal occurs, as he realizes: 'Then farewell heat, and welcome frost' (II.vii.75). Having chosen the wrong casket, he bids farewell to the heat of desire, and welcomes the frost of chastity. Ironically, he came seeking the 'icicles' of the North, and returns to the heat of his home country with the ice of his choice. As he leaves, Portia adds another comment, breathing a sigh of relief that the dark-complexioned Morocco has made the wrong choice: 'Let all of his complexion choose me so' (II.vii.79).

Unlike Morocco, Bassanio knows that he loves Portia and she loves him in return. She pleads with him to delay in making his choice, 'for in choosing wrong/ I lose your company' (III.ii.1–2). She also agonizes over whether she should help him: 'I could teach you / How to choose right, but then I am forsworn' (10–11). When he insists, 'But let me to my fortune and the caskets,' she replies: 'Away then! I am locked in one of them; / If you do love me, you will find me out' (III.ii.39; 40–1). In a passage quoted earlier, she invokes the help of young Alcides or Hercules to free her from 'the sea monster' (55–7). She finally encourages him, 'Go, Hercules! / Live thou, I live' (60–1), and sends for music. One should bear in mind the argument of some scholars that, unlike Morocco and the other suitors, Bassanio gets hints from the song that is sung as he makes his choice.[30] This song points to lead through rhyme – 'bred,' 'head,' 'red,' 'fed' – and through the tolling bell (III.ii.63–72). The subliminal song plants images of lead in his mind.

Like Morocco, Bassanio invokes Hercules (III.ii.85) and associates representation with both life and death. He too relies on interpretation of material culture. In a conversation with Antonio, he referred earlier to Portia's Golden Fleece; since that is what he seeks, he now considers the significance of golden hair. Gold reminds him of golden hair, and he focuses his interpretation on the manufacture of wigs:

> Look on beauty,
> And you shall see 'tis purchased by the weight,
> Which therein works a miracle in nature,
> Making them lightest that wear most of it:
> So are those crispèd snaky golden locks,
> Which maketh such wanton gambols with the wind

Upon supposèd fairness, often known
To be the dowry of a second head,
The skull that bred them in the sepulchre.

(III.ii.88–96)

The pursuit of the golden fleece alone leads one to 'the skull that bred them in the sepulchre.'[31] As he indicates, he also knows that 'The world is still deceived with ornament' (74). He thinks of specific examples in law and religion. In law, for example, 'a gracious voice' can cover up a tainted and corrupt plea, 'the show of evil' (75–7). Likewise, he adds, 'In religion,/What damned error but some sober brow/Will bless it and approve it with a text,/Hiding the grossness with fair ornament?' (77–80). He concludes that, if appearances deceive in law and religion, why not then in material culture?

Unlike Morocco, the text suggests, Bassanio can fashion an identity for himself as he makes the choice. Although earlier he had referred to Portia as being 'richly left' and as the 'Golden Fleece' that he desires, he puts aside his desire for Portia's gold. Should he pursue the riches of this world, the gold casket, he would expect to find 'carrion death'; in the simple, dull, unimportant lead, he expects to find Portia's representation. Predictably, bodies are encased in lead, where Portia's father has placed her representation. The subliminal song sung in preparation for his attempt at the lottery of the caskets, his own understanding of European cultural practices, values and assumptions, and his knowledge of funeral practices guide Bassanio toward the right answer.

The double representation found in the gold and lead caskets suggests the European practice of placing two sculptures on funeral monuments: one represents the person in life; the other, the skeletal remains, represents the person in death. A magnificent example of such funeral effigies (Plate 6) can be found in the tomb of Robert Cecil in the Salisbury Chapel, Hatfield House:

On a slab of black marble supported at each corner by white figures representing the cardinal virtues of Justice, Prudence, Temperance and Fortitude, lies the figure of the dead man clad in his Lord Treasurer's robes and with his actual Treasurer's staff in his hand. Beneath the slab a rough pallet props up his skeleton, macabre witness to the condition to which all mortal greatness must in the end come; and awaiting the verdict to be delivered on him by his Creator on the final Day of Judgment.[32]

The inscriptions on the casket and the pictorial representations and inscriptions within seem to be closely intertwined with English funeral practices.[33] The emphasis on these may also reflect Shakespeare's awareness of Francesco Sansovini's observation about Venetian funeral customs: 'Likewise there is no part of the world, where the funerals even of the meanest citizens are solemnized with greater ceremony and expense.'[34] Thus Bassanio's knowledge of and experience in European cultures, as well as his genuine love for Portia, guide him through textual and ethnographical interpretation to arrive at the representation of Portia. Morocco, however, though relying on some knowledge of European cultures, does not have the depth of ethnographical knowledge of Bassanio and hence arrives at the wrong answer.

The second major fragment of the legend of the Golden Fleece lies behind the Jessica–Lorenzo subplot. Bassanio, Gratiano, and Jessica – all three who allude to the legend of the Argonauts – have forgotten an important part of it. The legend follows the familiar pattern of both myth and history: European adventurers set sail for remote alien territory. With the help and love of an alien princess, they bring home prizes in the form of treasure, merchandise, or alien slaves and mistresses. We recall, for example, that in his conquest of Mexico in 1521, Hernán Cortés counted on the help of a native woman; similarly, Jason was helped by Medea, who fell in love with him. As Euripides' *Medea* puts it, she killed the serpent that kept watch over the Golden Fleece, betrayed her father, and committed murder – all to help Jason. Many years later, however, when he wants to marry King Creon's daughter, Jason sees Medea as an alien with no rights or privileges. As he rationalizes his abandonment of her, he reminds her of her alien status and heritage: 'you left a barbarous land to become a resident/ Of Hellas; here you have known justice; you have lived/ In a society where force yields place to law.'[35] Condescendingly, he belittles all women: 'If only children could be got some other way/ Without the female sex!' (p. 34). Enraged by the condescending tone and ingratitude, Medea murders Jason's new bride Glauce, Creon, and her own children.

Shakespeare's comedy mentions neither Jason's rejection of Medea nor Medea's murderous nature; nonetheless, Jessica's story echoes Medea's, not at the later stage of Medea's life, but rather when Jason appeared in Colchis to fetch the Golden Fleece. The daughter of the rich Jew Shylock, Jessica complains about her father's behavior: 'Our house is hell' (II.iii.2); and she is ashamed to be her father's child. Having fallen in love with the Christian Lorenzo, she plans to renounce her Jewish heritage: 'I shall end this strife,/ Become a Christian and thy loving wife!' (II.iii.20–1). When Venetian maskers, or as Shylock puts it, 'Christian fools with varnished faces,' come to fetch her, Jessica steals property from her father: 'I will make fast the doors, and gild myself/ With some moe ducats, and be with you straight' (II.vi.49–50). As she escapes to Belmont, she strews not pieces of a brother's body, as Medea does, but rather Shylock's money and precious stones on the trail behind her. Apparently loving his gold more than his own daughter, Shylock feels pain as he hears of her prodigality: she gives away a diamond that cost two thousand ducats, and trades a turquoise, a gift from her mother Leah to Shylock, for a monkey. This betrayal, though not involving murder, seems to be for the same reasons as Medea's.

Ironically, despite her conversion, Launcelot Gobbo jokingly raises the question of whether Jessica, as a Christian convert, will be able to break the fetters of heredity; in other words, whether she, like Medea, will be forever perceived as an alien. Shylock, we recall, tried to establish that fundamental link between himself and her: 'I say my daughter is my flesh and my blood' (III.i.32). In Act III, scene ii, presumably despite her conversion, Gratiano refers to her as a foreigner, when he asks Nerissa 'cheer yond stranger; bid her welcome' (III.ii.237). This underscores that conversion alone will not change Jessica's status.[36] Later, Launcelot returns to the point when he argues that 'the sins of the father are to be laid upon the children' (III.v.1–2). Always 'plain' with her, he says that he has concluded that she is 'damned' unless she is not 'the Jew's daughter,' what he calls 'a kind of bastard hope.' He adds that 'you are damned both by father and mother' (III.v.13). When Lorenzo enters, Jessica explains to him what Launcelot has just said:

> He tells me flatly there's no mercy for me in heaven because I am a Jew's daughter; and he says you are no good member of the commonwealth, for in converting Jews to Christians you raise the price of pork.
>
> (III.v.29–32)

Since it is Launcelot rather than another more serious character who raises the issue, the conversation diffuses a very important point: the question of Jessica's betrayal of her father and people. Jessica thus complements Portia's association with the legend.

Lorenzo wins Jessica's hand without having to negotiate textual interpretations with aliens. I believe, however, that even this part of the play is consistent with Shakespeare's understanding of the textual basis for cross-cultural encounters because texts will ultimately govern and determine the interaction between Jessica's father Shylock and the Venetians. As in the lottery subplot, the written word ultimately leads to Shylock's defeat, of which Lorenzo becomes the primary beneficiary. Through textual interpretation, Portia embodies Venetian traditions and values.

Jessica's betrayal of her father and her heritage and her alliance with the Christians anticipate many other problems for Shylock. From what we know of the history of European Jews, Shylock had to negotiate a difficult position in Venetian society, whereby he was barely tolerated and not easily assimilated. Cantarini suggests, however, that there is no nation except Venice 'where straungers find better entertainment, and live with greater security,' where 'some forrain men and strangers have beene adopted' into Venetian citizenry: 'eyther in regard of their great nobility, or that they had beene dutiful towardes the state, or els had done unto them some notable service.'[37] Cantarini declares that Venice had special judges to handle legal matters between Venetians and strangers: 'But if the question bee betweene straungers, or that if any citizen will sue a stranger that commeth to lodge in *Venice* for some fewe dayes, those Judges must then bee repayred unto that are appoynted to heare the causes of straungers, and have thereof their proper nomination and tytle.'[38] Obviously, this is a complex issue. In *Shakespeare and the Jews*, James Shapiro reviews the Jewish presence in Europe, arguing for its impact upon the English national psyche: 'Even as England could be defined in part by having purged itself of Jews, English character could be defined by its need to exclude Jewishness.'[39] What follows, then, serves as a brief overview of the situation of European and English Jews.

Jews played a prominent role as financiers in commercial centers such as Venice. The Jews could not very easily assimilate into medieval and Renaissance European societies where they lived either openly or clandestinely; yet they performed an indispensable function in some societies and enjoyed a special, perhaps privileged, status in others.[40] Primarily restricted to the practice of usury and denied other economic activities, some Jews could accumulate assets that proved amazingly tempting to European sovereigns: 'Because of the church's policy of forbidding any Christian from indulging in money-lending or virtually any form of commercial speculation, the Jews were given free rein in this lucrative area.'[41] Yet the status of the Jews undoubtedly varied considerably from place to place.[42] Two sixteenth-century English travelers, Fynes Moryson and Thomas Coryat offer invaluable descriptions of European Jews.[43] Moryson observes that, although the Jews had been banished out of some Christian kingdoms such as England, France, and the Netherlands, 'they lurke disguised' in various places. In some countries, however, they are allowed to dwell openly, although their economic activities and social status are curtailed:

> They live upon usury and selling of Fripery wares, as Brokers, therein permitted by Christian Princes for private gayne to use horrible extortions upon their subjectes, but are not allowed to buy any lands, howses, or stable inheritances, nether have they any Coyne of their owne, but use the Coynes of Princes where they live.[44]

The Jews were despised for not being Christians; in Italy, they were financially punished if they converted, as Coryat explains:

> All their goodes are confiscated as soone as they embrace Christianity: and this I heard is the reason, because whereas many of them doe raise their fortunes by usury, in so much that they doe not only sheare, but also flea many a poore Christians estate by their griping extortion; it is therefore decreed by the Pope, and other free Princes in whose territories they live, that they shall make a restitution of their ill gotten goods, and so disclogge their soules and consciences, when they are admitted by holy baptisme into the bosome of Christs Church. Seeing then when their goods are taken from them at their conversion, they are left even naked, and destitute of their meanes of maintenance, there are fewer Jewes converted to Christianity in Italy, than in any country of Christendome.[45]

The penalties discouraged conversion for appearance's sake or to ensure one's personal safety in a hostile world. Jewish persons, upon conversion, lost their means of support.

Occasionally, Coryat seems sympathetic in his representation of the Jews; although often he dispels a stereotype, only to create another:

I observed some fewe of those Jewes especially some of the Levantines to bee such goodly and proper men, that then I said to my selfe our English proverbe: To looke like a Jewe (whereby is meant sometimes a weather beaten warp-faced fellow, sometimes a phrenticke and lunaticke person, sometimes one discontented) is not true. For indeed I noted some of them to be most elegant and sweet featured persons, which gave me occasion the more to lament their religion.[46]

The Jewish women he found 'as beautiful as ever I saw, and so gorgeous in their apparel, jewels, chaines of gold, and rings adorned with precious stones, that some of our English Countesses do scarce exceede them, having marvailous long traines like Princesses that are borne up by waiting women serving for the same purpose.'[47] Coryat reports that the Jews are 'distinguished and discerned from the Christians by their habites on their heads.'[48] According to him, the Jews born in Europe wear red hats, but those born in the East wear yellow turbans to distinguish them from the Turks, who wear white ones. He describes a religious service, refers to the circumcision practiced by the Jews, and reports on a theological discussion he had with a rabbi.

In some detail, Fynes Moryson, too, describes Jewish customs in various European cities. He says that in Italy the Jews live

in less contempt of the people, and the Princes who extort upon their owne subjectes, doe also for gayne admit the Jewes into their Cittyes, and permitt them to use horrible extortion upon their subjectes, in the lending of mony, and in selling or letting out by the day or weeke upon use both mens and wemens apparrel and furnitures for horses, and all kyndes of Fripery wares.   (p. 488)

In Mantua, he says, they

have more priviledges then the Christian Citizens, keeping the cheefe shops in the very markett places, and hardly to be knowne from Christians, being only tyed to weare a litle snipp of yellowe lace upon the left syde of their Clokes, which some weare on the insyde of their Clockes, or so, as (they being foulded under the left arme) the marke cannot be discerned.   (p. 489)

In Prague, he found 'free liberty of all Religions being permitted;' the Jews enjoyed many privileges (p. 489). According to him, the Jews practice such 'oppressive usury, as it seemed wonderfull the magistrate would suffer them so to devoure Christians' (p. 491). He discusses Jewish circumcision, observation of the Sabbath, fasting, wedding and funeral practices, beliefs, etc.[49] He notices a similarity between Jews and Christians: 'their divine service (save that they dispise the newe testament) is not unlike ours, for it consists of Psalmes, and two lessons, one out of the lawe, the second out of the Prophetts (which last a boye reades, they lesse esteeming them then the lawe)' (p. 493). Moryson notes, for example, that the citizens of Prague treat the Jews 'more like doggs then men'; therefore, he notes, the Bohemian Jews should move to Italy, 'where they live in better fashion, and where the Devill himselfe bringing stoore of mony may be welcome and reverenced' (p. 490).

The history of Jews in England takes an altogether different turn. Apparently the first Jews to arrive in England came with William the Conqueror: 'King William brought the Jewes from Rhoane to inhabite here, he received homage, oth of fidelite, and pledges of the nobles. . . . .'[50] By the middle of the twelfth century, writes Glassman, Jews were able to amass large sums of money, and 'Aaron of Lincoln, a Jewish financier, was supposedly the wealthiest member of the commercial classes.'[51] Glassman argues that 'the king used his Jewish subjects as a kind of sponge to absorb the wealth of his people.'[52] King John extorted large sums of money from the English Jews:

> The King commanded all the Jewes both men and women to be imprisoned and greevouslie punished, because he would have all their mony, some of them gave all they had, and promised more, to the ende they might escape so manie kinds of torments as he did put upon them, for every one of them had one eie at the least pulled out: amongst whome, there was one, which being tormented many waies, would not ransome himselfe, till the king had caused everie daie one of his great teeth to be pulled out by the space of 7. daies, and then he gave the king 10000. markes of silver, to the end they should pull out no more.[53]

From this incident, King John, according to Stow, netted 66,000 marks. In societies where Christians could not practice usury, the Jews occupied a liminal space and performed taboo functions that the Christians could not. No other alien group had such an indispensable role in Christian kingdoms. The 'special' status of the Jews inevitably attracted malice and envy.

The anti-Jewish sentiment flared up from time to time as Christians spread malicious rumors. During the reign of Edward I, Parliament banished the Jews from England; records suggest, however, that some continued to live in England, although it is difficult to determine the precise changes in their status over the next three centuries.[54] The most famous of such Jews was Dr Rodericke Lopez, a Portuguese Marrano, who became Queen Elizabeth's private physician. Though innocent, Dr Lopez was, in 1593–4, arrested, put on trial for treason for trying to poison the Queen, found guilty and executed. Dr Lopez and the co-conspirators were 'hanged, cutte downe alive, holden downe by strength of men, dismembred, bowelled, headed and quartered, their quarters set on the gates of the citie.'[55] The highly sensational trial of Dr Lopez fueled the anti-Jewish sentiment, which may have manifested itself in a revival of Marlowe's *The Jew of Malta*. Cecil Roth writes: 'A miniature anti-Semitic storm was nevertheless aroused in England. During the period between the sentence and its execution the most popular play on the London stage was Marlowe's *Jew of Malta*, the extravagances of which seemed to anticipate the character as well as the fate of Dr Lopes.'[56] The interest in the trial persisted well into the seventeenth century. The fourth edition of *A Thankfvll Remembrance of Gods Mercie* (1630), by George Carleton, Bishop of Chichester, includes a cartoon depicting Dr Lopez and his co-conspirator Stephen Ferreira da Gama. This is the earliest Anglo-Jewish portrait (Plate 7).[57]

For knowledge of the Jewish people, most Elizabethans relied on literary representations rather than everyday interaction. In these representations, the Jews, through hatred of all Christians, re-enact the crucifixion of Christ. Shakespeare's Shylock may be reflecting these accounts when he describes the mutual hatred, 'the ancient grudge,' that he and Antonio feel toward each other: 'I hate him for he is a Christian' (I.iii.37). When Shylock is about to go to dinner with the Christians, he observes, 'But yet I'll go in hate to feed upon / The prodigal Christian' (II.v.14–15). In various accounts, Christians perceive the Jews as bloodthirsty, incapable of avoiding a desire to crucify every Christian. Jewish identity seems at once trapped in and by representation, perhaps, as James Shapiro has pointed out, because of the belief that 'Jews, like actors, were skilled at exploiting representation itself.'[58]

Many writers perceived the rejection of Jesus as the Messiah as the quintessential mark of Jewish identity. Andrewe Boorde, in his 1542 *The Fyrst Boke of the Introduction of Knowledge*, offers a compendium of various nations and ethnic groups of the world. In chapter 29, he defines what he judges to be the Jewish character and offers a picture of a generic middle-aged man wearing a tunic and scarf. The caption under the picture reads: 'I am an Hebrycyon, some call me a Jew/ To Jesu Chryst I was never trew.'[59] He describes Palestine as a noble and fruitful country; but he says that there are no Jews there: 'there doth never a Jue dwel in at Jury, for it was prophised to them bi theyr lawe, that yf they would not believe in Messias which is christ, they should be expelled out of their countrey.' He adds that the 'Jewes do dwell amonge christian people in divers cities & townes, as in Rome, Naples, Venis, and diverce other places, and for asmuch as our Lorde did suffer death at Jerusalem.' Although, according to Boorde, the Jews are a people without a country, like the Egyptians/Gypsies, they are nonetheless human, not monsters.

Others offer a much harsher picture. Edward Fenton, in his 1569 translation of Boaistuau's *Certaine Secret Wonders of Nature*, is unabashedly anti-Semitic. Fenton places the Jews among medical freaks, other monsters, and strange phenomena of nature. The descriptions and the illustrations underscore the sensational nature of the material. Fenton reports, for example, that in England in 1552, a monster was born, 'a childe, which had two bodies, two heades and foure hands, and yet had but one belly and one navell: On one syde of the bodye came two perfect leggs, and on the other, but one, the same having one foote made like two, tyed the one gainst the other with ten toes.'[60] Another section depicts a pygmy born in France: 'It was a childe rough or hairy on all the body, having the navell in the place where the nose would stand, and the eyes where naturally should stand the mouth' (fol. 146). Amid the menagerie of freaks, one finds the portrait of a Jew (Plate 8). The picture is dominated by three figures: a Jew, a fountain, and a child on a large cross. The Jew, on the left-hand side, shares the foreground with the crucifix, which stands on the right-hand side. The Jew holds a bag, presumably full of poison, which he threatens to drop into the fountain. Unlike the other freaks, which are one of a kind, the Jew belongs to a 'wicked secte,' known for molesting 'our Christian publike weale,' and committing 'cruell blasphemies & abhominable execrations.' The Jew is thus of double status as a member of a human group and as a unique monstrous phenomenon of nature.

In their apparent rejection of the Christian Messiah, Fenton suggests, the Jews annually sacrifice a Christian boy. He writes of one particular incident that occurred during the reign of King Philip:

> These wicked people in the despite of the passion of Jesus Christe, upon good Friday, when they judged that the Christians were most occupied in celebrating that day, they inclosed them selves yearely in a cave, where having stolne a yong chylde, they whipte him, crounyng him with thornes, makying him to drinke gall, and in the end crucified him upon a crosse.
>
> (fol. 27)

It is clear that the crucifix of the picture illustrates the alleged incident. Similarly, he describes another crime committed by the Jews, who having 'allied them selves in consorte wyth divers Lepers,' made a concoction of blood, urine, and poisonous herbs, with which they poisoned a well and spread the plague throughout Europe. Although the Jews look human, Fenton suggests, they are like the other monsters, and harbor a desire to kill all humans.

Other accounts, less sensational but thoroughly prejudiced, offer a similar picture of the Jews as practitioners of 'ritual murder.'[61] During the reign of Henry III, 103 Jews from Lincoln were accused of crucifying a child, named Hugh of Lincoln:

> The child which they had so crucified was named Hugh, about an eight yeares of age. They kept him ten daies after they got him into their hands, sending in the meane time unto diverse other places of the realme, for other of their nation to be present at the crucifying of him.[62]

The child's mother found the body behind the Jew's house: 'she had learned, that hir sonne was lastlie seen plaieng with certeine Jews children of like age of him, before the dore of the same Jew' (p. 437). In the same vein, Chaucer's Prioress narrates the story of Hugh of Lincoln, who used to sing '*O Alma redemptoris*' as he walked through the Jewish quarter, until the Jews 'kitte his throte, and in a pit hym caste.'[63] The Prioress and other sources believe that, out of hatred, the Jews compulsively re-enact the crucifixion of Jesus and the crime of Herod against the Holy Innocents.

Even the practice of circumcision was believed to be a bloody re-enactment of the Crucifixion. Fynes Moryson observed a boy being circumcised:

> Then the Chyldes linnen Clothes being opened, the Rabby cutt off his prepuce, and (with leave be it related for clearing of the Ceremony) did with his mouth sucke the blood of his privy part, and after drawing and spitting out of much blood, sprinckled a red powder upon the wounde. The prepuce he had at the first cutting cast into a guilt sylver bowle full of wyne, whereof the Rabby the Father and the Godfather did drincke, sprinckling some drops into the Chyldes mouth. Then the pre-puce or foreskinne was taken out, and putt into a box of salt to be buryed after in the Churchyearde.[64]

Thomas Coryat points to what he considers a fundamental urge that the Jews possess to engage in seemingly endless repetition: 'One thing they observe in their service which is utterly condemned by our Saviour Christ, Battologia, that is a very tedious babling, and an often repetition of one thing, which cloied mine eares so much that I could not endure them any longer, having heard them at least an houre.'[65] Shylock's presence is thus doubly textual: he is not only a character in Shakespeare's play but also an echo of previous and contemporaneous representations of Jews in history and in literature.

Shakespeare's Shylock is not, however, simply a stereotype out of these texts or historical accounts about European Jews; rather, he becomes an individual, a reader and interpreter of texts in his own right. Like Morocco, he matches wits with Venetians in a fierce battle of textual interpretation. His status in Venice, his faith, and his fortune are at stake. As in the casket subplot, where Portia's father encodes the inscription in such a way as to defeat Morocco and other undesirable aliens, Portia eventually emerges as the champion of Venetian traditions, values, and interests by defeating Shylock and confiscating his 'Golden Fleece.' Shylock's interaction with Christians hinges upon the interpretation of four texts: the Venetian City Charter, Genesis 27–30, the bond, and decrees against aliens.

Like Morocco, Shylock wrongly assumes a level playing field, an assumption apparently derived from what turns out to be a com-monly held belief, as Antonio explains:

> The Duke cannot deny the course of law;
> For the commodity that strangers have
> With us in Venice, if it be denied,
> Will much impeach the justice of the state,
> Since that the trade and profit of the city
> Consisteth of all nations.
>
> (III.iii.26–31)

In this passage, Antonio suggests that the charter codifies and governs all transactions in Venice. Apparently the equivalent of a Bill of Rights, the Charter extends its protection to Venetians and foreigners alike, who feel confident that they enjoy equal recourse to the Law. Shylock, for example, does not hesitate to invoke the Charter (IV.i.39). Even Antonio readily resigns himself to death because of the inviolability of the agreement into which he and Shylock have entered under Venetian Law. Until Portia appears in the courtroom, no one argues that the Charter should discriminate alien from citizen. Thus, although Venetian life and commercial interests intersect alien reality and markets, the Charter presumably offers an umbrella of protection for both Venetians and aliens and ensures harmonious mercantile transactions. Foreigners and Venetians seem to agree on the interpretation of the Charter.

The next text opened for interpretation is Genesis 27–30. As in the legend of the Golden Fleece, Shakespeare splits the Genesis account into two segments, one involving Shylock and the other Jessica. The story of Jacob, Laban, and Laban's daughters Leah and Rachel must have been in the back of Shakespeare's mind as he conceived of a context for the characterization of Shylock. *The Merchant of Venice* contains seven allusions to the biblical Jacob, six of which occur in Act I, scene iii, and two references to Jacob's father Abraham. Except for a brief reference in *Measure for Measure*, the name occurs nowhere else in Shakespeare's canon. Shylock's wife, like Jacob's first wife, was also called Leah. The story of Shylock's daughter Jessica and Lorenzo echoes Jacob's. Shylock seems to consider Jacob a hero in his ability to make Laban's sheep multiply so that both he and Laban benefit from it: 'This was a way to thrive, and he was blest;/ And thrift is blessing if men steal it not' (I.iii.85–6).[66]

Like the Legend of the Golden Fleece, the biblical story also contains a subtext that Shylock does not remember. Laban repeatedly breaks his promises: he offers Jacob the wrong wife and then cheats his son-in-law out of the promised share of the herds. Tired of broken promises, Jacob escapes with his two wives, Leah and Rachel, his children, and his slaves. Like Jessica, Rachel steals from her father, although there is no clear explanation as to why she does so: 'When Laban the Aramaean had gone to shear his sheep, Rachel stole her father's household gods, and Jacob deceived Laban, keeping his departure secret.'[67] Yet, we should remember that, for a nomadic tribe with few possessions, the household gods probably had not only emotional but also monetary value.[68] When Laban sets forth in pursuit of Jacob and the stolen property, he arrives where the fugitives have pitched their tents. He unsuccessfully searches for the household gods until he enters Rachel's tent:

> Now she [Rachel] had taken the household gods and put them in the camel-bag and was sitting on them. Laban went through everything in the tent and found nothing. Rachel said to her father, 'Do not take it amiss, sir, that I cannot rise in your presence: the common lot of woman is upon me.' So for all his search Laban did not find his household gods.
>
> (Gen. 31: 32–5).

As in the Golden Fleece legend, the daughter deceives her father to help her husband.

For Shylock, the biblical text presumably proves that the Scriptures sanction 'thrift': he ignores the implications of Rachel's deceit. Shylock and Antonio compete over the interpretation of this text. Antonio seems puzzled as to the purpose of Shylock's story:

> This was a venture, sir, that Jacob served for,
> A thing not in his power to bring to pass,
> But swayed and fashioned by the hand of heaven.
> Was it inserted to make interest good?
> Or is your gold and silver ewes and rams?
>
> (I.iii.87–91)

Antonio doubts Jacob's ability to control the outcome of the sheep-raising venture; as a matter of fact, Antonio too denies the uncertainty of his own investments. He assumes that, for Shylock, Jacob's story serves to justify charging interest on loans. Then he attacks Shylock's ability and credibility as an interpreter of texts: 'The devil can cite Scripture for his purpose./ An evil soul producing holy witness/ Is like a villain with a smiling cheek,/ A goodly apple rotten at the heart' (I.iii.95–8). Antonio refuses to take the ewes and rams as metaphors for the gold and silver pieces that can multiply. Divergent interpretations clearly separate Antonio from Shylock and foreshadow the courtroom battle with Portia.

The third and perhaps most important text is the bond, a duly notarized legal document that both Antonio and Shylock sign, as Shylock notes: 'Then meet me forthwith at the notary's;/ Give him direction for this merry bond,/ And I will go and purse the ducats straight' (I.iii.168–70). Shylock seems utterly puzzled as to why Antonio would turn to him for a loan:

> You come to me and you say,
> 'Shylock, we would have moneys' – you say so,
> You that did void your rheum upon my beard
> And foot me as you spurn a stranger cur
> Over your threshold!
>
> (I.iii.111–15)

If he is held in so much contempt, Shylock reasons, how can Antonio want to borrow money from a cur or a 'bondman'? Since Antonio insists on having the loan, 'lend it rather to thine enemy' (131), Shylock names his conditions. The document, presumably drawn up according to the laws of Venice, becomes a test of the rights of all in the city.

When Antonio fails to repay the loan and Shylock insists on exacting the penalty, Salerio suggests that Shylock 'plies the Duke at morning and at night,/ And doth impeach the freedom of the state/ If they deny him justice' (III.ii.277–9). Venice, as a commercial center and world metropolis, perpetuates the myth that it offers protection for both citizens and aliens. An alien tests this legal umbrella of protection. Shylock succeeds awhile, as his desire for revenge energizes him and the seeming fairness of the Venetian Law empowers him. Antonio, the man who has spurned and spit on him, remains at his mercy. In the process, however, Shylock exposes his own hatred and intransigence. As Shylock matches wits with Antonio, as an interpreter of a Venetian text, he temporarily prevails.

Like the story of the caskets, the bond plot depends upon the interpretation of a written text. When Portia emerges as a textual interpreter, however, the bond does not prove liberating for Shylock.[69] Assuming equal protection under the Venetian charter, Shylock offers a literal interpretation of the bond. When Portia herself insists on the literal interpretation, she entraps Shylock in the text and demonstrates to the court that he is the enemy of the Christians. Instead of winning the case, Shylock emerges from the courtroom as the Jew who seeks the life of Christians, desiring the crucifixion of Antonio, always unable to rise above the stereotype.

The fourth text consists of a secret decree presumably hidden in the archives of Venice. Not open for scrutiny or interpretation, for no one except Portia knows of its existence, the decree codifies xenophobia, singling out foreigners for harsh punishment:

> It is enacted in the laws of Venice,
> If it be proved against an alien
> That by direct or indirect attempts
> He seek the life of any citizen,
> The party 'gainst the which he doth contrive
> Shall seize one half his goods; the other half
> Comes to the privy coffer of the state;
> And the offender's life lies in the mercy
> Of the Duke only, 'gainst all other voice.

(IV.i.346–54)

Like Antonio in his dispute with Shylock about the biblical passage, Portia attempts to exclude Shylock from the community of interpreters by attacking his character. Other laws apply to everyone; this decree applies only to aliens. Shylock could interpret the first three texts, even if his interpretation differed from everyone else's, but not here. The decree distinguishes citizen from alien, insider from outsider, Self from Other. Peering into the gold casket, Morocco discovered 'carrion death'; Shylock, by probing the Venetian legal system, has discovered utmost prejudice.[70] In the courtroom, Portia affirms and reinforces Shylock's status as an alien.

The Christians exchange other texts, which further empower them. Portia, though impersonating a lawyer, gains power from Doctor Bellario's letters and other writings that the two have consulted together. Antonio's desperate letter to Bassanio in Act III elicits help from Portia and Bellario. At the end of the play, Portia brings Antonio letters reporting that he has not lost everything after all. Antonio appropriately thanks Portia: 'Sweet lady, you have given me life and living!' (V.i.286). Also Lorenzo and his newly Christian wife stand to benefit from other Venetian writings. Nerissa, speaking as the lawyer's clerk, unexpectedly reveals that Shylock was forced to draw up documents through which he has surrendered his possessions to Lorenzo and Jessica: 'There do I give you and Jessica/ From the rich Jew, a special deed of gift,/ After his death, of all he dies possessed of' (V.i.291–3). These texts bring about the 'happy' resolution for the Christians. Portia's father, in the caskets subplot, and Portia, in the pound-of-flesh plot, demonstrate the power of written texts in eventually advancing and protecting Venetian interests.

Morocco and Shylock find themselves at the threshold of European life, but like the 'threshold dog' of Shylock's allusion, they do not gain acceptance in Venice. Presumption of equality, which initially permits Morocco to contend for Portia's hand and Shylock to enter into a legal agreement, proves itself an illusion. Both Morocco and Shylock encounter texts that defeat them. Portia's textual negotiations with these aliens, however, expose what the Venetians want to hide: xenophobia and racial and religious prejudice. In male disguise, she undertakes Antonio's rescue and replicates the 'magic' of her father's caskets: like her father, she creates a textual barrier, which Shylock cannot finally overcome. Her 'victory' far exceeds what she apparently set out to do: it saves Antonio's life, allows Antonio to demand Shylock's fortune and conversion, and underwrites the marriage of Lorenzo and Jessica. As a seemingly passive heiress whose father devised a lottery to protect her from undesirable aliens and as a cross-dressed Italian attorney who clashes with a Jewish male, Portia thus becomes the ideological center of a cultural battle, which Venice fights by means of texts and which yields fundamental displacements of identity. Through textual encodings, her culture confronts, defeats, or keeps at bay what Coryat refers to as 'barbarous Ethnickes.'

4

Textual Intersections:
Titus Andronicus and *Othello*

For mine owne part, when I heare the Africans evil spoken of, I wil affirme myselfe to be one of Granada; and when I perceive the nation of Granada to be discommended, then will I professe my selfe to be an African.

Leo Africanus, *A Geographical Historie of Africa* (1600)

On 13 May 1888, Princess Isabel, Regent of the Empire of Brazil, signed into law the emancipation of all slaves in the country, and masses of her subjects took to the streets of Rio de Janeiro to celebrate. Two years later, Brazilians, now under a provisional republican government, witnessed another momentous event in the history of African slavery. On 14 December 1890, Rui Barbosa, Minister of Finance and Internal Affairs, ordered a thorough search of the archives that had been kept by the Portuguese colonial authorities and later by the Imperial government.[1] All records pertaining to slavery were to be located and burned. Barbosa hoped to remove a blot from the national character. If, as Michel de Certeau suggests, 'writing *produces history*,' then Barbosa single-handedly succeeded in wiping out much of the history of millions of Brazilians of African descent.[2]

This experience has an ideological precedent in an account written in 1453, at the dawn of the Atlantic slave trade. The Portuguese chronicler Gomes Eanes de Azurara recorded the capture of the first African slaves and the ideology that justified it. In a passage quoted earlier, Azurara remarked that 'after they [the Africans] had come to this land of Portugal, they never more tried to fly, but rather in time forgot all about their own country, as soon as they began to taste the good things of this one.'[3] Barbosa and Azurara apparently differ in their intentions: the actions of one derive from embarrassment for his country's past; whereas the actions of the other stem from arrogant and Eurocentric self-confidence. Yet Barbosa and Azurara

97

converge in their belief that the comforts of Europe or the bonfires of the newly proclaimed Brazilian Republic would obliterate the cultural and historical memory of the African slaves. Undoubtedly, without memory, only puzzled faces, feeling a profound sense of displacement, would remain.

This chapter focuses on cross-cultural encounters as dramatic fictions in which Africans communicate a profound sense of cultural displacement in *Titus Andronicus* and *Othello*. As they interact with members of European cultures, Aaron and Othello function as displaced representatives from geographically remote and culturally exotic places. These two characters, however, have incomplete, partial, or no cultural memory and, therefore, contrast with Europeans, who are embroiled in historical enterprises. Their presence invites ethnographical recovery and reconstruction. Shakespeare situates his African characters at the intersections of European and alien cultures, dramatizing what Claude Lévi-Strauss refers to as 'the problem of writing the history of a present without a past.'[4] My discussion will center first on *Titus Andronicus* and then on *Othello*.

I

Lévi-Strauss argues that both history and anthropology share a common goal, 'a better understanding of man'; he adds, however, that 'They differ, principally, in their choice of complementary perspectives: History organizes its data in relation to conscious expressions of social life, while anthropology proceeds by examining its unconscious foundations.'[5] In *Titus Andronicus*, Shakespeare pursues these complementary perspectives in his portrayal of a Moor displaced in the Roman culture. The Romans make history and celebrate a collective act of remembering; and even Tamora, a white woman and a prisoner of war, enters the public life of Rome. Aaron, however, has no memory and cannot participate in the making of history; rather, he epitomizes the unconscious foundation of an ethnographical fantasy that his presence generates.

In his edition, Gustav Cross calls *Titus Andronicus* 'a ridiculous play,' nothing more than a 'gallimaufry of murders, rapes, lopped limbs, and heads baked in a pie, lavishly served with the rich purple sauce of rhetoric.'[6] In *Palladis Tamia: Wit's Treasury* (1598), Francis Meres, however, praised *Titus Andronicus* as 'our best for Tragedie' and lamented that greater plays could have been written if patrons like Augustus, Octavia, or Mecaenas 'were alive to rewarde and countenaunce' the playwrights.[7] Indeed, I believe that the notable RSC production directed by Deborah Warner, which I saw on 1 July 1988, vindicated Meres's assessment and proved the extraordinary power of this drama on the stage.[8] In the intimacy of the Pit at the Barbican Centre, this production with Brian Cox in the title role, truly lived up to the promises of Stanley Wells' program notes: 'The theatrical experience of *Titus Andronicus* shows that it has retained its power to move and disturb audiences by the characterization of both major and minor roles, by the verbal rhetoric of Marcus and Titus and the dumb rhetoric of the stricken Lavinia, and by the climactic horrors of the final holocaust.'[9] I can also testify to the interest that the play elicits in the classroom, and the emotional vigor with which my students approach it through performance, discussion, and other assignments. Further, I believe that the play also retains its historical importance in Shakespeare's exploration of the cross-cultural experience.

Shakespeare may have written *Titus Andronicus* in order to cap-italize on the audience's growing interest in things African, as a review of contemporary plays makes apparent. The play may be in part indebted to George Peele's *The Battle of Alcazar* (*c.* 1589), which recounts the historical events of the famous battle of Alcazarquivir on 4 August 1578, when Dom Sebastian (1554–78), the last king of the Aviz dynasty of Portugal, lost his life fighting Muslims in Mor-occo.[10] Peele creates a character, the Moor (Muly Mahamet), who is not unlike Shakespeare's Aaron. Eldred Jones writes:

> [Muly] is the type of the cruel Moor who is usually portrayed, as he is here, as black. Historical accident thus combined with pop-ular rumour to produce Muly, who headed a line of black Moors on the stage, a line which included notably Aaron in *Titus Andron-icus* (1589–1590), Eleazer in *Lust's Dominion* (1599), and, in a strik-ing reversal of the traditional portrayal, the hero of *Othello* (1604).[11]

But in terms of plot, *The Battle of Alcazar* and Shakespeare's tragedy have little in common: one takes place in the distant deserts of Barbary; the other, in ancient Rome, although Peele's play reflects an interest in Dom Sebastian – his death, fanaticism, and the legend prophesying his messianic return to found a new kingdom. In England, this interest was sustained into the end of the seventeenth century when John Dryden wrote his play, *Don Sebastian*, and in Brazil, into the end of the nineteenth century with the messianic rural uprising at Canudos (1893–7), led by Antônio Conselheiro.[12]

In *Lust's Dominion*, by Thomas Dekker, we encounter Eleazar, a displaced Moor who has become the paramour of the Queen Mother of Spain and who resembles Aaron in his evil nature. Eleazar is married to a white noblewoman, who apparently is unaware of his schemes and of his love affair with the Queen Mother. Whether Dekker's play in fact derives from *The Battle of Alcazar* or *Titus Andronicus*, we cannot ascertain; but the Moor, like Aaron, has a white lover with whom he plans to gain the throne and to destroy his Spanish arch-enemies. The presenter, throughout Peele's play, curses the Moor, who is described as 'this Negro moore' (II. Prol. 278) and as the 'barbarous Moore,' who was 'Chased from his dignitie and his diademe,/And lives forlorne among the mountaine shrubs,/And makes his food the flesh of savage beasts' (II. Prol. 307–10). Although evil, both Eleazar and Aaron are indeed quite different. Eleazar is a deposed African prince who tries to avenge his father whom the Spaniards killed in combat. His desire for revenge stems from an indisputable grievance. Conversely, Aaron harbors no specific grudge, and on the surface, he seems to act out of a motiveless malignancy. Further, unlike these other plays, *Titus Andronicus* highlights a clash between a society that makes history by conquering alien nations and a displaced African without history.

In fact, Aaron reveals a stronger kinship to Africans depicted in medieval and Renaissance art than to those in the drama of the period.[13] Most of these representations are highly stylized, similar to the Ethiopian that appears on the shield of the Knight of Sparta, a suitor to Thaisa in Shakespeare's *Pericles*: 'And the device he bears upon his shield/Is a black Ethiope reaching at the sun;/The word, 'Lux tua vita mihi'' (II.ii.19–21). Jean Devisse and Michel Mollat discuss in detail the image of the Black in Western art, tracing 'a wealth of themes and myths [that] grew up around the color black, the *Aethiops*, Prester John, the Queen of Sheba, and the Magi.'[14] They also trace the 'emergence and development of the image of St. Maurice' and discuss the families that 'included the black in their armorial bearings.'[15] Aaron's portrayal depends to a large extent on images associated with the color black and therefore emerges out of ethnographical fantasies.

In his paintings, Paolo Veronese (1528–88) captures well the Africans' profound sense of displacement. In *Christ and the Centurions*

(Plate 11) (Nelson-Atkins Museum of Art, Kansas City, Missouri),[16] Veronese presents a dramatic scene, dominated by two groups: on the left, Christ, surrounded by the disciples, and on the right, Roman centurions. Providing the focal point, one centurion kneels before Christ, while the others try to pull him away. From behind the centurions emerges the turbaned head of an African, making the scene more poignant and dramatic. The African seems enigmatic, puzzled, somewhat melancholy, utterly displaced, as if realizing that nothing but slavery awaits him. In *The Finding of Moses* (Andrew Mellon Collection, National Gallery), Veronese depicts a female African page holding a basket. This time the African appears in the foreground, interposed between the viewer and the Pharaoh's daughter and her servants. Whether the page found Moses or simply had to transport him, the scene does not explain. She, however, no longer holds the infant in her hands: her role is not clear, except as a silent observer. In *Cena in casa di Levi* (Venice, Gallerie dell'Accademia), the face of another African onlooker appears from behind a column, as though, in Veronese's imagination, an African face will emerge wherever shadows are to be found.[17] Emblems of ethnographical fantasy, these silent and melancholy faces reach across the canvas, seemingly unable to tell their story or to establish an identity. I am not, however, suggesting that Veronese provided a source for Shakespeare; rather, Veronese's paintings serve as an emblem for Africans standing at the margins of history. I will argue that, from the margins, Aaron explores cultural concepts associated with the color black and the violent fantasies that he finds in Roman texts – out of which, he shapes an identity for himself.

In *Titus Andronicus*, conquest of foreign nations brings into the same space a racially diverse group: Romans, Goths, and a Moor. Emily Bartels writes that 'Before Titus hands the rule to Saturninus, the bounds between Romans and Goths are clearly and absolutely in place'; but 'When Saturninus takes command, however, the differentiation between the two worlds, between inside and outside, self and other, is disrupted, and with it the idea of right and what is right in Rome.'[18] I see the situation in the play differently, however. I believe that, although the Romans assimilate the foreign Tamora and crown her as their empress, they, nevertheless, maintain strong racial boundaries, exaggerate cultural and racial differences, and in fact never accept Aaron on any level. As a European, Tamora enters the historical consciousness of Rome in ways that Aaron, as an African, never can.

In Shakespeare's play, the 500-year-old mausoleum of the Andronici symbolizes the culture and history of a country, where glory depends upon spectacular acts of violence – killing, plundering, conquering – committed to expand Roman dominion over barbarous nations. Act I centers on the family tomb. This site provides the focal point for Titus's triumphal march bearing the Goths as slaves to Rome, for the sacrifice of Tamora's first-born son, Alarbus, and for the funeral of another son of Titus, killed in the wars against the Goths. As Titus indicates, the dead and the living intermingle: to this place are brought together 'the poor remains' of living warriors who are to be rewarded with the love of Rome, and of dead ones who are to find 'burial amongst their ancestors' (I.i.84–7). As Titus believes, no higher honor can be achieved but in military service to Rome, 'Knighted in field, slain manfully in arms,/In right and service of their noble country' (I.i.199–200). The cross-cultural encounter entails violent subjugation of alien nations, through which the Romans achieve feats of glory and write their bloody history. One should also bear in mind that the Romans of the play make racial distinctions between the 'fair queen' (I.i.266) of the Goths and the 'raven-colored' Aaron (II.iii.83).

Tamora has a contradictory double status in Rome as both captive barbarian and empress, through which she comments on Roman customs and beliefs. When Lucius demands that Alarbus, 'the proudest prisoner of the Goths,' be turned over, so 'That we may hew his limbs and on a pile/Ad manes fratrum sacrifice his flesh' (I.i.99–100), she offers 'a mother's tears in passion for her son' (I.i.109), hoping that the family-centered Romans will hear her pleas. Like Cleopatra later, she also resents being put on display as the centerpiece of Titus's triumph:

> Sufficeth not that we are brought to Rome
> To beautify thy triumphs and return,
> Captive to thee and to thy Roman yoke;
> But must my sons be slaught'red in the streets
> For valiant doings in their country's cause?
>   (I.i.112–16)

Ironically, she points out that Alarbus, too, served his country. She appeals to compassion: 'sweet mercy is nobility's true badge' (I.i.122). After the Romans carry out the human sacrifice, Tamora comments: 'O cruel irreligious piety!' (I.i.133); Chiron retorts: 'Was never Scythia half so barbarous' (I.i.134).

To counter the brutality of Rome, Tamora puts forward an alternative ethos as a mother. Although Titus remains unmoved by her pleas and displays no sympathy for her, Saturninus responds in a very different way. In an aside, Saturninus is quite struck with Tamora, whom he describes as 'a goodly lady' who, he adds, will not be 'made a scorn in Rome' (I.i.268). Later, when he offers to marry her and create her empress of Rome, she responds: 'If Saturnine advance the Queen of Goths,/She will a handmaid be to his desires,/A loving nurse, a mother to his youth' (I.i.333–5). For a good part of the play, she pretends to be the loving nurse and mother. She also intervenes in Saturninus and Bassianus's dispute over the first 'rape' of Lavinia, advising the two brothers: 'pardon what is past' (I.i.434); and she mediates between the Emperor and Titus, although she really seeks their destruction (IV.iv.88–92). From a barbarous slave, she becomes a Roman, as she points out to Titus: 'Titus, I am incorporate in Rome,/A Roman now adopted happily' (I.i.464–5). She is wife, empress, nurse, mother, and advisor to the Roman emperor. This is a meteoric rise, indeed.

This is not, however, her ethos; she only fills a perceived affective void in Rome. She realizes that to destroy Titus, she must use stratagem and subterfuge: 'Dissemble all your griefs and discontents'; she adds, 'I'll find a day to massacre them all/And race their faction and their family,/The cruel father, and his traitorous sons,/To whom I suèd for my dear son's life' (I.i.446; 453–6). She counsels her sons to kill Bassianus and rape Lavinia, both of whom taunt her about her love affair with Aaron. Having been accepted into the public life of Rome, Tamora differs from Aaron, who remains a shadowy, marginalized figure.

Yet Tamora and Aaron represent complementary perspectives: she finds a niche in Rome's conscious expressions of social life, whereas he seems lodged in its unconscious foundation. Taken captive along with the Goths, Aaron is not the usual barbarian against whom the Romans wage war. Rather, he follows his masters and his lover, the Queen of the Goths. As a black man among the Goths, he was already displaced in ways that none of the African characters in Peele's or Dekker's plays could possibly be. In fact, I believe that Henry Peacham's drawing (*c.* 1595) misrepresents the point of the play.[19] In this drawing, apparently to illustrate the scene in which Tamora begs Titus to spare her son's life, Aaron appears on the right-hand side, to the right of Tamora and her two sons. The Goths are on their knees, but Aaron is upstanding, defiantly brandishing a sword and pointing his finger at Titus. In the play, however, Aaron inconspicuously remains in the background, moving like a shadow. Peacham's Aaron is openly defiant while Shakespeare's character resorts to subterfuge and secrecy. Aaron of the play understands that he occupies the space at the margins of the Roman world, where there is no accountability, where acts of villainy are perpetrated with impunity.

From his first appearance, Aaron is an enigmatic figure. The stage direction in Act I, scene i in part reads: '*[Enter] Tamora, the Queen of Goths, and her two sons, Chiron and Demetrius, with Aaron the Moor, and others as many as can be.*' Except for a brief exit, Aaron remains on stage for the rest of the act, but he has nothing to say. Gustav Cross comments: 'Again, it is curious, to say the least, that Aaron, the demonic force behind most of the action of the play, should be silent during the entire first act.'[20] Although Aaron witnesses a contest between mighty opposites, he blends in with the shadowy background.[21] As a cultural shadow, Aaron bears closer resemblance to Veronese's African figures, who usually lurk from behind the principals, rather than Peacham's Moor.

Blackness defines every aspect of Aaron's character. The connection between his black skin and his identity preoccupies him, as he asks the telling question: 'What signifies my deadly-standing eye,/ My silence, and my cloudy melancholy,/My fleece of wooly hair that now uncurls/Even as an adder when she doth unroll/To do some fatal execution?' (II.iii.32–6). This is understandable, considering that the Romans are obsessed with his blackness. Just before her rape, Lavinia and Bassianus taunt Tamora and Aaron. They refer to Aaron as Tamora's 'swart Cimmerian' (II.iii.72), 'barbarous Moor' (77), and 'raven-colored love' (83). Titus himself refers to Aaron as the 'raven' (III.i.158). For the Romans, the darkness of the woods corresponds to the color of Aaron's skin. In fact, long before he discovers the identity of Lavinia's rapists, Titus assumes that Aaron was involved in her rape. Similarly, Marcus gratuitously kills a fly, apparently because it 'comes in likeness of a coal-black Moor' (III.ii.79).

Nothing but the blackness of his skin seems to link Aaron to a place of origin. Unlike Othello, Aaron displays no sense of a cultural past and seems to possess no memories: he mentions neither parents nor homeland. The only reference to his origins occurs when he searches for a white child to take the place of his and Tamora's black son: 'Not far one Muliteus my countryman / His wife but yesternight was brought to bed; / His child is like to her, fair as you are' (IV.ii.153–5). Although he apparently identifies with a native country, Aaron, unlike Morocco of *The Merchant of Venice*, Eleazar, and even Othello, remains amazingly reticent about his origins – he has no fond recollection or even painful memories for that matter. Without a past, his identity centers almost exclusively on his blackness and on Roman perceptions of him, which he tries to mould in a threefold way: 'Vengeance is in my heart, death in my hand, / Blood and revenge are hammering in my head' (II.iii.38–9). He views his blackness as the measure and the very essence of his difference, as he states: 'Aaron will have his soul black like his face' (III.i.205). No wonder, then, that Aaron turns to the Romans in order to understand what blackness means. He reaches deeply into the unconscious of his Roman oppressors, where he discovers cruelty, pillage, violence, precisely what the Romans associate with blackness; hence, he sets out to make these the mark of his difference.

In this regard, Aaron differs from Fernando, an African who appears in the Portuguese play *Frágua d'Amor* (1525), by Gil Vicente. This character desires to assimilate into Portuguese culture, to be initiated into the privileges of European life, and to gain acceptance as the sexual partner of white women. Nevertheless, he can fulfill none of these desires because of the color of his skin and because he speaks an African creole known as *fala da Guiné* rather than standard Portuguese. One day, as he daydreams, singing a song in *fala da Guiné*, he comes across the goddess Venus, who is disguised as a mortal. Quite taken with this white woman's beauty but well aware of the impossibility of any sexual relationship with her, he offers to become her slave. As such, he will run errands and steal for her – whatever she needs or desires. In search of her son Cupid, Venus wonders whether Fernando has heard the news about a shop that her son has set up in Castile. She explains that Cupid has built a *frágua* or blacksmith's shop, to which she guides Fernando. At the *frágua*, which is managed by four gods, any person can be made over into whatever shape or form that he or she desires. An elderly person may turn into a youth, or a black man into a white man. Even a friar, unhappy with his religious calling, has been transformed into a layman. In fact, Mercury, the shopkeeper, brags in Castilian, *'todo se pude hazer'* (anything can be done). With his hopes raised, Fernando asks to be transformed into a white man, so that he will escape servitude and gain acceptance into white society: *'Fazê-me branco, rogo-te, homem,/asinha, logo, logo, logo:/mandai logo acendere fogo,/e minha nariz feito bem,/e fazê-me beiça delgada, te rogo'* (Make me white, I beg you, man,/Quickly, soon, soon, soon./ Kindle the fire soon./And make my nose well,/And make my lips thin, I beg you.)[22] Jupiter wonders how he wants his body reshaped; Fernando answers in Portuguese: *'Branco como ôvo de galinha'* (white like a chicken egg).

At this point, Fernando enters Cupid's smithy and comes out as a *'muito gentil homem branco'* (a very refined white man). He joins a different world, the rules of which he does not entirely understand. To his horror, Fernando discovers that, although he has become white, his former identity can be easily recognized whenever he opens his mouth. He still speaks *fala da Guiné*:

> *Já mão minha branco estai,*
> *e aqui perna branco é,*
> *mas a mi fala guiné:*
> *se a mi negro falai,*
> *a mi branco para quê?*
> *Se fala meu é negregado,*
> *e não fala portugás,*
> *para que mi martelado?*

> (My hand is already white,
> and my leg is white.
> But I still speak 'Guiné'.
> If I speak black speech,
> what is the use of being white?
> If my speech is black,
> and I don't speak Portuguese,
> why did you 'hammer' me?)

(p. 349)

Language enfetters him to a former identity that skin color cannot erase: he is a black man trapped in a white body. He feels more displaced than ever before. Mercury explains that the gods can do nothing else to help him: *'No podemos hazer más,/lo que pediste te han dado'* (There is nothing we can do;/what you requested has been granted) (p. 349). Desperate, Fernando passionately begs Mercury to restore him to his original appearance:

Dá ca minha negro tornai:
se mi falá namorado
a moier que branco sai,
êle dirá a mi – 'bai, bai,
tu sá home o sá riabo [diabo]?'
A negra, se a mi falai,
dirá a mi: 'Sá chacorreiro!'
—Oiai, seoro ferreiro,
boso meu negro tornai,
como mi saba primeiro.

(Let me be black.
If I speak as a lover
to a white woman
she'll say – 'Go away! Go away!
are you a man or the devil?'
A black woman, if I talk to her,
will say to me: 'Are you kidding?'
Look, Senhor Blacksmith,
change me back into a black man,
As I was at first.)

Fernando realizes that white women will take him for an incubus pretending to be a white man, a white body possessed by the devil; black women will not take him seriously, assuming that he mocks them. Language retains his original identity intact, even when all other markers of difference have been removed: it possesses the body and inscribes it with cultural markers. Understandably, Fernando wants to become inconspicuous in a hostile world; instead, *Frágua d'Amor* suggests that we not only possess language but language possesses us, replicating chains of servitude and helping define our identity in ways similar to the color of our skin.

Unlike Fernando, Aaron does not try to hide his blackness; rather, from early on in the play, he views his black skin as the fundamental marker of his difference. Yet, like Fernando, Aaron seeks to transform himself and to gain recognition by white society. He realizes that his fate depends upon his 'charm' over Tamora and hers over Saturnine. With Tamora's help, he too aspires to climb Mount Olympus and intermingle with the gods:

Upon her wit doth earthly honor wait,
And virtue stoops and trembles at her frown.

> Then, Aaron, arm thy heart and fit thy thoughts
> To mount aloft with thy imperial mistress,
> And mount her pitch whom thou in triumph long
> Hast prisoner held, fett'red in amorous chains,
> And faster bound to Aaron's charming eyes
> Than is Prometheus tied to Caucasus.

(II.i.10–17)

He will shake off his 'slavish weeds and servile thoughts' (I.i.18); and, therefore, transform himself: 'I will be bright and shine in pearl and gold,/To wait upon this new-made empress' (II.i.19–20). To do so, he needs more than Tamora's help. As the references to Greco-Roman mythology of this passage imply, he will research Roman texts in order to discover how he can shine brightly in pearl and gold.

With apparently no memories, Aaron turns to Latin literature and mythology in order to grasp the significance of his blackness. As a matter of fact, all the aliens brought into Rome seem to know Roman culture very well. Tamora advises Saturninus on Roman values, when she points out that Rome deems ingratitude to be 'a heinous sin' (I.i.450–1). She also displays her knowledge of Roman mythology when she sarcastically threatens to change Bassianus into a deer, as Diana once did to Actaeon (II.iii.61–5). Aaron, however, believes that texts encapsulate the heinous side of the Roman character. He studies these texts, lectures on them, and even has Chiron and Demetrius reenact them in 'real' life. In his revenge, Aaron remembers the literary precedents for rape and mutilation: Lucrece, who was raped by Tarquin, and Philomel, who was raped by Tereus. A number of familiar sources contained these stories. Accounts of the rape of Lucrece were to be found in Ovid's *Fasti* and Livy's *Ab urbe condita*. Shakespeare's own poem on the subject, based on these ancient sources and on versions from William Painter's *Palace of Pleasure* and Chaucer's *Legend of Good Women*, was printed in quarto in 1594. The story of Philomel's rape, based on the Greek myth, was available in Ovid's *Metamorphoses*. Aaron notices that Lavinia resembles Lucrece in her virtue: 'Lucrece was not more chaste/Than this Lavinia, Bassianus' love' (II.i.108–9); therefore, like Tarquin, Chiron and Demetrius can rape her. Similarly, he points out to Tamora that Bassianus' 'Philomel must lose her tongue to-day,/Thy sons make pillage of her chastity/And wash their hands in Bassianus' blood'

(II.iii.43–5). But Aaron wants to outsmart Tereus in his cruelty, thereby leaving his imprint upon the Roman myth. To outdo the myth, he suggests an additional act of cruelty: chop off Lavinia's hands so that, unlike Philomel, Lavinia cannot weave the names of her rapists into a tapestry.

Thus, in his crimes against Lavinia, Aaron communicates through texts to the Romans. When Marcus first encounters his niece Lavinia, he immediately draws the lesson from literature: 'But sure some Tereus hath deflow'rèd thee,/And, lest thou shouldst detect him, cut thy tongue' (II.iv.26–7). Marcus also realizes that Lavinia's fate is worse than Philomel's: 'A craftier Tereus, cousin, hast thou met,/ And he hath cut those pretty fingers off/That could have better sewed than Philomel' (II.iv.41–3). This provides the initial clue to decipher the identity of Lavinia's assailants.

Lavinia herself turns to books, through which she hopes to tell her story. In Act IV, scene i, she frightens Lucius' son, following him around, trying to grab his books. Titus reassures the boy that Lavinia means no harm, and in fact, she loves literature: 'Ah, boy, Cornelia never with more care/Read to her sons than she hath read to thee/ Sweet poetry and Tully's Orator' (IV.i.12–14). When Lucius's son, who has read of Hecuba's madness, drops the books he has been reading, Lavinia frantically attempts to turn the pages over with her stumps. Titus concludes, 'Marcus, what means this?/Some book there is that she desires to see' (IV.i.30–1). He guides Lavinia to his library: 'Come and take choice of all my library,/And so beguile thy sorrow, till the heavens/Reveal the damned contriver of this deed' (IV.i.34–6). The boy finally identifies the object of her attention: 'Grandsire, 'tis Ovid's *Metamorphosis*./My mother gave it me' (42– 3). Titus reads and summarizes the appropriate passage: 'This is the tragic tale of Philomel/And treats of Tereus' treason and his rape;/ And rape, I fear, was root of thine annoy' (IV.i.47–9). Reading Ovid together, Titus and his family reconstruct and interpret what befell Lavinia. Titus also accentuates the similarity between Lavinia and Philomel:

> Lavinia, wert thou thus surprised, sweet girl,
> Ravished and wronged as Philomela was,
> Forced in the ruthless, vast, and gloomy woods?
> See, see!
> Ay, such a place there is where we did hunt
> (O had we never, never hunted there!)

Patterned by that the poet here describes,
By nature made for murders and for rapes.

(IV.i.51–8)

Another Tarquin has once again re-enacted Tereus' crime: 'What Roman lord it was durst do the deed./Or slunk not Saturnine, as Tarquin erst,/That left the camp to sin in Lucrece' bed?' (IV.i.62–4). Taking the stick into her mouth and guiding it with her arms, Lavinia writes the names of Chiron and Demetrius in the sand. Obviously, Aaron replicates Ovid's tale, encoding the crime in such a way as to permit the Romans to decipher it by using their own literary knowledge.

In turn, Titus also communicates with Lavinia's assailants through the written word. He scribbles a message on a scroll, which he asks Lucius' son to carry to Chiron and Demetrius, along with some 'weapons of his armory' (IV.ii.11). Demetrius reads the message in Latin: ' "Integer vitae scelerisque purus/Non eget Mauri iaculis nec arcu" ' (IV.ii.20–1), meaning 'one of upright life and free from crime does not need the javelins or bow of the Moor.'[23] Chiron at once identifies the passage, 'I know it well./I read it in the grammar long ago' (22–3); and Aaron concurs, 'Ay, just; a verse in Horace; right, you have it' (24).[24] In an aside, Aaron comments that there is more to this message than Chiron and Demetrius can grasp: 'the old man hath found their guilt,/And sends them weapons wrapped about with lines/That wound, beyond their feeling, to the quick' (IV.ii.27–8), although he does not warn his companions of the danger that the message carries.

Aaron can even forge Roman texts. In Act II, scene iii, he buries gold coins under a tree and gives a 'fatal-plotted scroll' (47) to Tamora for her to convey to Saturninus. In the next scene, Tamora hands Saturninus the letter, who promptly reads a message, supposedly written by Martius and Quintus, disclosing the location of the gold coins and the plan for the murder of Bassianus. Aaron reads Roman literature, re-enacts Roman myths, and forges Roman letters. He even digs up bodies and scribbles notes on the decomposing flesh in order to torment the survivors: 'And on their skins, as on the bark of trees,/Have with my knife carvèd in Roman letters/"Let not your sorrow die, though I am dead" ' (V.i.138–40). For him, writing symbolizes racial prejudice, violence, rape, and conquest. Although he cannot, on his own, bring the Roman empire down, he terrorizes

the Romans, focusing his revenge on representative Romans, especially Lavinia and Titus, whose bodies he seeks to ravage, rape,
mutilate, and above all render unable to write. He even chops off
Titus's hand, the source of the violence and destruction with which
Rome writes its violent history. Aaron seems to succeed, for, as Titus
recognizes, Lavinia's ravished and mutilated body becomes a 'map
of woe' (III.ii.12).

From Roman texts, Aaron discovers the dark side of the Roman
character, through which he forges his own identity. He concludes
that the Romans are 'furious,' 'impatient,' and jealous. Behind their
facade of civility, Aaron discovers that the Romans perpetrate horrifying crimes, especially those committed beyond the borders of
Rome and in spaces hidden from public view, such as the hunting
grounds outside the city. He thus decides to claim this as his space, a
place of darkness and villainy. In defining his identity in opposition
to Roman values, Aaron resembles Satan in Milton's *Paradise Lost*,
who observes:

> To do aught good never will be our task,
> But ever to do ill our sole delight,
> As being the contrary to his high will
> Whom we resist.[25]

Aaron discovers Rome's worst traits, which he adopts in his revenge.
Therefore, he advises Tamora's sons to behave in the Roman fashion:
'That what you cannot as you would achieve,/You must perforce
accomplish as you may' (II.i.106–7). Further, he adds, the forest
provides the necessary cover for acts of villainy: 'The forest walks
are wide and spacious,/And many unfrequented plots there are,/
Fitted by kind for rape and villainy' (II.i.114–16). In contrast, he
remarks, 'The emperor's court is like the house of fame,/The palace
full of tongues, of eyes and ears:/The woods are ruthless, dreadful,
deaf, and dull' (II.i.126–8). Aaron astutely notices that the palace and
the woods reflect two conflicting and irreconcilable parts of the
Roman psyche. The forest comes to symbolize a repressed dimension
of the Roman character. Since the Romans loathe the color black,
Aaron sets out to defend it, knowing that the Romans always assume
the worst about him and expect the worst from him. Therefore,
through acts of violence, Aaron hopes to hold the mirror up to Rome.

When Aaron's child is born and others want to put it to death,
Aaron asks, 'is black so base a hue?' (IV.ii.71). Like Shylock in his

famous speech in *The Merchant of Venice* about his ethnicity, Aaron points out the power of the color black:

> Coal-black is better than another hue
> In that it scorns to bear another hue;
> For all the water in the ocean
> Can never turn the swan's black legs to white,
> Although she lave them hourly in the flood.

(IV.ii.99–103)

Aaron proudly notes his 'seal' stamped upon his son's face, his blackness dominating Tamora's whiteness, and wants to bring the son up 'To be a warrior and command a camp' (IV.ii.181). When taken prisoner by Lucius, who points out that the child is the 'growing image of thy fiend-like face' (V.i.45), Aaron will do anything, even sacrifice his own life, in order to save his son's, to defend his 'seal' and heritage.

A keen observer, Aaron perceives changes that may be sweeping through the Roman world, as, for example, when he comments on Lucius's religious beliefs and the rise of Christianity: 'Yet, for I know thou art religious / And hast a thing within thee callèd conscience, / With twenty popish tricks and ceremonies / Which I have seen thee careful to observe' (V.i.74–7). But even as he appeals for Christian forgiveness, he denies his own beliefs, and paints a horrifying picture of his acts, curses, murders, rapes, false accusations, and perjury. This he has done 'As willingly as one would kill a fly' (142), as if aware of Titus's earlier statement. When Lucius wants to dismiss him as the devil, Aaron retorts: 'If there be devils, would I were a devil, / To live and burn in everlasting fire, / So I might have your company in hell / But to torment you with my bitter tongue!' (V.i.146–50). At the end of the play, he vows to repent for any *good* act that he has ever performed in his life. Even here, Aaron constructs an identity in opposition to Christianity; and apparently aware that Christians associate blackness with the devil, he takes Satan as his model.

Aaron thus views the cross-cultural encounter as a textual experience; therefore, he re-enacts Latin texts and leaves his own scriptural markings. Unlike Tamora, who joins Rome's public life, Aaron has no power to influence history, except through crimes committed upon a dominant and violent culture. Aaron refuses to become like

Veronese's silent bystanders; rather, he enacts a literary rape and mutilation, mutilates Titus' body, and defiles Roman corpses. The Romans, in contrast, constantly make history. In their raids against those they consider barbarous, Titus Andronicus and his sons write history. If Titus's wounds symbolize Roman expansion, Aaron creates a horrifying parody of the Romans as he mutilates and inscribes Roman bodies in order to leave a mark of his identity.[26] Unlike the illiterate Jack Cade, Aaron does not destroy books, but rather uses books to destroy. He remains, however, at the mercy of others, a text seemingly written 'not in tables of stones, but in fleshy tables of the heart' (2 Cor. 3.2–3).

II

In contrast, Othello has cultural memories, however partial they may be, gains acceptance into Venetian society, and even marries a Venetian noblewoman. In *Othello*, Shakespeare creates a character who can also shift between a European and an alien identity. In some ways, Othello resembles Leo Africanus, a Moor born in Granada, Spain (see Plate 10). Africanus' book, *A Geographical Historie of Africa*, presents a first-hand account of his travels in Africa. It circulated in Latin, Italian, and French; John Pory's English translation appeared in 1600 and was, of course, available for Shakespeare to consult.[27] In this work, Africanus shows a remarkable awareness of his double identity, which can shift between Europe and Africa: 'For mine owne part, when I heare the Africans evil spoken of, I wil affirme myselfe to be one of Granada; and when I perceive the nation of Granada to be discommended, then will I professe my selfe to be an African.'[28] I contend that Othello, too, oscillates between two different cultures, but in the process, loses the sense of who he is. Shakespeare dramatizes this oscillation as a narrative shift between history and ethnography.

We must bear in mind that everything in *Othello* is, of course, dramatic fiction; yet Shakespeare creates the semblance that actual historical events in the Venetian–Turkish wars serve as the foundation for his play. For his fictional premise, he turned to Giovanni Battista Giraldi Cinthio's *Gli Hecatommithi* (1566), where he found the intrigue of an ensign to destroy the Moor and his beloved Disdemona. Into this fictional narrative, he inserted a matrix based on historical sources, creating a two-layered dramatic narrative situated simultaneously in a fictive and a historical world. Stephen Greenblatt recognizes one dimension of this phenomenon when he observes that 'in *Othello* the characters have always already experienced submission to narrativity' and that Othello himself 'comes dangerously close to recognizing his status as a text.'[29] He refers to the narratives that Othello and Iago generate in order to fashion their identities. I suggest, however, that in another sense Shakespeare simultaneously grounds his play in history and fiction, perhaps realizing what modern historians have come to recognize: 'narrative form in history, as in fiction, is an artifice, the product of individual imagination.'[30]

The stage history of *Othello* intertwines with historical events. The play was first performed by the King's Men for King James's Court at Whitehall on 1 November 1604.[31] Earlier in the same year, on 15 March, the pageant for King James's entry into London took place. In Gracious Street, the Italian merchants erected the triumphal arch 'filled with paintings and carved figures rather than live actors.'[32] In his text of the pageant, Thomas Dekker describes the arch, which contained a square on the back of which was portrayed the picture of Apollo:

> With all his Ensignes and properties belonging unto him, as a *Sphere*, *Bookes*, a *Caducaeus*, an *Octoedron*, with other *Geometricall* Bodies, and a Harpe in his left hand: his right hand with a golden Wand in it, poynting to the battle of *Lepanto* fought by the *Turks*, (of which his Majestie hath written a *Poem*).[33]

The designer of the arch, as well as Dekker, remembered that King James was very much interested in the Venetian–Turkish wars of 1571; so may have Shakespeare been when he wrote *Othello*. This may explain why *Othello* was chosen to be performed at Whitehall.

In 1585, King James, then 19 years old, wrote a poem entitled *Lepanto*, to celebrate the victory of Don Juan of Austria, the illegitimate half-brother of the King of Spain. Don Juan put together a Christian armada which decisively defeated the Turkish naval force at the battle of Lepanto in 1571 but only temporarily halted the ultimate conquest of Cyprus by the Turks. King James sang of the battle 'Which fought was in LEPANTOES gulfe / Betwixt the baptiz'd race, / And circumsised Turband Turkes.'[34] Although the victory of the Christians was much celebrated, it was short-lived; for later that year Venice permanently lost her Mediterranean possessions to the

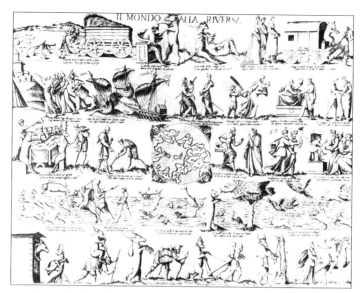

1. 'Il mondo alla riversa' ('World Upside Down'), probably Venetian, 1560s.

2. 'Magdalena Ventura with Her Husband and Son' ('La mujer Barbuda'). Oil on canvas, 1631. Jusepe de Ribera, lo Spagnoletto.

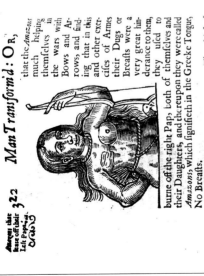

that the *Amazons* much helping themselves in the wars with Bows and Arrows, and finding that in this and other exercises of Armes their Dugs or Breasts were a very great hinderance to them, they used to burne off the right Pap, both of themselves and their Daughters, and thereupon they were called *Amazons* which signifieth in the Greeke Tongue, No Breasts.

Amazons that burne off their Left Paps.

Purch. Pilgr. 3. lib. 7.

Pigafetta in hys relation of Congo,

The chiefe of the Guard of the King of *Corgo* are left-handed *Amazons*, who feare off their left Paps with a hot Iron, because it should be no hinderance to them in their shooting, *Pigafetta* in his reports of the Kingdome of *Congo*, makes the like mention of these

3. Left-handed and Right-handed Amazons with Corresponding Breasts Seared off. John Bulwer, *Anthropometamorphosis* (London, 1653).

Of the Kingedome of Amazony whereas dwelleth none but women.

4. Two Amazons Ready for Battle. *The Voiage and Travayle of Sir John Maundeville* (London, 149–?). Reprint 1887.

5. Ednei Giovenazzi as Shylock (left) and
   Heleno Prestes as Tubal in Limite 151's
   1993 production of *The Merchant of Venice*.

6. Funeral monument of Robert Cecil, the Salisbury Chapel,
   Hatfield House.

7. Dr Rodricke Lopez and Stephen Ferrera de Gama. George Carleton, *A Thankful Remembrance of Gods Mercie* (London, 1627).

8. A Jew dropping poison into a fountain and a Christian boy crucified. P. Boaistuau, *Certaine secrete wonders of nature*, translated by Edward Fenton (London, 1569).

9. A gypsy woman and child. Cesare
Vecellio, *Habiti antichi, et moderni di
tutto il mondo* (Venice, 1598).

10. Moro di conditione (A Moor). Cesare
Vecellio, *Habiti antichi, et moderni*.

11. 'Christ and the Centurions', c. 1575. Oil on canvas. Paolo Caliari, called Veronese, and workshop.

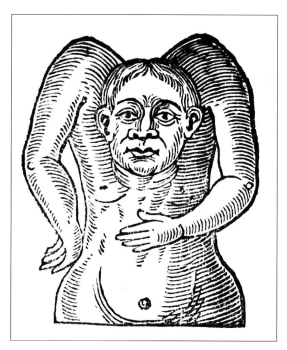

12. A human monster. John Bulwer,
Anthropometamorphosis (London, 1653).

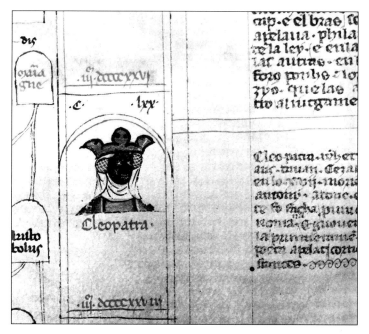

13. Black Cleopatra. Egerton MSS 1500, Folio 15v.

Ioan. Stradanus invent.

Theodor. Galle fecit.   Phls Galle excud.

14. 'America'. An allegorical depiction of Vespucci's encounter with America. Engraving by Théodore and Philippe Galle. In Jan van der Straet, *Nova reperta* (Antwerp, c. 1600).

Ottomans. In this battle, the Turkish leader, Ali Basha, was 'killed by a common soldier who cut off his head and gave it to Don John'; and 'the commander-in-chief caused it to be fixed at the mast-head of his galley.' The report adds, 'when the Turks saw it stuck there they broke and fled.'[35] King James's poem was well-known and much celebrated. In *A Brief Letter* (1593), Gabriel Harvey refers to 'The glory of such an immortal memorial as some noble and royal wits have bestowed upon the ever-renowned *Lepanto*'; and he again mentions the poem in *Pieces Supererogation* (1593), alluding to Lepanto first as an important historical event and second as the subject of a king's poem, 'first the glory of Christendome against the Turke, and now the garland of a soveraine crowne.'[36] Richard Barnfield in *Poems in Divers Humours* (1598) cites *Lepanto* as evidence of the King's poetical talents; so does Francis Meres in *Palladis Tamia* (1598).[37]

For a historical account of the Venetian–Turkish wars, Shakespeare may have turned to Richard Knolles's *History of the Turks* (1603). Interestingly enough, as Geoffrey Bullough notes, Richard Knolles also dedicates his book to King James, and he too remembers the King's poem *Lepanto*: 'When he introduced the Turkish war and went to some trouble to get his facts right Shakespeare must have known that he was meeting one of the King's interests.'[38] Bullough adds that Knolles's reference to King James's 'Heroicall Song' 'would encourage Shakespeare to set his tragedy in the period shortly before the great and glorious victory.'[39] By avoiding any suggestion of the eventual defeat of the Christian forces, Shakespeare thus underscores King James's own celebration of Lepanto as a watershed victory of Christians over infidels. History and fiction seem closely connected indeed.

Thus, Shakespeare remembers the battle, but his memory is mediated by the King's poem. King James may have also influenced Shakespeare's choice of hero for his play. In 1585, King James *chose* to write of Lepanto as a major Christian victory, not a single battle in a war that the Venetians eventually lost. In 1603–4, Shakespeare *chose* to set his play before Lepanto, and could thus have the Turkish fleet scattered in an event reminiscent of the Spanish Armada of 1588. Furthermore, he chose to create a fictional Moorish general to lead the Venetians rather than to use Don Juan. In the preface to his poem, King James had, in fact, found it necessary to defend his choice of a Catholic hero for the poem: *'And for that I knowe, the special thing misliked in it, is, that I should seeme, far contrary to my degree and Religion, like a Mercenary Poët, to penne a worke,* ex professo, *in praise of a forraine Papist bastard.'*[40] Later he adds, *'what so ever praise I have given to* DON-JOAN *in this Poëme, it is neither in accompting him as first or second cause of that victorie, but onely as of a particular man, when hee falles in my way, to speake the truth of him.'*[41] Shakespeare could avoid political and religious controversy by creating a fictional hero rather than depicting a real-life Catholic.

In deciding to center his tragedy on a heroic Moor, Shakespeare, furthermore, had the authority both of his fictional source and of Venetian historical practice on his side. Giraldi Cinthio notes that the Moor of his *novella* was 'a very gallant man, who, because he was personally valiant and had given proof in warfare of great prudence and skillful energy, was very dear to the Signoria, who in rewarding virtuous actions ever advance the interests of the Republic,' and furthermore, 'It happened that the Venetian lords made a change in the forces that they used to maintain in Cyprus; and they chose the Moor as Commandant of the soldiers whom they sent there.'[42] History corroborates Cinthio's assumption that there was nothing unusual about Venice having a Moorish general. In *The Commonwealth and Government of Venice* (1599), Gasper Cantarini writes that the general of the Venetian army is 'alwaies a straunger.'[43] Fynes Moryson, who traveled extensively in Europe and who was in Venice, Cyprus, and Constantinople in 1596–7, writes of Venice's troubles with the Turks and reveals some specific military customs of the Venetians:

> Besides that this State is not sufficiently furnished with men and more specially with native Commaunders and Generalls, nor yet with victualls, to undertake (of their owne power without assistance) a war against the Sultane of Turky. This want of Courage, & especially the feare lest any Citizen becoming a great and popular Commaunder in the Warrs, might thereby have meanes to usurpe uppon the liberty of their State, seeme to be the Causes that for their Land forces *they seldome have any native Comaunders, and always use a forrayne Generall.*[44]

Moryson observes, the Venetians 'seldome have any native Comaunders, and always use a forrayne Generall.' David C. McPherson, who has explored this question in some detail, also suggests that historically there is nothing unexpected about the fact that a Moor has become the commander of the Venetian army: apparently, 'The idea was to prevent military *coups d'etat.'*[45] In this regard, Shakespeare strives for historical accuracy.

Moreover, Shakespeare endows Othello with an extraordinary historical consciousness. If writing produces history, Othello seems particularly aware that he is being written about, that these writings will be added to the Venetian archives, and that he produces history. From early in the play, he views his life as a matter of public memory, public reports, history. He is confident, for example, that 'My services which I have done the signiory / Shall out-tongue' Desdemona's father's complaints (I.ii.18–19). When he appears before the Duke to receive his commission, Othello is primarily concerned with setting the record straight. Such state matters tend to generate records; therefore, while he admits to having taken away 'this old man's daughter' (I.iii.78), he reminds the Venetians of his accomplishments (I.iii.81–7). Othello offers his own recollections of the events – what he remembers should be added to the report that is presumably being produced. He also sends for Desdemona to present 'her report': 'let her speak of me before her father' (I.iii.116). Desdemona's testimony provides first-hand evidence that Othello did not use magic to win her love. In his dealings with the Republic of Venice, Othello seems very much aware that reports most likely to survive are those preserved in state archives.

His communications with the Venetian state also hinge on written documents. In Act IV, scene i, Lodovico, an emissary from Venice arrives in Cyprus with letters containing new orders for Othello. Othello receives the letters, 'I kiss the instrument of their pleasures' (213) and reads the words, first silently, then aloud: '"This fail you not to do, as you will – "' (224). When the Duke and Senate order his immediate return to Venice, Othello assumes that Desdemona has been conspiring to install Cassio in his place. A little later, Othello in private with Desdemona gives voice to his thoughts, when her face becomes a metaphor for the paper upon which he will write: 'Was this fair paper, this most goodly book, / Made to write "whore" upon?' (IV.ii.71–2). The two passages underscore the power of writing and, in a sense, his own powerlessness.

Finally, at the end of the play Lodovico asks, 'O thou Othello that wert once so good, / Fall'n in the practice of a damnèd slave, / What shall be said to [of] thee?' (V.ii.291–3). Othello's initial response is: 'Why, anything: / An honorable murderer, if you will; / For naught did I in hate, but all in honor' (V.ii.293–5). Othello suddenly remembers, however, that, on the one hand, the Venetians will say anything they please; on the other, he hopes that they will strive for fairness and accuracy. His place in history depends upon the accuracy of the report; therefore, he decides to amend his statement, as he explains to Lodovico:

> Soft you! a word or two before you go.
> I have done the state some service, and they know't.
> No more of that. I pray you, in your letters,
> When you shall these unlucky deeds relate,
> Speak of me as I am. Nothing extenuate,
> Nor set down aught in malice.

(V.ii.338–42)

The letters in the national archives will outlast the memory of any eyewitness. His life combines with the public life of Venice; but reports extenuate, distort, denigrate, malign. He thus finds himself at the mercy of Lodovico's ability to interpret the events in Cyprus. Other writings, produced by Iago and Roderigo, and Cassio's report corroborate Othello's statements. In the fictional world of this drama, the historians will have much evidence by which to reconstruct the history of Venice's colony.

As I have demonstrated, Shakespeare posits that Othello's life in Venice is thus the domain of history: it leaves scriptural traces; it is a matter of state archives. His life preceding his European experience, however, is the domain of orality, which when written about and interpreted by fieldworkers becomes an ethnography. European fieldworkers have, of course, crisscrossed the cultural map of the world, producing indelible written impressions of various cultures. Thus, ethnography can be described as the perception of one culture by another. As Certeau argues, 'Even if they are the products of research, observation, and practices, these texts are nonetheless a tale and a milieu as told to its members.'[46] Othello's presence elicits an ethnographical enterprise whereby his pre-European culture is subjected to reconstruction. In his play, then, Shakespeare creates a dramatic fiction in which the cross-cultural encounter seems to occur not only on a historical level but also on an ethnographical one. We need to remember, however, that the experience across cultures, as James A. Boon writes, creates a 'sense of exaggeration.'[47] Again, I believe, Shakespeare grasps the dynamics of ethnographical representation, as he does of historiography.

Throughout the play, Othello himself and other characters remind us of Othello's background in a world elsewhere. Although this world is never explicitly described, a number of characters attempt to reconstruct it. The primary informant about himself and his country, Othello carefully controls the data that he conveys about his homeland. Therefore, we need to distinguish Othello's narrative apparently based on his memory and the narratives based on fantasies. I will examine these fantasies first because they offer insights into how various characters – Brabantio, Desdemona, and Iago – perceive Othello's culture. I will then examine the narrative that Othello himself generates.

Brabantio has a small yet crucial role in re-creating Othello's cultural past; yet he associates witchcraft with Moors, thus creating a lasting impression of his son-in-law. Roused out of bed in the middle of the night with news of Desdemona's elopement, Braban-tio remarks, 'This accident is not unlike my dream' (I.i.141). This statement reveals deep-seated fear and prejudice. In his defense before the Duke and Senators, however, Othello contradicts his father-in-law: 'Her father loved me, oft invited me;/Still questioned me the story of my life/From year to year – the battles, sieges, fortunes/That I have passed' (I.iii.128–31). Considering the dream of Desdemona's betrayal, why then did Brabantio invite Othello to dinner? Obviously on some level, he, like his daughter, was fascin-ated with Othello's narrative.

Brabantio accentuates magical practice as the most questionable element in Othello's background. Ironically, no one else, not even Iago, believes that Othello practices witchcraft. Brabantio may have read about witchcraft in books, as his question to Roderigo suggests, 'Is there not charms/By which the property of youth and maid-hood/May be abused? Have you not read, Roderigo,/Of some such thing?' (I.i.170–3). In the next scene, he confronts Othello and accuses him of binding Desdemona 'in chains of magic': 'That thou hast practiced on her with foul charms,/Abused her delicate youth with drugs or minerals/That weaken motion' (I.ii. 73–5). Later, before the Senate, he directly accuses Othello of casting a spell on Desdemona:

> She is abused, stol'n from me, and corrupted
> By spells and medicines bought of mountebanks;
> For nature so prepost'rously to err,
> Being not deficient, blind, or lame of sense,
> Sans witchcraft could not.
>
> (I.iii.60–4)

For Brabantio, the relationship between a father and daughter hinges on obedience, as he makes clear when he questions Desdemona: 'Come hither, gentle mistress./Do you perceive in all this noble company/Where most you owe obedience?' (I.iii.178–80). Only witchcraft could have broken the fetters of obedience. Once he realizes that his daughter has a mind of her own, he gives up, muttering that he would rather adopt a child than beget one.

Like her father, Desdemona focuses on obedience, but unlike him, she believes that she owes a duty to her husband, not her father – a dilemma which also confronts Cordelia in *King Lear*. Although Desdemona considers her father the 'lord of duty,' she admits that hers is a divided duty: 'But here's my husband;/And so much duty as my mother showed/To you, preferring you before her father,/So much I challenge that I may profess/Due to the Moor my lord' (I.iii.185–9). Later, as a way of solving the crisis in her marriage, she again returns to obedience: 'Whate'er you be, I am obedient' (III.iii.88–9). When Lodovico arrives in Cyprus, Othello sarcastically questions her obedience: 'And she's obedient; as you say, obedient,/Very obedient' (IV.i.247–9).

Predictably, Desdemona exhibits curiosity about Othello's racial and cultural difference, and she attempts to understand his cultural origins; but unlike Disdemona in Giraldi Cinthio's *Gli Hecatommithi*, she displays no prejudice. While trying to have the Corporal reinstated, Cinthio's Disdemona states to the Moor: 'He has not committed so serious an offence as to deserve such hostility. But you Moors are so hot by nature that any little thing moves you to anger and revenge.'[48] Almost as if to confirm her prejudice, the Moor becomes 'more enraged' and vows 'such revenge for any wrongs done to me as will more than satisfy me!'[49] From this the Ensign suggests to an already despondent and enraged Moor that 'The woman has come to dislike your blackness' (245). The source character's latent prejudice prepares the way for the Ensign's intrigue. Iago, however, is careful first to 'prove' to Othello that Desdemona is having an affair; only then does he introduce the question of race.

Desdemona's fantasy takes the form of ethnographical speculation, possibly in an attempt to understand how a Moorish woman would relate to her husband: would a Moorish wife be obedient or defiant? Two separate passages reveal Desdemona's own assumptions about the nature of blackness and a possible answer to this question. The first one occurs in Act II, scene i. When they first arrive in Cyprus, Desdemona and Iago engage in a discussion of the nature of women. At one point they talk about a witty black woman. 'How if she be black and witty?' asks Desdemona; Iago responds, 'If she be black, and thereto have a wit,/She'll find a white that shall her blackness fit' (II.I.132–3). Her question and Iago's double entendre leave her more puzzled than ever: how is the black woman to find a white man that will 'fit' her?

Imagine, for a moment, that the woman whom Desdemona and Iago are discussing is an African from the Niger who married a Frenchman, Anselme d'Ysaguier, and followed her husband to Toulouse. There she raised a son and three daughters. This African, accompanied by a daughter named Martha, slaves, and three eunuchs, landed at Marseille in 1413 and proceeded to Toulouse; 'as wife of Ysaguier she had a notable position in Toulouse, where her husband was member of Parliament.'[50] One of her daughters in turn married another Frenchman Eugène de Faudoas, '*jeune homme d'une des meilleures familles de Toulouse.*'[51] Obviously, the hypothetical witty black lady of the conversation could be any African woman or no one in particular; but, like the woman from the Niger, she would find a white man who would complement her blackness. Had Desdemona known about this relationship, she would have apparently found a model interracial marriage to follow as an example. She would thus have presumably been better equipped to counter opposition to her relationship.[52] But in her culture interracial marriages are apparently rare or do not exist; therefore, she does not have a positive role model after which she could pattern her own marriage.

In another passage, Desdemona reveals her own ideas and prevailing misconceptions about Othello's original culture. Trying to interpret Othello's changed behavior and in answer to Emilia's question, 'Is he not jealous?,' Desdemona offers a theory to explain the absence of passions in Othello's heart: 'Who? he? I think the sun where he was born/Drew all such humors from him' (III.iv.29–31). In view of her interest in the narrative of Othello's past, one imagines that Desdemona would have read all the sources that she could find on Africa and Africans. These sources, being outrageously prejudiced and predominantly inaccurate, contained much misinformation. As Eldred Jones and others have documented, some of the ideas circulating about Africa went back to antiquity, especially Pliny. These descriptions focused on the 'strangeness' of Africa, especially the 'fantastic specimens of human and sub-human life in Africa.'[53] In *The Cosmographical Glasse* (1559), William Cuningham writes that much of Africa was not inhabited because of 'th'extreme heat': 'being under the burning zone, the Sone draweth all the moister of th'earth from it, so that for want of water no man can there live.'[54] Azurara, for example, writes in his account of D. Francisco de Almeida's voyage in 1505–6 to India that the Garamantes and Ethiops are black because they live near the heat of the sun.[55] As Desdemona seems to believe, these sources explained blackness as the direct effect of the heat of the sun.

Finally, Desdemona remembers her mother's maid, Barbary: 'She was in love; and he she loved proved mad/And did forsake her. She had a song of "Willow";/An old thing 'twas; but it expressed her fortune,/And she died singing it' (IV.iii.25–31). Whether the maid was Moorish, Desdemona does not say; but the maid's name could suggest the Barbary states of North Africa, especially if we take into account that the conversation becomes a cultural fantasy about women's sexual habits and mores around the world. In the back of her mind, Desdemona has fused the story of Barbary and her own, even repeating Barbary's defense of her love, 'Let nobody blame him; his scorn I approve' (IV.iii.50). The fantasy that begins with Barbary extends to women all over the world, women who 'abuse their husbands/In such gross kind' (60–1). She turns to Emilia, 'Wouldst thou do such a deed for all the world?' (IV.iii.66). Barbary was obedient, meek, patient, self-sacrificing; Desdemona may have patterned her life after this woman to give Othello what she thought he expected.

Like Brabantio and Desdemona, Iago engages in ethnographical fantasies about Othello, speaking most explicitly about Othello's origins. In Act IV, scene ii, he convinces Roderigo to kill Cassio, so that Othello will not be able to leave Cyprus: 'O, no; he goes into Mauritania and takes away with him the fair Desdemona, unless his abode be lingered here by some accident; wherein none can be so determinate as the removing of Cassio' (IV.ii.221–4). Ironically, Iago offers some of the best insights into Othello's character. These insights occur in soliloquies, when Iago has no reason to lie. He confesses that 'The Moor is of a free and open nature' (I.iii.393); and later, he says:

> The Moor, howbeit that I endure him not,
> Is of a constant, loving, noble nature,
> And I dare think he'll prove to Desdemona
> A most dear husband.

(II.i.282–5)

Iago recognizes that, left to their own devices, Desdemona and Othello will remain a happy couple. He consciously decides to weave a plot, to disseminate misinformation about Desdemona and Cassio; in other words, to create an identity for them that does not exist except in his own mind: 'Hell and night/Must bring this monstrous birth to the world's light' (I.iii.397–8). Alone he cannot conceive this monstrous creature; he and Othello must together conceive and give birth to it.

In the cover of night, Iago incites Roderigo to awake Brabantio with the revelation that his daughter has eloped with the Moor. To Brabantio and Roderigo, Iago emphasizes the oversexed nature of Moors:

> Even now, now, very now, an old black ram
> Is tupping your white ewe. Arise, arise!
> Awake the snorting citizens with the bell,
> Or else the devil will make a grandsire of you.

> (I.i.88–91)

He suggests to Brabantio that 'you'll have your daughter covered with a Barbary horse; you'll have your nephews neigh to you; you'll have coursers for cousins, and gennets for germans' (I.i.110–13); further, he adds, 'your daughter and the Moor are now making the beast with two backs' (I.i.115–16).

Additionally, Iago convinces Roderigo that 'These Moors are changeable in their wills' (I.iii.344–5), echoing Cinthio's Disdemona. His theory of sexuality also applies to Desdemona, 'when she is sated with his body, she will find the error of her choice' (I.iii.347–8). He promises Roderigo: 'If sanctimony and a frail vow betwixt an erring barbarian and a supersubtle Venetian be not too hard for my wits and all the tribe of hell, thou shalt enjoy her' (I.iii.352–4). Consistent with this view, he exaggerates the intensity of Othello's sexual desire, assuming that 'it is thought abroad that 'twixt my sheets/H'as done my office' (I.iii.381–3). But all of these assumptions, he suggests, are the fabrication of his brain, 'I know not if't be true;/But I, for mere suspicion in that kind,/Will do as if for surety' (I.iii.382–4). Iago focuses his reconstruction on Othello's sexuality and the unpredictability of the nature of Moors.

Amateur ethnographers try to describe and inscribe Moorish culture. Brabantio concentrates on magic, Desdemona on obedience, and Iago on sexuality. Even Othello himself seems aware that the interest in his life is both ethnographical and historical. On the one hand, Othello affirms his otherness (after all his reputation in Venice depends on his military expertise and foreign experience); on the other, he wants to erase it. Neither Desdemona nor the other characters, except Iago, perceive Othello as easily given to expression of passions. In fact, when Othello strikes Desdemona in Act IV, scene i, Lodovico, who has just arrived from Venice with letters instructing Othello to return and instate Cassio in his place in Cyprus, doubts his own eyes:

> Is this the noble Moor whom our full Senate
> Call all in all sufficient? Is this the nature
> Whom passion could not shake? whose solid virtue
> The shot of accident nor dart of chance
> Could neither graze nor pierce?

> (IV.i.257–61)

Lodovico is quite incredulous, 'Are his wits safe? Is he not light of brain?' (IV.i.262). And he concludes by saying, 'I am sorry that I am deceived in him' (275).

Like the other characters, Othello seems confused about his own origins. He assumes that everyone accepts him as he is: his origins, his abilities, his service. He dazzles Desdemona with the story of his life, 'From year to year – the battles, sieges, fortunes / That I have passed' (I.iii.129–31). This becomes the basis for their relationship; for, as he says, 'She loved me for the dangers I had passed, / And I loved her that she did pity them' (I.iii.167–8). No other witchcraft did he use but a powerful personal narrative. Desdemona understood that this man's memory could transport her to the far corners of the earth, places that as a European woman of high birth she was unlikely to see.

But Othello's own perception of his culture is mediated through the European experience. Through the centuries, Africa has fired the European imagination with the wildest fantasies and prejudices about the nature of humanity. 'Africa always produces new and monstrous things,' wrote Rabelais in *Pantagruel*.[56] Cuningham describes the people as 'blacke, savage, Monstrous, & rude', some of whom are veritable monsters:

> Divers also (yea right grave authors) make mention of certaine
> deformed that dwell in Africk, as men with dogges heades, called

Cynocephali, some with one eye & that in the forehead, name Monoculi, others without heades, & theyr face in the breast, with divers such like which I suppose rather fables than any truth.[57]

Othello uncritically adopts a Eurocentric perspective when he enumerates the wonders, exotic otherness, and monstrosities (Plate 12) that he himself has encountered in his travels, including 'the Cannibals that each other eat,/The Anthropophagi, and men whose heads/Do grow beneath their shoulders' (I.iii.143–5).

Travelers also report not only promiscuity but also a lack of correspondence, according to European standards, between sex and gender: the males behaved like females; females, like males. We have already encountered in Chapter 1 reports of African Amazons on the Mountains of the Moon. Andrew Battell, who was in Angola between 1589 and 1607, reports that 'the men of this place weare skinnes about their middles, and beads about their neckes. They carrie Darts of Iron, and Bow and Arrowes in their hands. They are beastly in their living, for they have men in womens apparell, whom they keepe among their wives.'[58] Another account from Angola reports the discovery of 'certayne Chibadi, which are Men attyred like Women, and behave themselves womanly, ashamed to be called men; are also married to men, and esteeme that unnaturall damnation an honor.'[59]

Whether there is any truth to the reports from Angola, we cannot ascertain. I suggest, however, that in *Othello*, Shakespeare also registers a similar sex/gender dichotomy. Michael Neill writes that '*Othello* is a tragedy of displacement' and that 'the fetches of Iago's policy are designed to expose the essential savagery of his "stranger" general; but what they produce is an Othello remade in Iago's own monstrous image.'[60] Instead, I believe, the tragedy of displacement results from a clash between two assumptions about gender, Venice's and Othello's, and these are represented by Othello's two contradictory accounts of the history of the handkerchief that he gave Desdemona.[61]

In Cinthio's *Gli Hecatommithi*, the origin of the handkerchief is straightforward: '[The Moor's wife] carried with her a handkerchief embroidered most delicately in the Moorish fashion, which the Moor had given her and which was treasured by the Lady and her husband too.'[62] From this one myth, Shakespeare creates two, introduced in III.iv.55–68 and V.ii.214–18, respectively. Both narratives reveal Othello's ethnographical background; when combined, they localize a marital and a cross-cultural conflict.

In the first version, an Egyptian charmer who 'could almost read/ The thoughts of people' discovered the power of a handkerchief to subdue men and then passed the secret on to Othello's mother. While Othello's mother kept the handkerchief, it would 'make her amiable and subdue my father/Entirely to her love; but if she lost it/Or made a gift of it, my father's eye/Should hold her loathèd, and his spirits should hunt/After new fancies' (III.iv. 55–63). In a strict sense, females hold a form of power; males become their pawns. But for reasons unexplained, Othello's mother breaks the magic chain when she gives the handkerchief to Othello for temporary safekeeping until he finds a wife:

> She, dying, gave it me,
> And bid me, when my fate would have me wive,
> To give it her. I did so; and take heed on't;
> Make it a darling like your precious eye.
> To lose't or give't away were such perdition
> As nothing else could match.

> (III.iv.63–8)

In this gender configuration, males temporarily hold control, only until they surrender themselves to their wives.[63]

The second myth, told after Othello has killed Desdemona, presents a radically different story:

> Cassio confessed it;
> And she did gratify his amorous works
> With that recognizance and pledge of love
> Which I first gave her. I saw it in his hand.
> It was a handkerchief, an antique token
> My father gave my mother.

> (V.ii.213–18)

Othello does not mention the gypsy; instead, he states that his father obtained the handkerchief and gave it to Othello's mother. Here males initiate a contractual arrangement similar to the giving of a betrothal ring. Women play a more submissive and passive role.

A dichotomy thus arises between public life, where Othello is thoroughly acculturated into a patriarchal European ethos, and his private life, where he reverts to his parents' relationship and to his original cultural values, assumptions, and expectations. Indeed, Othello and Desdemona bring entirely different cultural assumptions into their marriage. She expects to be 'obedient'; yet, consciously or not, he demands that she break with custom and disobey her father. Since Brabantio later condemns her interracial marriage, this was probably the only way for Othello and Desdemona to be together. In the first part of the play, Othello and Desdemona reach a tacit understanding between them: she vouches to be obedient, but in fact she is not. Despite her statement, 'Whate'er you be, I am obedient' (III.iii.89), Desdemona becomes defiant. As a Venetian woman, she is expected to obey; but Othello does not expect her blind obedience. I posit, however, that Othello's cultural background requires independence and assertiveness on the part of women, a model based upon the relationship of Othello's parents.

Although Othello seems confident that he can handle Brabantio's rage because 'My parts, my title, and my perfect soul / Shall manifest me rightly' (I.ii.31–2), he does not rely on merit alone for his defense. Rather, he explains, Desdemona took an active role in their relationship, and in her own indirect way, she became the wooer: 'She thanked me; / And bade me, if I had a friend that loved her, / I should but teach him how to tell my story, / And that would woo her' (I.iii.164–6). Perceiving this 'hint,' Othello proposed to her. Othello sums up his defense by turning to Desdemona: 'Let her witness it' (170). When the Duke suggests that Desdemona should stay in her father's house while Othello goes to Cyprus, Brabantio and Othello disagree. Considering herself their equal, she retorts: 'Nor I. I would not there reside, / To put my father in impatient thoughts / By being in his eye' (I.iii.241–3). Desdemona affirms her 'downright violence' (I.iii.249) in loving Othello and defiantly says that she sees 'Othello's visage in his mind' (I.iii.252). Later, she becomes an outspoken advocate for Cassio, who, as she observes, 'came a-wooing with you, and so many a time, / When I have spoke of you dispraisingly, / Hath ta'en your part' (III.iii.71–3). Othello's appropriately masculine term of endearment for her is 'my fair warrior' (II.i.180); and she refers to herself as his 'unhandsome warrior' (III.iv.151). As Iago indicates, Othello's 'soul is so enfettered to her love / That she may make, unmake, do what she list' (II.iii.328–9), and for her love Othello might even 'renounce his baptism'

(II.iii.326). Iago also suggests to Cassio that 'Our general's wife is now the general' (II.iii.300–1).

Desdemona and Othello thus work at cross purposes. In his public, historical persona as a Venetian general, he requires his wife's obedience; yet in his private life, he reverts to what seem original cultural expectations in which his wife must assume power and control. Likewise, Desdemona shifts between submissiveness and defiance, never quite sure which Othello expects. Othello and Desdemona desperately love each other and could be perfectly happy together like many other interracial couples, such as Anselme d'Ysaguier and his African wife. However, their cultural expectations of each other do not coincide. Since they seem neither to understand nor to communicate these different expectations, they become easy preys to Iago's racial prejudices. Shakespeare thus dramatizes this irreconcilable oscillation of perspective as a narrative shift between historiography and ethnography.[64]

The Merchant of Venice connects ethnic identity and textuality, encoding cultural confrontation as textual interpretation. *Titus Andronicus* grounds ethnic identity in the textual foundation of a culture, wherein Aaron, who seems to have no memory, seeks to discover his identity and the significance of his blackness. In *Othello*, Shakespeare demonstrates that Othello's historical identity clashes with his ethnic heritage: Othello's public, historical role collides with ethnographical assumptions about the culture of Moors. Fact and fiction, history and ethnography, combine to shape the assumptions that are carried into cross-cultural expectations.

5

Habitat, Race, and Culture in *Antony and Cleopatra*

[Egyptian] women in old tyme, had all the trade of occupying, and brokage abrode, and revelled at the Taverne, and kepte lustie chiere: And the men satte at home spinnyng
Joannes Boemus, *The Fardle of Facions* (1555).

Although *Antony and Cleopatra* was entered in *The Stationer's Register* on 20 May 1608, it did not appear in print until the 1623 folio.[1] Scholars conjecture that the play was written and produced sometime between late 1606 and 1608, a period which, I will demonstrate, coincides with a heightened interest in Egyptian ecology.[2] By this time, Shakespeare had already represented cross-cultural conflicts involving historical, mythological, and fictional figures: biracial couples in *Titus Andronicus* and *Othello*; a clash between Amazons and Athenians in *A Midsummer Night's Dream*; the conflict between Jews and Christians in *The Merchant of Venice*; and political and ideological confrontations between French and English societies in the first tetralogy. In this chapter, I will argue that in *Antony and Cleopatra*, Shakespeare seizes the uniquely Elizabethan construct of the Egyptian identity as a composite of ancient Egyptian culture and habitat, gypsies, and English vagabonds in order to interrogate his own culture's understanding of Egyptians and Romans.

He does not, however, merely confront the matter of identity: he reconstructs an Egyptian ecology and suggests that the gypsy identity is intertwined with an Egyptian/gypsy habitat. When the Romans interact with the Egyptian/gypsy culture and habitat, they themselves undergo a transformation, most noticeable in Antony, whereby the Roman soldier becomes a self-indulgent guest of the Egyptians and a gypsy vagabond. Cross-cultural negotiation, based on a system of binary oppositions, inevitably precipitates an identity exchange: the Egyptians/gypsies not only invert Roman values, they also subvert them. By defining the Egyptians as gypsies, the Romans also redefine themselves. In the process, Shakespeare shakes the foundations of any ideological certainty based upon notions of cultural superiority.

For the purposes of discussion, I have divided my analysis into three segments: Egyptians, gypsies, and Romans, suggesting that in *Antony and Cleopatra* all three groups simultaneously engage in various cross-cultural encounters. The Egyptian identity subsumes a dynamic interplay between habitat and hospitality, in which human habitation turns into a wild habitat. The gypsies, with whom the Egyptians were confused, add the notions of the idle, lascivious, and foul vagabond to Egyptian hospitality. Both Egyptians and gypsies undercut and subvert the identity of the Romans, who view themselves as the opposite of both Egyptians and gypsies.

The cross-cultural encounter in *Antony and Cleopatra* rests in an Egyptian habitat, both as a physical environment and as an ideological construct transformed by Egyptian hospitality. Entrance into this wondrous and yet alien ecology predicates the Roman understanding of the Egyptian cultural identity. According to both ancient and Elizabethan formulations, which I will proceed to review, habitat, a physical space, joins with hospitality, a cultural practice, in order to shape and differentiate the Egyptians.

Early Egyptology and ecology overlap in fascinating ways. Although as a modern science Egyptology did not develop until the nineteenth century, Egyptian studies date back to Herodotus, who saw Egypt as a wondrous ecology regulated by the annual floods of the River Nile, without which Egyptian life and civilization would not have been possible.[3] Ecology, a branch of modern biology, studies the mutual relations of organisms to their habitats, habits, and modes of life. 'Habitat,' from third person singular, present tense of Latin *habitare*, literally meaning 'it inhabits,' was originally a term used in books of flora and fauna written in Latin to designate the natural place of growth or occurrence of a species, especially where a living organism finds shelter, water, and food.[4] Human ecology focuses on the complex and dynamic relations of humans and of culture to habitat. From the earliest period, Egyptian civilization could not be understood without reference to the ecological system created by the Nile.

An English translation of *The Famous History of Herodotus* appeared in 1584 and served to reinforce a confusion between pharaonic and contemporary Egypt.[5] Herodotus, ironically known as both the father of history and a master of lies, created the myth of Egypt as a land of inversion. This became the most enduring marker of the Egyptian identity.[6] According to him, Egypt formed the inverted geographical, ecological, and cultural image of Scythia, a region between Europe and Asia. To reach this conclusion, he apparently relied on Ionian maps that, according to François Hartog, organized the world symmetrically on either side of an equator.[7] As Hartog observes, 'If one accepts, as the Ionians did, that the frontier between Asia and Libya was marked by the Nile, then one has to consider Egypt as a land between Asia and Libya' (pp. 17–18). Egypt formed an inverted image of its European–Asian counterpart: 'Before Sesostris, the space of Egypt was an open range, as were the Scythian expanses, but after him Egypt came, quite astonishingly and artificially, to resemble what Scythia was naturally: "For their country is level and grassy and well-watered and rivers run through it not much less in number than the canals of Egypt".'[8] The Egyptians, originally nomads, became sedentary when the Pharaoh Sesostris drained the swamps and made the land habitable.

Directly linked to its habitat, Egyptian culture evolved in symmetrical opposition to Scythian/Greek culture, as Herodotus writes:

> The Egyptians themselves in their manners and customs seem to have reversed the ordinary practices of mankind. For instance, women attend market and are employed in trade, while men stay at home and do the weaving. In weaving the normal way is to work the threads of the weft upwards, but the Egyptians work them downwards. Men in Egypt carry loads on their heads, women on their shoulders; women pass water standing up, men sitting down. To ease themselves they go indoors, but eat outside in the streets, on the theory that what is unseemly but necessary should be done in private, and what is not unseemly should be done openly.... Sons are under no compulsion to support their parents if they do not wish to do so, but daughters must, whether they wish it or not. Elsewhere priests grow their hair long; in Egypt they shave their heads.[9]

This passage, often quoted by Renaissance writers, contains the basic elements of the cultural inversion associated with the Egyptians and the many activities that the Egyptians were believed to perform in the contrary way.

From a land of inversion, Egypt mutates into a land of monsters and fantastical phenomena in *Mandeville's Travels*, which was written in French about 1357. In Thomas East's 1568 and subsequent editions, Mandeville has, as Michael C. Seymour puts it, 'fertilized the minds and kindled the hearts of generations of poets and playwrights.'[10] In the section on Egypt, Mandeville defines 'monster,' of which his account contains many examples, as 'a thing disformed ayen kynde bothe of man or of best [beast] or of any thing elles' (p. 33). He refers to the encounter between an Egyptian hermit and a monster, half man, half goat, with horns on his head (p. 33). He speaks of the wondrous Phoenix, of gardens 'that han trees and herbes the whiche beren frutes vii. tymes in the yeer,' of the artificial incubation of eggs, of the cultivation of balm, of the cisterns of Alexandria (p. 34). He believes that the pyramids used to be the granaries of Joseph, rather than funeral monuments, but nowadays they have become dens 'fulle of serpentes': 'And sum men seyn that thei ben sepultures of grete lordes that weren somtyme, but that is not trewe' (p. 37). Ironically, he associates crocodiles not with Egypt but with a mysterious island in the East (p. 144). Mandeville perpetuates the image of Egypt as an exotic and fantastical ecology.

Like Herodotus and Mandeville, other Renaissance writers emphasize Egypt's cultural inversion. Joannes Boemus, in *The Fardle of Facions* (1555), writes of the Egyptians: 'Their women in old tyme, had all the trade of occupying, and brokage abrode, and revelled at the Taverne, and kepte lustie chiere: And the men satte at home spinnyng, and woorkyng of Lace, and suche other thynges as women are wonte.'[11] Boemus, in *The Manners, Lawes, and Customes of all Nations* (1611), amplifies the concept of Egyptian inversion, listing the same inversions that he found in Herodotus.[12] Even Henry Blount, though aware of contemporary Egyptian history, confuses modern Egyptians with Herodotus's:

> Now as for the *Justice*, and *Governement*, it is perfectly *Turkish*, and therefore not to bee set downe apart; onely it exceeds all other parts of *Turky* for *rigour*, and extortion; the reason is because the *Turke* well knowes the *Egyptian* nature, above all other *Nations*, to be *malicious*, *trecherous*, and *effeminate*, and therefore dangerous, not fit for Armes, or any other trust; nor capable of being ruled by a sweet hand.[13]

Blount suggests that, reflecting the nature of their habitat, the Egyptians are malicious and treacherous like the crocodile, and, because of the customary Egyptian exchange of gender, the Egyptian men are 'effeminate.'

In the early seventeenth century, Egyptian ecology and culture gain additional prominence, beginning with the publication of two books in 1600. John Leo Africanus, who travelled extensively in Africa in the early sixteenth century, seems to rely on first-hand observation of Egypt, although he does not hesitate to restate old myths.[14] Unlike Mandeville, Leo Africanus presents an evocative, factual description of the country: 'As we sailed farther we sawe great numbers of crocodiles upon the bankes of Islands in the midst of Nilus' with the jaws wide open, 'whereinto certaine little birdes about the bignes of a thrush entring, came flying foorth againe presently after.'[15] He describes the race of the Egyptians: 'the countrey people are of a swart and browne colour: but the citizens are white' (297). His knowledgeable commentary displays aptness and wit: 'the inhabitants are of an honest, cheereful, and liberall disposition' (297); and 'the inhabitants of Cairo are people of a merrie, jocund, and cheerfull disposition, such as will promise much, but performe little' (p. 313). Like Leo Africanus, George Abbott in *A Briefe Description of the Whole Worlde* (1600) stays with the known facts about Egypt. He speaks of the wonders of Egypt: the ancient cradle of learning, the hieroglyphics, the pyramids – 'one of the 7. wonders of the worlde' – Cairo. Modern Egypt, he indicates, remains 'wholy under the Turke.'[16] He also marvels at the fertility of the country – 'a land most fruitfull, as any almost in the world.' The annual flood of the Nile, he says, 'is one of the greatest miracles of the world' (sig. K1).

Further, during the period of composition of *Antony and Cleopatra*, England experienced a heightened interest in Egyptian zoology with the publication of two works about the fauna of the world. In 1607, Edward Topsell published his *The Historie of Foure-footed Beastes*, shortly followed by *The Historie of Serpents* in 1608.[17] These massive works, masquerading as scientific studies, continuously blur the boundaries between science and legend. They nonetheless underscore the notion of magnificent ecological systems, of which Egypt constitutes one of the most wondrous. *Foure-footed Beastes*, for example, begins with descriptions of apes, monkeys, and baboons, which are presented as monsters bearing a striking resemblance to humans even in their anatomy and sexuality. Illustrations depict male monsters with large erect penises, and the females with exaggerated breasts and prominent genitalia. In *Historie of Serpents*, intended as a sequel to the previous work, Topsell studies 'serpents,' loosely defined as including a variety of animals – dragons, reptiles, certain mammals, and even insects. He veers off from his scientific purpose to present myths, among other things, about the serpents and crocodiles of Egypt.

Topsell blurs the line dividing human and reptilian natures. In *Historie of Serpents*, human desire is intertwined with the sexuality of serpents, telling a fascinating story of a sexual desire that cuts across the boundaries of species:

> We reade also in *Plutarch* of certaine Serpents, lovers of young Virgins, who after they were taken and insnared, shewed all manner of lustfull, vitious, & amorous gestures of uncleanenes and carnalitie; and by name, there was one that was in love with one *Aetolia* a Virgin, who did accustome to come unto her in the night time, slyding gentlie all over her body never harming her, but as one glad of such acquaintance, tarried with her in that dalliance till the morning, and then would depart away of his owne accorde: the which thing beeing made manifest unto the Guardians and Tutours of the Virgin, they removed her unto another Towne. The Serpent missing his Love, sought her uppe and downe three or foure dayes, and at last mette her by chance, and then hee saluted her not as he was wont, with fawning, and gentle slyding, but fiercely assaulted her with grimme and austere countenaunce, flying to her hands, and binding them with the spire of his bodie fast to her sides, did softly with his tayle beate upon her backer parts. Whereby was collected, some token of his chastisement unto her, who had wronged such a Lover with her willfull absence and disappointment.   (sig. B3)

The snake desires the virgin and gives her pleasure without compromising her virginity; the virgin desires the snake. This passage brings to mind Hermia's erotic dream about trying 'to pluck this crawling serpent from my breast' (II.ii.146), as well as the deaths of Cleopatra, Iras, and Charmian, with the asps crawling upon and biting their breasts.

Topsell studies the asps and crocodiles of Egypt, explaining their habitats, habits, and metaphoric signification. He tells us that 'the kings of *Egypt* did weare the Pictures of Aspes in their crownes: whereby they signified the invincible power of principality in this creature, whose wounds cannot easily be cured' (sig. F4). The water cobra, for example, lives 'in the bankes of *Nylus* all the yeare long, as in a house & safe Castle, but when they perceive that the water will over flow, they forsake the bankes sides, & for safegard of their lives, betake them to the Mountaines' (sig. F5). The crocodiles, he notes, 'are exceeding fruitefull and prolificall, and therefore also in Hieroglyphicks they are made to signifie fruitfulnes' (sig. M6), which, we recall, corresponds to the Egyptian women's reputed fertility. He explains the temperament of the crocodile:

> The nature of this beast is to be fearefull, ravening, malitious, and trecherous in getting of his prey, the subtiltie of whose spirit, is by some attributed to the thinness of his blood, and by other to the hardnes of his skin and hide. (sig. M6)

The crocodile, he adds, can also weep and dissemble, hence the proverbial crocodile's tears:

> The common proverbe also, *Crocodili lachrimae*, the crocodiles teares, justifieth the treacherous nature of this beast, for there are not many bruite beasts that can weepe, but such is the nature of the Crocodile, that to get a man within his danger, he will sob, sigh & weepe, as though he were in extremitie, but suddenly he destroyeth him. Others say, that he crocodile weepeth after he hath devoured a man. (sig. N2)[18]

Egypt, the land of Cleopatra, acquires metaphoric signification as the land of lustful serpents, deadly asps, and treacherous, dissembling crocodiles.

In *Historie of Serpents*, hospitality, a cultural practice, and habitat, a place, converge. Topsell suggests that 'the Egyptians lived familiarly with Aspes,' worshipping them and welcoming them into their homes as household gods. The Egyptians, writes Topsell, having learned to cohabit with serpents, blurred the boundaries between human habitation and wild habitat:

> By meanes whereof the subtill serpent grewe to a sensible conceit of his owne honour and freedome, and therefore would walke up and downe and play with their children, doing no harme, except they were wronged, and would come and licke meate from the table, when they were called by a certaine significant noyse, made by knacking of the fingers. For the guests after theyr dinner,

would mix together hony, wine and meale, and then give the signe, at the hearing whereof they would all of them come foorth of their holes; and creeping up, or lifting their heads to the table, leaving their lower parts on the ground, there licked they the said prepared meate, in great temperance by little & little without any ravening, and then afterward departed when they were filled.[19]

Humans and serpents live together in a harmonious way, the serpents moving freely as if they were not guests but hosts. The Egyptians' guests, however, have to become hosts to the serpents, feeding them as required. The guests constantly live on the edge of danger; if they make one false move, the serpents will strike and kill them. When one accepts shelter in an Egyptian house, one must dwell with dangerous serpents. In an ecological and cultural reversal, human habitation becomes a wild habitat. Culture gives way to ecology. Egyptian identity hinges on a dynamic and complex interplay between cultural and environmental imperatives.

In *Antony and Cleopatra*, Shakespeare investigates the dynamic and mutual relations of character to habitat, of culture to ecology and to the environments that shape us and which we inhabit, manipulate, exploit, or control. To do so, he sets up cultural and environmental binary oppositions between Egypt and Rome. Egypt becomes a land of exotic, lustful, fruitful, and feminine people dependent upon a sumptuous and luxuriant habitat; Rome, however, emerges as an austere, military, masculine culture accustomed to and dependent upon deprivation. These opposites drift toward each other, as the Romans, feeling a sense of incompleteness and tempted by Egyptian hospitality, enter and appropriate the Egyptian habitat. In this regard, Cleopatra functions simultaneously as the center of a culture and an ecosystem; Antony represents the deprived Roman soldier, sidetracked by the comforts and pleasures of Egyptian life.

Thus, Shakespeare carefully scatters images of Egyptian culture: Isis, the Nile, the Ptolemies, the pyramids, and the cisterns of Alexandria. Eight references establish Isis, the goddess of earth, fertility, and the moon, as the deity presiding over Cleopatra's kingdom.[20] The prodigious fertility of the land parallels that of the Egyptian women, as Peter Heylyn suggests: 'very fruitful in child bearing, and quickly of dispatch when they are in labour: some of them having three or four children at a Birth; those that are born in the eighth moneth living to good Age, and not in danger of death, as in other countries.'[21] The Nile creates and regulates a wondrous ecology. We learn, from the play, that the Egyptians 'take the flow o'th'Nile' (II.vii.17) to determine the size of the next crop; that the heat of the sun 'quickens Nilus' slime' (I.iii.69) or might 'Melt Egypt into Nile' (II.v.78). A reference to 'A cistern for scaled snakes' (II.v.95) evokes the famous cisterns of Alexandria, where the scarce water was collected for year-round use. The ecology of Egypt emerges with accuracy in references to crocodiles, serpents, heat of the desert, and the annual floods of the Nile. Cleopatra speaks of the 'flies and gnats of Nile' (III.xiii.166) and ravenous 'waterflies' (V.ii.59). The Nile spreads its fertile mud; the asp leaves a trail of slime upon fig leaves: 'This is an aspic's trail, and these fig leaves/Have slime upon them, such as th'aspic leaves/Upon the caves of Nile' (V.ii.349–51). The Nile is also the natural habitat of the crocodile, and the play contains two references to it (II.vii.24–7; 40–50).[22]

Like previous writers, Shakespeare appropriates Egypt's exotic ecology and strange hospitable practices. The cross-cultural encounter in the play connects hospitality and habitat in fascinating and dangerous ways. As Cleopatra pines for Antony, she imagines what is happening to him:

> He's speaking now,
> Or murmuring, 'Where's my serpent of old Nile?'
> (For so he calls me). Now I feed myself
> With most delicious poison.
>
> (I.v.24–7)

As host, she provides hospitality; but as an Egyptian serpent, she devours and is devoured. Like Lady Macbeth and Timon of Athens, Cleopatra is defined, to a large extent, by a cultural practice – her hospitality and her imagination as host – and by her role in Egypt's ecological system.[23] Rules of hospitality require her to provide entertainment, food, and shelter. As host, Cleopatra entertains and feeds the guest; as the venomous serpent, the guest entertains and feeds her. Each of these roles is grounded in the Egyptian ecosystem. As in Topsell's account, a tension exists in the host–guest relationship, especially when it involves a demanding Cleopatra or the deadly Egyptian cobra.[24]

In addition to its ecological function, the Nile becomes the stage for Egyptian hospitality, through which Cleopatra transforms the

landscape of her country into a magnificent pageant; Enobarbus
describes the exoticism of Cleopatra's imagination:

> The barge she sat in, like a burnished throne,
> Burned on the water: the poop was beaten gold;
> Purple the sails, and so perfumèd that
> The winds were lovesick with them; the oars were silver,
> Which to the tune of flutes kept stroke, and made
> The water which they beat to follow faster,
> As amorous of their strokes. For her own person,
> It beggared all description: she did lie
> In her pavilion, cloth-of-gold of tissue,
> O'erpicturing that Venus where we see
> The fancy outwork nature. On each side her
> Stood pretty dimpled boys, like smiling Cupids,
> With divers-colored fans, whose wind did seem
> To glow the delicate cheeks which they did cool,
> And what they undid did.

(II.ii.192–206)

Antony watches from a distance: 'Antony,/Enthroned i'th'market
place, did sit alone,/Whistling to th'air; which, but for vacancy,/
Had gone to gaze on Cleopatra too,/And made a gap in nature'
(II.ii.215–19). Cleopatra, the Nile, the wind, and the barge blend into
a theatrical spectacle, with Antony as spectator.

The Nile also permits the production of a great abundance of food
required for Egyptian feasts. The Romans of the play, seemingly
leading a life of deprivation, admire Cleopatra's feasts. Maecenas
has heard a rumor that in Egypt eight wild boars were roasted
whole for the breakfast of twelve guests (II.ii.180–1); Enobarbus
reports that they 'had much more monstrous matter of feast'
(II.ii.182–3). After her excursion on her barge, Antony offered to
provide a feast for his hostess; but, as Enobarbus reports, Cleopatra
would hear none of it:

> Upon her landing, Antony sent to her,
> Invited her to supper. She replied,
> It should be better he became her guest;
> Which she entreated. Our courteous Antony,
> Whom ne'er the word of 'no' woman heard speak,

Being barbered ten times o'er, goes to the feast,
And for his ordinary [meal] pays his heart
For what his eyes eat only.

(II.ii.220–7)

In Enobarbus' fertile imagination, Cleopatra is a woman of 'infinite variety,' and a most unusual hostess: 'other women cloy/The appetites they feed, but she makes hungry/Where most she satisfies' (II.ii.237–9). For a meal, Cleopatra exacts a price.

Cleopatra cannot separate the Nile ecosystem from Egyptian hospitality. The Nile provides both entertainment and sustenance for herself and her guests, who in turn become entangled in an inescapable web of interconnected food chains. To while away the time in the absence of Antony, she goes on an imaginary fishing expedition, which reminds her of past exploits:

Give me mine angle, we'll to th'river: there,
My music playing far off, I will betray
Tawny-finned fishes. My bended hook shall pierce
Their slimy jaws; and as I draw them up,
I'll think them every one an Antony,
And say, 'Ah, ha! y'are caught!'

(II.v.10–15)

Antony becomes the fish that she draws out of the Nile. She can also manipulate the food chain, whereby food becomes entertainment. Charmian reminds her of another fishing expedition, in which Antony was Cleopatra's guest when Cleopatra commanded a diver to 'hang a salt fish on his hook' (II.v.17). In her own space, Cleopatra's hospitality and the attendant theatrical representations depend upon the ecology of Egypt.

At the end of the play, Cleopatra, following Egyptian practice, provides hospitality to the asp, 'the pretty worm of Nilus there,/That kills and pains not' (V.ii.243–4). The Clown warns her not to befriend the naja of Africa because the 'worm is not to be trusted but in the keeping of wise people,' and not to feed it, 'for it is not worth the feeding' (V.ii.263 ff.). When Iras falls and dies after Cleopatra kisses her, Cleopatra imagines herself as the deadly asp: 'Have I the aspic in my lips? Dost fall?' (V.ii.292). As she applies the asp to her breast, the asp becomes her child, 'Dost thou not see my baby at my breast,/That sucks the nurse asleep' (309–10). She is both the asp and its mother, a metaphoric association reminiscent of Topsell's story of Egyptian children playing harmlessly with the cobra of the Nile. The daily proximity between humans and asps may account for Cleopatra's fascination with death.

Egyptian hospitality exacts its price; it reverses common cultural practices, as Enobarbus notes, 'we did sleep day out of countenance and made the night light with drinking' (II.ii.178–9). It can prove dangerous for host and guest alike. Antony surrenders himself as a guest to a feast, as a spectator to Cleopatra's theatrical spectacle, and as an organism to the Egyptian ecosystem. Cleopatra surrenders herself to her Roman and reptilian guests. Egyptian hospitality is thus embedded in a fragile and dangerous ecosystem.

In *Antony and Cleopatra*, Shakespeare proposes that, not unlike other dominant, expansionist cultures, the Romans define their cultural identity in opposition to that of the Egyptians, whose habitat and culture the Romans desire to appropriate. To accomplish this ideological formulation, the Romans demonize the Egyptians and demythologize Cleopatra by transforming the Egyptians into gypsies and Cleopatra into their vagabond queen. In the process, however, categories fall apart, as the Romans experience a symbolic exchange of gender, culture, and identity. Presenting Egypt's inhabitants simultaneously as ancient Egyptians and Elizabethan gypsies/vagabonds, Shakespeare reinterprets and reshapes his own culture's concept of racial and cultural identity. As yet unrecognized by the commentators of the play, I believe that this constitutes his unique and original contribution to the Cleopatra legend.

Shakespeare's classical and medieval sources represent Cleopatra as a white woman of Macedonian ancestry. Chaucer, in 'The Legend of Good Women,' describes Cleopatra as 'fayr as is the rose in May.'[25] Although Plutarch, in Sir Thomas North's translation of *Lives of the Noble Grecians and Romanes* (1579), does not mention her race, he seems well aware of her European heritage, tracing her line of descent from Ptolemy I Soter (d. 282 BC), one of the generals of Alexander the Great. This is especially apparent when he writes that Cleopatra could speak many languages, whereas her Macedonian ancestors could barely master the Egyptian tongue, and 'many of them forgot to speak the Macedonian.'[26] Like Plutarch, Lucan (39–65), in *Pharsalia*, condemns her character but admires her bejeweled whiteness:

Her *snowy breasts* their *whitenesse* did display
Thorough the thinne Sidonian tiffenay
Wrought, and extended by the curious hand
Of Aegypts workemen.[27]

According to the anonymous thirteenth-century *I Fatti di Cesare* (*The Deeds of Caesar*), Cleopatra presided over a multiracial court: 'the attendants and the slaves were as various as the flowers of the fields: some blonde as gold, others black beyond measure, some young, some old, some small, some tall'; but Cleopatra herself, the Italian writer believes, was white: 'She had at her throat a circlet of splendid gold, which heightened the *whiteness* of her neck.'[28]

Other writers either question or reject outright Cleopatra's whiteness; in them, Shakespeare found support for the Elizabethan perception of the Egyptians' dual racial nature. In the Countess of Pembroke's translation of Robert Garnier's *Tragedie of Antonie* (1592, 1595, etc.), Cleopatra speaks of the nations over which she might rule:

O that I had beleev'd! now, now of *Rome*
All the great Empire at our beck should bende.
All should obey, the vagabonding *Scythes*,
The feared *Germaines*, back-shooting *Parthians*,
Wandring *Numidians*, *Brittons* farre remov'd,
And tawny nations scorched with the Sunne.[29]

Cleopatra does not seem to include Egypt among 'Tawny nations scorched with the Sunne,' although this would fit the stereotypical Elizabethan view of Africa. A fourteenth-century manuscript from southern France or Italy, now at the British Library, depicts Cleopatra as a black African (Plate 13).[30] Even Shakespeare's Cleopatra may be indicating that she is black when she says, 'Think on me,/That am with Phoebus' amorous pinches black' (I.vi.27–8). It is difficult to determine how widespread this view was; nonetheless, some in England thought that Cleopatra was black because George Abbott, in *A Briefe Description of the whole worlde* (1608), argues against this misconception, saying that the Egyptians were not 'blacke, but rather dunne, or tawnie. Of which colour, *Cleopatra* was observed to be.'[31]

English writers, however, though apparently uncertain about Cleopatra's race, also associate the queen of Egypt with the most undesirable elements of English society: vagabonds and the newly arrived gypsies. Such an alternate identity arose from an Elizabethan confusion between Egyptians and gypsies in the early sixteenth-century English imagination for whom these two unrelated ethnic groups became one. For the Elizabethans, the inhabitants of Egypt were not only ancient Egyptians but also gypsies – deceitful, shiftless vagabonds or wanderers. As Kenrick and Bakewell point out, the Europeans have two contradictory images of the gypsies: 'the image of the mysterious and attractive wanderer' and 'the image of the repulsive and dirty vagabond.'[32] Cleopatra comes to represent both of these ideas.

Signs of this development can be found in Samuel Daniel's *Tragedy of Cleopatra.* Although Daniel writes of 'Misterious Egypt, wonder breeder,/strict Religions strange observer,' and does not identify the race of the Egyptians, he attributes to Cleopatra a restless nature that finds expression in her 'vagabond desires.'[33] As his Cleopatra says: 'My vagabond desires no limites found,/For lust is endlesse, pleasure hath no bound.'[34] This tradition identifies Cleopatra not as European or a black African but rather as a 'vagabond,' a gypsy (see Plate 9), confusing Egyptians with 'gypsies,' who appeared in the British Isles in the early sixteenth century. I will therefore briefly examine the history of the gypsies in order to explain how the ancient Egyptians, gypsies, and English vagabonds blend together to form the distinctive character of Shakespeare's Egyptians.

The historic gypsies originated not in Egypt but in northwest India, and 'probably they existed as a loose confederation of nomadic craftsmen and entertainers following a pattern similar to groups such as the Banjara and Sapera in modern India.'[35] In Renaissance England, the gypsies were thought to have come from Egypt. Calling themselves Romany, the gypsies were of Hindu origin and spoke a corrupted dialect of Hindi. They made a living as entertainers, basket-makers, horse dealers, and fortune-tellers. They were wanderers, but not all gypsies were nomads, although 'nomadism is a part of Gypsy identity and distinguishes them from a Gorgio,' or non-gypsy.[36]

Expelled from France in 1504, the gypsies appeared in Scotland in 1505 and in Lambeth, England, in 1514.[37] Throughout the sixteenth and seventeenth centuries, the words 'gypsy' and 'Egyptian' were interchangeable. 'Gypsy' is the aphetic form of 'Egyptian.' An Egyptian/gypsy identity emerges from the confusion. The first instance of the word 'Egyptian' to mean 'gypsy' recorded in the *OED* dates from 1514, shortly after the gypsies' arrival in the British Isles: 'It is ordayned agaynste people callynge themselves Egypcyans, that no such persons be suffred to come within this realme.'[38] According to the *OED*, the word 'gypsy,' however, entered the written language in a 1537 letter by Lord Thomas Cromwell: 'The Kings Majestie, about a twelfmoneth past, gave a pardonne to a company of lewde personnes within this realme calling themselves Gipcyans, for a most shamfull and detestable murder.'[39] Other examples illustrate the early usage of the word. Thomas Nashe, in *Martins Months Minde* (1589), writes, 'Hee wandring...in the manner of a Gipson...was taken, and trust up for a roge' (*OED*).[40] Edmund Spenser, in *Mother Hubberd's Tale* (1591), equates 'gipsen' and 'Juggeler.'[41] In *Romeo and Juliet*, Mercutio speaks in jest of Cleopatra as 'a gypsy' (II.iv.41). In *As You Like It*, Shakespeare creates a vivid image of the gypsies' skill at horsemanship: 'both in a tune, like two gypsies on a horse' (V.iii.13–14).

The gypsies, already confused with wandering Egyptians, became identified with Welsh and English vagabonds. By 1607 the confusion was so deeply ingrained in the British legal system that John Cowell, in *The Interpreter: or Booke Containing the Signification of Words* (1607), offers the following legal definition of 'Egyptians':

> *Egyptians* (*Egyptiani*) are in our statutes and lawes of *England*, a counterfeit kinde of roagues, that being English or Welch people, accompany themselves together, disguising themselves in straunge roabes, blacking their faces and bodies, and framing to themselves an unknowne language, wander up and downe, and under pretence of telling of Fortunes, curing diseases, and such like, abuse the ignorant common people, by stealing all that is not too hote or too heavie for their cariage.... These are very like to those, whom the Italians call *Cingari*....[42]

Cowell, as well as the law, questions the true ethnic identity of English gypsies; he assumes that they are English and Welsh thieves who disguise themselves (as Egyptians) in order to take advantage of ignorant people. English gypsies thus impersonate true gypsies, whom the Italians call *Cingari*. George Abbott makes a similar point when he questions the identity of the Egyptians, 'who goe up and downe the world under the name of Aegiptians, being in deed, but counterfeites, and the refuse or rascality of many nations.'[43]

The statutes against rogues and vagabonds offer a fascinating indirect account of the gypsies' presence in the British Isles. From the start, the British regarded the gypsies with much suspicion:

> The church resented the competition of palm readers, the Guilds the fact that the gypsies could undercut their prices, and the State wanted them to settle down, register their names and birthdates and occupy a fixed position in the system.[44]

The gypsies came to represent some of the most undesirable elements of the society: the homeless, traveling entertainers, wandering highwaymen, itinerant beggars, and masterless men and women. Laws were passed to deal with these new immigrants. In 1531, during the reign of Henry VIII, *An Acte concernying punysshment of Beggers & Vacabundes* stipulated that the vagabonds were to be tied naked to a cart and whipped 'tyll his Body be blody by reason of suche whyppyng.'[45] In 1547, during the reign of Edward VI, a more severe statute was adopted, and during the reigns of Elizabeth and James supplementary laws were passed. The Act of 1572 stipulates a jail penalty, whipping and burning 'through the gristle of the right Eare with a hot Yron of the compasse of an Ynche about, manifestinge his or her rogyshe kynde of Lyef.'[46] Subsequent offenses were deemed felonies and carried the death penalty. The Act of 1604, during the reign of King James, reaffirms the penalties of the previous Act. All of these laws suggest an obsession with finding a home and fixed employment for the gypsies. As Kenrick and Bakewell note, 'the extent to which these laws were applied varied from one part of the country to the other, but men and women were executed in Aylesbury, Durham and York for the sole crime of "being a Gypsy."'[47]

As one attempts to distinguish the ethnic gypsies from native wanderers or other itinerant groups, one may infer, based on these laws and accounts from later periods, that Elizabethan gypsies traveled from place to place, offering their services as fortune-tellers, palm-readers, and entertainers. In their occupation, they overlapped to a certain degree with other entertainers, such as traveling troupes.[48] The Act of 1598 offers an interesting description of the activities and occupations of the gypsies: 'all idle persons goinge aboute in any Countrie, either begginge, or usinge any subtile Crafte or unlawfull Games or Playes, or fayninge themselves to have knowledge in Phisiognomie Palmestry or other like craftye Science, or pretendinge that they can tell Destinies Fortunes or such other like fantasticall Imaginations.'[49]

To explain the phenomenon of the wandering 'Egyptians,' writers relied on Herodotus's belief that originally the Egyptians were a people without a country until the silting up of the Delta and Sesostris's canal-building project occurred. According to Herodotus, an ecological phenomenon predated and made possible Sesostris's drainage and canal-building project. Herodotus argues that 'there was a time when the Egyptians had no country at all; for I am convinced – and the Egyptians themselves admit the fact – that the Delta is alluvial land and has only recently (if I may so put it) appeared above water.'[50] Originally, the Egyptians had no country, at least not one that could sustain the flourishing of a great civilization. As the Nile silted up the delta, the Egyptians moved into the newly formed *terra firma*.

Sixteenth- and seventeenth-century writers, however, reverse the myth: the Egyptians have now reverted to their original state, becoming wanderers and vagabonds. Andrewe Boorde, in *The First Boke of the Introduction of Knowledge* (1548 and later editions), explains the absence of 'Egyptians' in Egypt:

The people of the country be swarte, and doth go disgisyd in theyr apparel, contrary to other nacyons: they be lyght fyngerd, and use pyking [picking and stealing]; they have litle maner, and evyl loggyng, & yet they be pleas[a]unt daunsers. Ther be few or none of the Egipcions that doth dwel in Egipt, for Egipt is repleted now with infydele alyons [aliens].[51]

Here he perpetuates the stereotype of the dirty gypsy thief or the seductive dancer. Since Egypt was overrun by infidel aliens, his logic suggests, the Egyptians have been wandering throughout the world, eventually reaching England.

Two works by Peter Heylyn reveal the extent of the confusion about ancient and modern Egyptians, gypsies, and home-bred English rogues and vagabonds. In *Microcosmus: A Little Description of the Great World* (1625), Heylyn describes modern Egyptians as 'not black, but tawnie and brown,' and, like their forebears who invented the 'mathematicall Sciences,' they 'are still endued with a special dexterity of wit; but are somwhat slothfull, and given to riot and luxury.'[52] He reiterates the well-known ancient myths about the Egyptians. Of Cleopatra, he writes that during the tenth or eleventh year of her reign, 'the river increased not which was observed to be a fore-teller of the fall of two great Potentates, this *Cleopatra*, and her sweet-heart *Antonie*' (p. 746). He describes Cleopatra: 'a woman of most exquisite beauty she killed her selfe that she might not be ledd in triumph through Rome' (p. 761). By 1652, when he published his *Cosmographie in foure Bookes*, Heylyn had transformed Egyptians into the stereotypical gypsies, 'of a mean stature, tawnie of complexion, and spare of body, but active and quick of foot':

> ... to *Fortune-telling* great pretenders, by which, and by some *cheating-tricks* in which very well practised, great numbers of them wander from one place to another, and so get their lively-hood occasioning the *vagabonds* and straglers of other Nations, who pretend unto, the same false Arts, to assume their names. The whole body of the inhabitants now an *Hochpot* or medley of many nations, *Moors*, *Arabians*, *Turks*; the natural *Egyptian* making up the least part of the reckoning.[53]

Egyptian women become stereotypical gypsies, wearing 'bracelets and hoops of gold, silver, and some other Mettal' (p. 5).

Several elements of the gypsy identity stand out. This identity hinges on dispossession: Herodotus imagined Egypt to be the creation of the Nile and the original Egyptians to be a people without a country. The Elizabethans imagined the gypsies to be the descendants of the ancient Egyptians, who, after the Turkish conquest of their country, had reverted to their original wandering state. From the confusion with native rogues and vagabonds comes the idea that the gypsies represent idle, dirty vagabonds.

Shakespeare incorporates Elizabethan notions of the stereotypical gypsies into his representation of ancient Egyptians in *Antony and Cleopatra*. In this tragedy, Cleopatra in fact becomes both the attractive, mysterious gypsy and the idle, foul vagabond. Shakespeare presents this metamorphosis as a Roman ideological formulation, which he will deconstruct in order to unsettle all categories based upon demonization and binary opposition. In the opening scene, Philo introduces Cleopatra as both irresistibly attractive and repulsively foul, the very enemy of Rome, who ensnares his friend and great Roman soldier Mark Antony:

> Nay, but this dotage of our general's
> O'erflows the measure: those his goodly eyes
> That o'er the files and musters of the war

Have glowed like plated Mars, now bend, now turn
The office and devotion of their view
Upon a tawny front. His captain's heart,
Which in the scuffles of great fights hath burst
The buckles on his breast, reneges all temper
And is become the bellows and the fan
To cool a gypsy's lust.

(I.i.1–10)

Although when glossing the passage the play's editors point out that gypsy was a term for Egyptian and for a whore, they do not, however, recognize the extent to which Cleopatra's identity depends upon the confusion between gypsies and Egyptians.[54] Here, Philo introduces the recurring perception that Cleopatra's face, like the pharaonic Sphinx, marks Egypt as a 'tawny front' or frontier where the Roman legions meet with aliens. The bellows and the fan cannot, of course, 'cool' the fire of Cleopatra's lust; rather, they intensify the flame. As a gypsy, Cleopatra, consumed with an insatiable lust, demands Antony's attention, devotion, and energy and distracts her Roman lover from military conquest and colonial expansion.

Embittered by Cleopatra's betrayal at the battle of Actium, Antony, on the other hand, describes his lover as the stereotypical dirty, deceitful vagabond:

This foul Egyptian hath betrayed me:
My fleet hath yielded to the foe, and yonder
They cast their caps up and carouse together
Like friends long lost. Triple-turned whore! 'tis thou
Hast sold me to this novice, and my heart
Makes only wars on thee. . . .
O this false soul of Egypt! this grave charm,
Whose eye becked forth my wars, and called them home,
Whose bosom was my crownet, my chief end,
Like a right gypsy hath at fast and loose
Beguiled me to the very heart of loss.

(IV.xii.10–15; 25–9)

Cleopatra, in his bitter assessment, has lived up to her 'right' [true] character as the false, foul gypsy. Behind her swarthy front, he has found a 'triple-turned whore,' who slept with Pompey, Julius Caesar, and himself. Like the proverbial crocodile of her country, she has dissembled and betrayed him. He further develops the association by referring to the gypsies' reputation as con-artists with a large repertoire of cheating tricks, such as the 'fast and loose' game, which was played with a stick and a belt or string.[55] Thus, the attractive, alluring queen of Egypt shares an identity with the foul, dirty vagabond.

Similar images of the stereotypical gypsy appear and serve as markers of the Egyptians' cultural difference. The mysterious gypsy may also have created the 'strong Egyptian fetters' that Antony seems unable to break. This mysterious power may be linked to the gypsies' reputation as fortune-tellers. Early on, Shakespeare establishes fortune-telling as one of the occupations the gypsies were known for. The Act of 1598, we recall, mentions fortune-telling as a criminal offense: 'fayning themselves to have knowledge in Phisiognomie Palmestry or other like craftye Science, or pretendinge that they can tell Destinies Fortunes or such other like fantasticall Imaginations.'[56] The soothsayer, who like other gypsies specializes in palmistry, further establishes the gypsy nature of Cleopatra's court. Praised by Alexas to Cleopatra, the soothsayer brags, 'In nature's infinite book of secrecy / A little I can read' (I.ii.8–9). Both Iras and Charmian are interested in finding out about their future husbands and children. To Charmian's question, 'how many boys and wenches must I have?' (I.ii.35), the Soothsayer replies: 'If every of your wishes had a womb, / And fertile every wish, a million' (I.ii.36–7). Amidst jokes and *double entendres*, the soothsayer reads their palms and rightly predicts that their 'fortunes are alike' (I.ii.51).

Idleness and wandering also become dominant images associated with Cleopatra's court. Since the play's action occurs presumably before the gypsy diaspora, Shakespeare introduces the 'wandering' spirit as a marker of the gypsy character. The word 'beg' in its various forms and meanings occurs twelve times in the play and creates an echo chamber for the related ideas of wandering and idleness. Some of these occur as crucial metaphors in relation to Cleopatra's love or her status in relation to Rome. At Cleopatra's entreaty that Antony recount the ways of his love for her, he states, 'There's beggary in the love that can be reckoned' (I.i.15). At the end of the play, Cleopatra recognizes her predicament as a beggar, a queen without a kingdom, as she points out to Proculeius:

> If your master
> Would have a queen his beggar, you must tell him
> That majesty, to keep decorum, must
> No less beg than a kingdom.

> (V.ii.15–17)

After Proculeius warns her not to 'abuse my master's bounty' (43) by killing herself, Cleopatra blurts out: 'Where art thou, death?/Come hither, come: come, come, and take a queen/Worth many babes and beggars!' (V.ii.46–8). Death, then, more often killed infants and beggars than others, but Cleopatra's statement is rather puzzling. She measures her worth by 'babes and beggars' rather than by diamonds or crowns of gold. At such moments, she seems almost on the verge of a metadramatic awareness of her status as queen of the gypsies.

Egyptian idleness contrasts with Roman busyness. One has a purpose; the other does not. Perhaps with the gypsies in mind, Lafew establishes this distinction in *All's Well That Ends Well* when he insults Parolles: 'You are a vagabond, and no true traveller' (II.iii.254–5). The Egyptians rot in a mental wandering and aimlessness, while the Romans seek to accomplish specific missions. Octavius Caesar bears witness that idleness, perceived as the opposite of military action, creates uneasiness in the Romans and challenges their mode of life. Not only does he compare the wavering of the common people to 'a vagabond flag upon the stream' which 'Goes to and back, lackeying the varying tide,/To rot itself with motion' (I.iv.45–7), but he later admits the consequences of his own perceived idleness:

> 'Tis time we twain
> Did show ourselves i'th'field; and to that end
> Assemble we immediate council. Pompey
> Thrives in our idleness.

> (I.iv.74–7)

The conflict between two seemingly opposite value systems finds expression in Antony's own wavering. Antony defines Egypt as his 'space'; there, he yearns to wander aimlessly in the streets, the favorite pastime of the Egyptians, as he suggests to Cleopatra: '…all alone/To-night we'll wander through the streets and note/

The qualities of people' (I.i.52–4). For Antony, Cleopatra personifies idleness:

> ANTONY: But that your royalty
> Holds idleness your subject, I should take you
> For idleness itself.
> CLEOPATRA: 'Tis sweating labor
> To bear such idleness so near the heart
> As Cleopatra this.

> (I.iii.91–5)

But the perceived idleness disturbs Antony, challenging his Roman nature. His reaction to Fulvia's death underscores his cultural conflict:

> I must from this enchanting queen break off:
> Ten thousand harms, more than the ills I know,
> My idleness doth hatch.

> (I.ii.124–6)

As we have seen, this idleness, from the Roman perspective, keeps Antony from engaging in military conquest and colonial expansion.

Paradoxically, despite constant movement and wandering in Egypt, the Egyptians seem to rot in aimlessness and idleness, unable to escape the luxuriousness of their habitat, trapped in their roles as entertainers for the pleasure-seeking Romans. With Antony's impending return to Rome, Cleopatra worries about being forgotten, 'O, my oblivion is a very Antony,/And I am all forgotten' (I.iii.90–1). In Antony's absence, stasis sets in; and a quasi-narcoleptic state emerges, as one struggles to stay awake. Cleopatra asks for a drink of 'mandragora,' a narcotic, 'That I might sleep out this great gap of time/My Antony is away' (I.v.4; 5–6). Even without the narcotic, however, Egypt remains sleepy, like the crocodile basking in the hot Egyptian sun. In this atmosphere, Cleopatra fantasizes about sexual acts with Antony. Like her eunuch Mardian, Cleopatra bemoans her own temporary eunuch-like condition:

> I take no pleasure
> In aught an eunuch has: 'tis well for thee

That, being unseminared, thy freer thoughts
May not fly forth of Egypt.

(I.v.9–12)

Mardian, though acknowledging his 'fierce affections' and thoughts
about 'what Venus did with Mars,' underscores his impotence and
stasis: 'Not in deed, madam; for I can do nothing/But what indeed
is honest to be done' (I.v.15–16). This depiction of Egypt assumes
that the Egyptians lack the virility of Rome.

In contrast to Egypt, Roman women do not sit idly by but rather
assume some of the masculine qualities of their culture. Antony's
lingering in Egypt provokes Fulvia to take to the battlefield, against
his brother Lucius. Soon, however, Fulvia joins forces with Lucius
against Caesar in an attempt to make Antony return to Rome.
Antony expects the messenger to rail at him 'in Fulvia's phrase'
(I.ii.103), and he suggests that she can raise 'garboils' (I.iii.61). Later
he admits that Fulvia has, although a bit too late, succeeded in
making him return to Rome: 'The business she hath broachèd in
the state/Cannot endure my absence' (I.ii.167–8). Octavia seems
much more passive than Fulvia; but even she, of her own 'free
will,' returns to Rome from Athens in an attempt to appease her
brother Octavius Caesar (III.vi.57).

Like Bizet's Carmen, another gypsy *femme fatale* of nearly three
centuries later, Cleopatra embodies the stereotype of the capricious,
unpredictable gypsy, who toys with her lover's emotions and fate
but without whom the lover cannot live. She often does the opposite
of what Antony expects, as she instructs Charmian: 'If you find him
sad,/Say I am dancing; if in mirth, report/That I am sudden sick'
(I.iii.3–5). Love governs her emotions and goals. She finds it incom-
prehensible that one should marry without love: 'Why did he marry
Fulvia, and not love her?' (I.i.41). At the same time, she associates a
certain amount of tyranny with marriage: 'What, says the married
woman you may go?' (I.iii.20). She knows of her power over Antony.
She even uses his fear of losing her as a weapon. At Charmian's suggestion, she fakes her death to see how 'he takes my death' (IV.xiii.10).

Antony, who has obviously repeatedly proven himself as a soldier,
seems to acquire the capricious or whimsical Egyptian quality, as he
insists on fighting Caesar at sea, rather than on land as Enobarbus
wisely advises him (III.vii). As Scarus explains, in the heat of battle,
however, Cleopatra abandons the fight:

> Yon ribaudred nag of Egypt –
> Whom leprosy o'ertake! – i'th'midst o'th'fight,
> When vantage like a pair of twins appeared,
> Both as the same, or rather ours the elder,
> The breese [stinging fly] upon her, like a cow in June,
> Hoists sails, and flies.

(III.x.10–15)

Antony, following her in retreat, discovers that love for Cleopatra dooms one to an endless quest through her caprices, sudden shifts, unpredictable desires. Having transformed Egyptians into stereotypical Elizabethan gypsies and vagabonds, the Romans encounter a repressed version of themselves, which they both desire and reject, resulting in a reconfiguration of the Roman character.

When cultures come together, they mingle, share, exchange, negotiate. What are the ideological consequences, however, when a dominant culture meets another, which it considers inferior? Shakespeare's Romans confront this question as they experience the compulsive nature of the cross-cultural exchange. When in Egypt, do as the Egyptians do. This becomes a dangerous proposition for a culture that fashions itself as superior. Thus, we find Antony trapped in Egyptian hospitality and 'gypsy' idleness, turned into what his culture has utterly rejected. He neglects affairs of state, cannot concentrate on his military goals, and even abandons the battlefield in order to follow Cleopatra. Something more pervasive, however, affects the Romans: they begin to imitate the Egyptians in many other ways. Seemingly lost in what they construe as lascivious hospitality and an inescapable ecology and, distracted from military conquest, the Romans emerge as what they themselves deem idle, lustful, effeminate.

Desire for and enjoyment of Egyptian hospitality collide with the Roman soldiers' ideals. For the Romans, preoccupation with Egyptian affairs turns into an obsession with Cleopatra: the Romans fantasize about her kingdom, talk about her, imagine what she and Antony are doing in Egypt, recreate her feasts, even try to capture and bring her to Rome as the centerpiece of Caesar's triumphal march. Speaking of Antony, Caesar offers a bizarre description of the ideals of manhood and military values, which may explain the Roman soldier's susceptibility to Egyptian habits and hospitality.

These ideals include doing manly things, such as drinking horse urine and eating putrefied meat:

> Thou [Antony] didst drink
> The stale of horses and the gilded puddle
> Which beasts would cough at. Thy palate then did deign
> The roughest berry on the rudest hedge.
> Yea, like the stag when snow the pasture sheets,
> The barks of trees thou browsed. On the Alps
> It is reported thou didst eat strange flesh,
> Which some did die to look on. And all this
> (It wounds thine honor that I speak it now)
> Was borne so like a soldier that thy cheek
> So much as lanked not.

(I.iv.61–71)

The soldier must be toughened in an inhospitable environment, away from the tempting comforts and ease of the Egyptian world. Resourcefulness, resilience, and independence mark the life of the soldier. Being the opposite of Roman deprivation, hospitality, in this view, transforms and undoes the soldier, for it makes him dependent on the comforts afforded by the host, fastidious as to what he requires to satisfy him, and unable to adapt to a hostile environment. His manhood threatened, the soldier grows soft, preferring the comfortable beds of the East, as Antony indicates (II.vi.50).

Furthermore, the Romans believe that Egyptian hospitality threatens the bond between males, what a servant calls 'great men's fellowship' (II.vii.11–12) because it diverts the soldiers from the fellowship of other soldiers. Pompey, in particular, fantasizes about Egyptian hospitality and condemns Antony for not fulfilling his duties as a soldier and for choosing to sit at dinner in Egypt rather than to fight (II.v.11–13). Speaking of Antony, Pompey observes that hospitality can permanently trap a great Roman general in Egypt:

> But all the charms of love,
> Salt [lustful] Cleopatra, soften thy waned lip!
> Let witchcraft join with beauty, lust with both!
> Tie up the libertine in a field of feasts,
> Keep his brain fuming. Epicurean cooks
> Sharpen with cloyless sauce his appetite,

> That sleep and feeding may prorogue his honor
> Even till a Lethe'd dulness –

(II.i.20–27)

Lust, witchcraft, feasts, and sleeping – all will combine to undo Antony's honor.

Ironically, the Romans become so dependent on Egyptian hospitality that they even propose to recreate an Egyptian feast when Pompey, Antony, and Lepidus meet in the port of Misenum. Pompey proposes a series of banquets, perhaps echoing his earlier statement about Egypt's conquest of Antony's appetite: 'We'll feast each other ere we part, and let's/Draw lots who shall begin' (II.vi.60–1). He gives Egyptian cuisine the prominence it deserves:

> No, Antony, take the lot:
> But, first or last, your fine Egyptian cookery
> Shall have the fame. I have heard that Julius Caesar
> Grew fat with feasting there.

(II.vi.64–6)

Enobarbus foresees a series of four feasts. These all-male feasts are ostensibly designed to solidify the bonds of fellowship between men; but in fact they mask cut-throat competitiveness, which Menas foregrounds when he offers to 'give thee all the world' to Pompey (II.vii.64):

> These three world-sharers, these competitors,
> Are in thy vessel. Let me cut the cable;
> And when we are put off, fall to their throats.
> All there is thine.

(II.vii.69–72)

Aboard Pompey's galley in the port of Misenum, the Romans mentally picture an Egyptian habitat in preparation for the Egyptian bacchanals. The drunken Lepidus seems fascinated by things Egyptian, such as the mysterious Nile, the 'strange serpents,' the crocodile, and the pyramids. Well versed in things Egyptian, Enobarbus and Antony take charge of recreating Egypt. Enobarbus proposes a dance in the Egyptian fashion: 'Shall we dance now the Egyptian Bacchanals/And celebrate our drink?' (II.vii.103–4). Antony and Enobarbus instruct their fellow soldiers to take hands; Enobarbus says:

> All take hands:
> Make battery to our ears with the loud music;
> The while I'll place you; then the boy shall sing.
> The holding every man shall bear as loud
> As his strong sides can volley.

> (II.vii.107–11)

As the music plays and the men dance, the all-male gathering represents the salient features of what they desire about Egypt. The Romans act out their fantasies of Egypt. Interestingly, for the Romans of history, Bacchanalia and Saturnalia were Latin festivals, but Shakespeare's fictional straight-laced Romans associate Bacchic and Saturnalian revelry not with themselves but with the Egyptians. The ahistorical transference serves to mark the distinction between Roman and Egyptian.

From the perspective of Shakespeare's Romans, the feast feminizes the soldier as previous Egyptian feasts had done to Antony. Amidst the celebrations, Caesar grows uncomfortable, sensing what he judges to be a feminizing effect: 'You see we have burned our cheeks. Strong Enobarb/Is weaker than the wine, and mine own tongue/Splits what it speaks' (II.vii.121–3). Two scenes later, the effect of the feast becomes even more apparent. Agrippa and Enobarbus comment on the feast:

> AGRIPPA: What, are the brothers parted?
> ENOBARBUS: They have dispatched with Pompey; he is gone;
> The other three are sealing. Octavia weeps
> To part from Rome; Caesar is sad, and Lepidus
> Since Pompey's feast, as Menas says, is troubled
> With the green-sickness.
> AGRIPPA: 'Tis a noble Lepidus.
> ENOBARBUS: A very fine one. O, how he loves Caesar!
> AGRIPPA: Nay, but how dearly he adores Mark Antony!

> (III.ii.1–8)

Both Agrippa and Enobarbus mock Lepidus, who loved the Alexandrian feast so much that he, like a young woman at puberty, is suffering from green-sickness. He now loves Caesar and adores Antony.

The Romans' recreation of Egypt mirrors Antony's own transformation during his sojourn in Egypt. Caesar worries about the effect of Egyptian hospitality on Antony:

> From Alexandria
> This is the news: he fishes, drinks, and wastes
> The lamps of night in revel; is not more manlike
> Than Cleopatra, nor the queen of Ptolemy
> More womanly than he; hardly gave audience, or
> Vouchsafed to think he had partners.

> (I.iv.3–8)

Caesar complains that Antony has forsaken his partners as lords of the world. Agrippa later recalls Cleopatra's effect on Julius Caesar: 'She made great Caesar lay his sword to bed; / He ploughed her, and she cropped' (II.ii.228–9). Canidius expresses his concern that Roman soldiers have become 'women's men' (III.vii.70). Enobarbus, moved to tears by Antony's fate, wishes, 'Transform us not to women' (IV.ii.36). All fear that Antony's passion for Cleopatra, his adoption of Egyptian manners, his sense of comfort at being in Egypt, and his abandonment of Roman values have led to a transformation, marked by a change of gender.

Unlike the Romans, the Egyptians, not confined by ideological superiority, share a more fluid notion of gender boundaries and cultural identity. In fact, the exchange of gender roles, anchored in ancient views of Egypt as a land of inversion, becomes a part of Egyptian hospitality. Cleopatra recounts an event when she and Antony cross-dressed in order to entertain themselves:

> That time – O times! –
> I laughed him out of patience; and that night
> I laughed him into patience; and next morn
> Ere the ninth hour I drunk him to his bed;
> Then put my tires and mantles on him, whilst
> I wore his sword Philippan.

> (II.v.18–23)

Antony, on that day, became the Queen of Egypt; Cleopatra, the Roman soldier who defeated Brutus and Cassius at Philippi. Cleopatra incorporates the cross-dressing role playing into the spectacle of her hospitality. The Egyptian court creates a make-believe world in which the host and guest exchange identity and act out sexual, political, and cultural fantasies. These fantasies subvert the identity of the Romans, who forget themselves, waver in their allegiance to Rome, and therefore lose certain culturally specific traits that they associate with masculinity.

The Romans, ideologically inflexible, seem ill-equipped to handle the effects of their encounter with the Egyptians. Unable to adapt and to accommodate difference, they seek to transform Cleopatra into a Roman puppet and to appropriate Egyptian culture and habitat. Cleopatra provides a vision of the future when she pictures herself as an exotic freak paraded through the streets of Rome: 'Shall they hoist me up / And show me to the shouting varletry / Of censuring Rome' (V.ii.55–7). To Iras, she paints the picture of a freak show:

> Thou, an Egyptian puppet, shall be shown
> In Rome as well as I: mechanic slaves
> With greasy aprons, rules, and hammers shall
> Uplift us to the view. In their thick breaths,
> Rank of gross diet, shall we be enclouded,
> And forced to drink their vapor.

> (V.ii.208–13)

The Egyptians will become one-dimensional puppets and reluctant guests in a feast provided by incompetent and inadequate hosts who know nothing of hospitality and follow a 'gross diet.' She deems this an unacceptable parody of her own refined hospitality. She also believes that other forms of cross-cultural representation will be equally unkind to her, Antony, and the Egyptians:

> Saucy lictors
> Will catch at us like strumpets, and scald rhymers
> Ballad us out o'tune. The quick comedians
> Extemporally will stage us, and present
> Our Alexandrian revels: Antony
> Shall be brought drunken forth, and I shall see

Some squeaking Cleopatra boy my greatness
I'th'posture of a whore.

(V.ii.214–21)

In this passage, metatheater meets cross-cultural representation. In her imagination, she pictures the Romans appropriating her identity and the nature of the Egyptian character. In the Roman version, she sees herself inescapably performing misunderstood, ridiculous, distorted, exaggerated versions of her story.

Ironically, Cleopatra, the accomplished entertainer – a profession associated with gypsies from the beginning of their history – resists becoming a spectacle devoid of the Egyptian cultural and ecological context. Therefore, she chooses to take her own life, and thus accomplish a feat of heroism that elevates her in the estimation of her Roman guests. Having dismissed her as a gypsy and a vagabond, Caesar now elevates her status as he orders her burial by the side of Antony: 'No grave upon the earth shall clip in it/A pair so famous' (V.ii.357–8). The Romans demonize the Egyptians but discover themselves transformed into images of their ideological fantasies.

In *Antony and Cleopatra*, Shakespeare arrived at a paradoxical identity that the Elizabethans had fashioned for the Egyptians, gypsies, and English vagabonds, whereby xenophobia and racism met in the uniquely English configuration of Cleopatra's ethnicity and of her country's ecology. In the process, he reshaped the famous love affair of Antony and Cleopatra into a cross-cultural encounter that subverts the commonly held image of Rome, showing that, by defining Egypt as the cultural, racial, and ecological opposite of Rome, the Romans define themselves: seemingly fixed opposites and cultural entities intermingle and exchange identities and gender roles. We do not know, of course, whether Shakespeare intended Rome to become a metaphor for England, but since the Egyptian/gypsy identity was an Elizabethan construct, we can conclude that he brackets and unsettles his or any society's self-satisfied notions of ideological superiority.

6
Cultural Re-encounters in *The Tempest*

> The latest news is of the Basha of Algiers, who in returning to
> Turkey was betrayed to the Neapolitans by his christian wife and
> is now in Naples.
>
> Aurelianus Townshend, letter to Sir Robert Cecil (1601)

In *The Tempest*, Shakespeare abides by the classical unities, and
therefore the action of this play covers a period of about six hours;
yet through various narratives, the play dilates its boundaries to
encompass events extending over a period of more than
two decades. These events include the witch Sycorax's trial and
expulsion from Algiers, the birth and youth of her son Caliban,
and her long tyrannous rule over the island; Prospero's troubles
as Duke of Milan, his overthrow and banishment, and his twelve-
year control of the island; the King of Naples' voyage to Africa to
marry his daughter Claribel to the King of Tunis, his voyage of
return and shipwreck, and the royal party's wandering on the
island; and the reunion of Prospero and his former enemies. In its
extended action, *The Tempest* centers on several cross-cultural
encounters and in some ways provides a synthesis for the salient
features of Shakespeare's representation of cross-cultural interaction
through gender inversion, textual negotiation, and alien habitats.
But it also offers the unique example of a character who negotiates
his cultural reintegration after exile in an alien space. I will argue
that the dual process of estrangement and reintegration relies on the
exaggeration of differences characteristic of Shakespeare's cross-
cultural representation.

Like Antony in *Antony and Cleopatra*, Prospero estranges himself
from his European cultural community and enters an alien environment. Prospero eventually, however, negotiates his permanent
return to his European community. The question arises, what
makes this reintegration possible and on what terms is it to take

place? Unlike Antony, Prospero neither seeks nor discovers a world of pleasures wherein he will lose himself; rather, he finds celibacy, estrangement, and the isolation of books. In an alien habitat of a desolate island, Prospero discovers how to bring about his return home. I will argue that, although his love of books precipitates his cultural and political isolation, his sojourn in an inhospitable alien world allows him to build a new identity for himself upon female figures through which he re-encounters his culture. His reintegration, however, entails a fundamental political and dynastic realignment for his dukedom.

Events in Milan twelve years before the opening scene center on Prospero's books and intertwine textual studies, gender politics, and a dynastic crisis, which resulted in the overthrow of Prospero as Duke of Milan and of Miranda as heir apparent to the throne. These events are couched in cross-cultural terms. Although Prospero is a native of Milan, the play suggests that Antonio succeeds in portraying his brother as an alien. Prospero identifies books as the cause of his undoing in Milan, whereby he lost his political position and almost his life and underwent profound alienation, ending up, in Victor Turner's phrase from another context, at 'the fringes and interstices of the social structure' of his time.[1] Having transferred the government to his brother Antonio, Prospero applied himself to scholarly pursuits: 'those being all my study,/The government I cast upon my brother/And to my state grew stranger, being transported/And rapt in secret studies' (I.ii.74–7). As he says, he neglected 'worldly ends, all dedicated/To closeness, and the bettering of...[his] mind' (I.ii.89–90). Enraptured by his texts and dependent on his untrustworthy brother, he became an outsider in his own country. Antonio seized the opportunity and, as Prospero reports, 'new-created/The creatures that were mine, I say, or changed 'em,/Or else new-formed 'em' (I.ii.81–3). Antonio wins over the loyalty of the citizens of Milan and engineers Prospero's overthrow.

We have scanty first-hand knowledge of Prospero's books, although we can reconstruct the nature of those texts and explain Antonio's success in shaping public opinion against Prospero. Again, we must read retrospectively. From his secret studies, Prospero acquired powers, which to Miranda he describes as 'magic' (I.ii.24); but in Act V, he describes something that resembles witchcraft ('rough magic' that is too 'terrible to enter human hearing'):

I have bedimmed
The noontide sun, called forth the mutinous winds,
And 'twixt the green sea and the azured vault
Set roaring war; to the dread rattling thunder
Have I given fire and rifted Jove's stout oak
With his own bolt; the strong-based promontory
Have I made shake and by the spurs plucked up
The pine and cedar; graves at my command
Have waked their sleepers, oped, and let 'em forth
By my so potent art.

(V.i.41–9)

In this description, Prospero's art bears striking and indisputable parallels to witchcraft.[2] As Keith Thomas explains, the 1604 Act of Parliament, which was repealed only in 1736, made it a felony 'to take up a dead body in whole or part for magical purposes,' and to '"consult, covenant with, entertain, employ, feed, or reward any evil and wicked spirit to or for any intent or purpose".'[3] According to the Act, Prospero would have committed a felony by disturbing corpses in their graves. 'Rough' acquires the specific meaning of *maleficium*, a crime for which many were hanged in England.[4] In this context, Prospero's books become the repository of arcane, forbidden knowledge.

Although Prospero never admits that Antonio accused him of witchcraft, his study of old texts, his practice of magical arts, and his eventual renunciation of magical power in Act V suggest that the study of magic was one reason he was expelled from Milan and that Antonio's accusation might have been sufficient to discredit Prospero. Indeed, that connection between Prospero's secret study and his expulsion may help to explain his brother's hostility. E. E. Evans-Pritchard concludes that 'the operation of witchcraft beliefs in the social life are also closely connected with the kinship system, particularly through the custom of vengeance.'[5] Alan Macfarlane observes that witchcraft accusations 'made by the young against the old tend to be provoked by desire for change.'[6] In fact, as Deborah Willis notes, Antonio embodies the seed of social unrest and discontent: 'Shakespeare fashions Antonio out of his culture's anxieties about factious and rebellious aristocrats, about the exclusion of younger brothers from power by primogeniture, and about aggression unmodulated by a sense of familial or communal bonds.'[7] To insinuate witchcraft would certainly have been an easy way to discredit a ruler more interested in secretive intellectual pursuits than the welfare of his government.

However Prospero's discrediting occurred, Antonio turns public opinion against Prospero and thus succeeds in advancing his own political ambitions, although in the process he had to surrender Milan's sovereignty, as Prospero laments:

> [Antonio] confederates
> (So dry he was for sway) with th'King of Naples
> To give him annual tribute, do him homage,
> Subject his coronet to his crown, and bend
> The dukedom yet unbowed (alas, poor Milan!)
> To most ignoble stooping.

> (I.ii.111–16)

To gain power, Antonio betrayed not only his brother but also his own country. Never given a chance to defend himself, Prospero is cast out of Milan under the cover of darkness.

Interestingly, *The Tempest* presents the conflict between Prospero and Antonio through metaphors of gender inversion. Prospero describes his brother as the wooer, who seduced his subjects by setting 'all hearts i'th'state / To what tune pleased his ear' (I.ii.84–5). Likewise, Prospero personifies his 'trust' as a woman impregnated by Antonio's evil nature, giving birth to an unruly offspring: 'And my trust, / Like a good parent, did beget of him / A falsehood in its contrary as great / As my trust was' (I.ii.93–6).[8] Further, Antonio decisively takes the reins of government: 'He [is] thus lorded, / Not with what my revenue yielded / But what my power might else exact,' says Prospero (I.ii.97–9). Prospero, on the other hand, must attend to child-raising and other domestic duties. He describes his expulsion under the cover of night:

> A treacherous army levied, one midnight
> Fated to th' purpose, did Antonio open
> The gates of Milan; and i' th' dead of darkness,
> The ministers for th' purpose hurrièd thence
> Me and thy crying self.

> (I.ii.128–32)

Prospero becomes father and mother to Miranda while attempting to protect himself and his throne. In part, Prospero here resembles Cymbeline who, finding his lost sons and daughter, sees himself as a mother: 'O, what am I?/a mother to the birth of three? Ne'er mother/Rejoiced deliverance more' (V.v.368–70).

Coppélia Kahn has examined the effect of the absent mother in *King Lear*: 'The aristocratic patriarchal families headed by Gloucester and Lear have, actually and effectively, no mothers. The only source of love, power, and authority is the father – an awesome, demanding presence.'[9] Kahn observes that 'the absence of the mother points to her hidden presence' and that in this 'tragedy of masculinity,' Lear attempts to find a mother in Cordelia.[10] Stephen Orgel argues that although Prospero's wife is 'missing as a character,' 'Prospero, several times explicitly, presents himself as incorporating the wife, acting as both father and mother to Miranda, and, in one extraordinary passage [I.ii.155–8], describes the voyage to the island as a birth fantasy.'[11]

Indeed, for Miranda, the experience becomes a second birth. The expulsion of the weeping child from the body politic seems analogous to the expulsion of the newborn from the mother's womb. But this time there is a parturient father, not mother, as the gates of Milan open and Miranda is born again, not into a world of light, but into the 'dead of darkness.' Miranda's comment seems appropriate: 'Alack, what trouble/Was I then to you!' (I.ii.151–2). Prospero responds in terms reminiscent of those of a mother who has gone through the pains of labor:

> O, a cherubin
> Thou wast that did preserve me! Thou didst smile,
> Infusèd with a fortitude from heaven,
> When I have decked the sea with drops full salt,
> Under my burden groaned: which raised in me
> An undergoing stomach, to bear up
> Against what should ensue.

> (I.ii.152–8)

These metaphors suggest that Prospero assumes the role of a woman caring for an infant daughter into exile. Secret study, family politics, and the politics of gender come together. Books thus symbolize the pursuit of arcane and forbidden knowledge and the transgression of cultural boundaries. Antonio's success attests that he may be culturally and politically better attuned than Prospero to the beliefs, values, and, more important, prejudices of his culture. It must be emphasized that the Milanese throw not only Prospero and his heir into exile but also his library. Prospero praises Gonzalo for allowing him to have his books: 'So, of his gentleness,/Knowing I loved my books, he [Gonzalo] furnished me/From mine own library with volumes that/I prize above my dukedom' (I.ii.165–8). These books make survival in a hostile environment possible; therefore, Prospero feels grateful to Gonzalo. But one must not forget that these books got Prospero in trouble in the first place. Whether naively or astutely, Gonzalo in fact succeeds in expunging dangerous volumes from Milan's royal library.

Later in his conspiracy with Trinculo and Stephano, Caliban recognizes the source of Prospero's power. Caliban advises Stephano to kill Prospero and 'cut his wesand with thy knife'; but, he adds, 'Remember/First to possess his books; for without them/He's but a sot, as I am, nor hath not/One spirit to command' (III.ii.88–91). In these texts, Prospero found the means of survival and from them he developed an art to control the environment and to subdue Ariel and Caliban. The island becomes an extension of the library in Milan. We may also infer that Caliban's suspicion of Prospero's books echoes Antonio's twelve years before.

Both the library and the island of Prospero's exile represent an alien habitat associated with Europe's undesirable figures, such as witches, savages, and aliens; they also symbolize cultural assumptions about the nature of difference. In the *Henry VI* trilogy, for example, we saw how habitat intertwines with ideological fantasy: Margaret of Anjou and Joan of Arc guide the action to the frontiers of culture, the fantastical locus of gender transgression and ideological subversion. In *Antony and Cleopatra*, Egypt represents an alien habitat, where cultural opposites intermingle and exchange identities. Likewise in *The Tempest*, Prospero interacts with an alien world through which he will change his own identity.

European experience in the New World provided the basis for Shakespeare's creation of *The Tempest*. The King's Men performed this play for King James's court at Whitehall on 1 November 1611. The performance followed on the heels of intense interest in Sir Thomas Gates's shipwreck and disappearance at sea in 1609 and his miraculous arrival in Virginia in 1610.[12] Pamphlets were immediately published to capitalize on the sensational incident and interest in the remarkable alien habitat in which the English colonists found themselves. In *A True Reportory of the Wracke* (1610), Strachey describes a storm so ferocious that 'we could not apprehend in our imaginations any possibility of greater violence'; yet they discovered that 'fury added to fury, and one storme urging a second more outragious then the former.'[13] The voyagers experienced profound disorientation: 'During all this time, the heavens look'd so blacke upon us, that it was not possible the elevation of the Pole might be observed: nor a Starre by night, nor Sunne beame by day was to be seene.'[14] To make matters worse, the ship sprang a leak. Although the colonists made a heroic effort to keep themselves afloat, the boat was rapidly sinking. When hope seemed lost, they sighted land and managed to struggle ashore with their lives and the possessions that they could salvage. Once ashore, they encountered an equally strange habitat. They sowed seeds of garden vegetables, which promptly sprouted but then mysteriously died, perhaps eaten or destroyed by birds, flies, spiders, black beetles; even wild 'hogs' broke in and uprooted the plants.[15] The English colonists had chanced upon the Bermuda islands, which Strachey describes as being 'often afflicted and rent with tempests, great strokes of thunder, lightning and raine in the extreamity of violence.'[16] He also indicates that these were the Devil's Islands, 'feared and avoyded of all sea travellers alive, above any other place in the world.'[17]

Yet a chain of seemingly miraculous happenings on sea and on land ensured the colonists' survival. During the ferocious storm, Sir George Summers 'had an apparition of a little round light, like a faint Starre, trembling, and streaming along with a sparkeling blaze, halfe the height upon the Maine Mast, and shooting sometimes from Shroud to Shroud, tempting to settle as it were upon any of the foure Shrouds'; the apparition kept them company for several hours.[18] The English travelers believed that this atmospheric phenomenon known as *ignis fatuus* or St Elmo's fire[19] was a providential sign of their survival. Indeed, having braved the tempestuous seas in a leaky vessel, they found *terra firma*, which though seemingly unsuitable to grow European crops, proved remarkably fertile, producing an abundance of food.

Like the English colonists in Strachey's pamphlet, the sea voyagers in Act I, scene i of *The Tempest* battle the tumultuous elements but also survive unscathed. Ironically, the Boatswain taunts Gonzalo, 'if you can command these elements to silence and work the peace of the present, we will not hand a rope more; use your authority' (I.i.20–2). As the royal court of Naples abandons the ship, Gonzalo wishes for a 'dry death' in 'an acre of barren ground – long heath, brown furze, anything' (I.i.61–3). In the next scene, Miranda tells us, however, that this is no natural storm: 'If by your art, my dearest father, you have/Put the wild waters in this roar, allay them' (I.ii.1–2); and Prospero himself assures her and us that 'There's no harm done' (15). Prospero thus resembles the forces that paradoxically threatened the English colonists and yet saved them. His power transforms the island into a stage and the environment into theatrical effects.[20] A threatening alien place transmutes into something inviting and forgiving. The environmental transformation of the island parallels Prospero's own transformation and refashioning of an identity acceptable to his European guests.

Prospero's magic controls and produces a meteorological spectacle, similar to the hurricane of 1609. Apparently through optical and kinetic illusion, Ariel simulates a hurricane of frightening proportions. According to Miranda's testimony, the storm stirs up the 'wild waters' of the sea, which 'mounting to th' welkin's cheek,/Dashes the fire out' (I.ii.4–5), a description reminiscent of Strachey's: 'the Sea swelled above the Clouds, and gave battell unto Heaven.'[21] Likewise, Francisco describes the fury of the waves and how Ferdinand bravely beat the surges (II.i.110–17). For Alonso, the storm has the imprint of his guilt:

> Methought the billows spoke and told me of it;
> The winds did sing it to me; and the thunder,
> That deep and dreadful organ pipe, pronounced
> The name of Prosper; it did bass my trespass.
> Therefore my son i'th'ooze is bedded; and
> I'll seek him deeper than e'er plummet sounded
> And with him there lie mudded.
>
> (III.iii.96–102)

The rain is not rain, the water does not soak the characters' clothes, which look 'fresher than before,' and the surges are but gentle waves. St Elmo's fire, which both the English colonists of history and the Neapolitans of *The Tempest* saw, was a theatrical illusion, as Ariel explains:

I boarded the King's ship; now on the beak,
Now in the waist, the deck, in every cabin,
I flamed amazement: sometime I'ld divide,
And burn in many places; on the topmast,
The yards, and boresprit would I flame distinctly,
Then meet and join.

(I.ii.195–200)

The magically-generated storm replicates the harshness of the original environment that Prospero found when he first arrived on the island. Before Prospero asserted control, the island was in a state of barbarism and chaos. As Caliban states, Prospero and Miranda needed his help to survive in this unfamiliar habitat: 'And [I] showed thee all the qualities o'th'isle,/The fresh springs, brine-pits, barren place and fertile' (I.ii.337–8). Later, Caliban speaks of an inhospitable environment:

But they'll nor pinch,
Fright me with urchin-shows, pitch me i'th'mire,
Nor lead me, like a firebrand, in the dark
Out of my way, unless he [Prospero] bid 'em; but
For every trifle are they set upon me;
Sometime like apes that mow and chatter at me,
And after bite me; then like hedgehogs which
Lie tumbling in my barefoot way and mount
Their pricks at my footfall; sometime am I
All wound with adders, who with cloven tongues
Do hiss me into madness.

(II.ii.4–14)

In this tropical habitat, insects, birds, monkeys, and snakes thrive; but humans must struggle to survive. Stormy and unpredictable, this environment seems unstable, as, for example, when Trinculo, Stephano, and Caliban apparently experience a natural storm in II.ii. Thus, Prospero has learned to control the physical environment and to make it amenable to European habitation; but despite his extraordinary magical power, he remains in exile, yet unable to return home.

Prospero's return depends on an accident of fortune and on his own ability to refashion a new identity for himself by discarding not only his books but also all that his European compatriots find alien and undesirable. Prospero indicates to Miranda that he has been waiting for the moment when 'bountiful Fortune/(Now, my dear lady) hath mine enemies/Brought to this shore' (I.ii.178–80). If he fails to act now, he concludes, 'my fortunes/Will ever after droop' (183–4). Although an accident of fortune brings his enemies to him, Prospero needs much more for a personal and political reintegration.

Prospero displays an astute understanding of the functions of gender in the cross-cultural encounter, and he uses this to his advantage. Interestingly, he chooses feminine not masculine agents to speak for him and to mediate between himself and the royal party from Italy. In fact, as I proceed to demonstrate, he relies on female agents to bring about his return to Italy. Through symbolic inversion reminiscent of *A Midsummer Night's Dream*, Prospero eventually succeeds in erasing an alien cultural system and recovering his own European identity. The females form two triads: Nymph–Ceres–Harpy and Miranda–Claribel–Sycorax. Each triadic structure reveals polar opposites, Nymph/Harpy, Miranda/Sycorax, with an intermediary tragic figure, Ceres and Claribel. Embedded in each group lie acts of violence.

As Prospero's agent, carrying out his wishes, Ariel presents three female roles: a water nymph, a harpy, and the goddess Ceres. These female roles may seem appropriate to Ariel, a figure so thoroughly androgynous and sexless that, in modern productions, it can be played by a male or female actor. Through the water nymph, Prospero re-establishes his contact with the Europeans. He instructs Ariel: 'Go make thyself like a nymph o'th'sea. Be subject/To no sight but thine and mine; invisible/ To every eyeball else. Go take this shape/And hither come in't' (I.ii.301–4). This cross-cultural encounter recalls 'America,' the well-known engraving by Theodore and Philippe Galle (*c.* 1600), allegorically depicting Vespucci's encounter with America (Plate 14).[22] In this engraving, America, represented by a naked woman, lies on a hammock attached to the trunks of two trees, and she is surrounded by dense vegetation and exotic animals of the New World. She seems to be about to rise and greet Vespucci. By inventing the figure of a nymph, Prospero seems to know his culture well: he expects his countrymen to find a young, beautiful woman non-threatening, hence the perfect object to attract and invite the Neapolitans to the island.

The sea-nymph, however, disappears, giving way to the violent storm with which the play opens. Then the sexually attractive, apparently harmless sea-nymph reappears and invites the royal party to a banquet where cultural fantasies, dreams, and fears come together. Several 'strange Shapes' bring in food, dance about the table, and salute the royal party. Sebastian and Antonio both agree that they now believe that unicorns and the phoenix really exist, for they are in the realm of the exotic. Antonio remarks: 'Travellers ne'er did lie,/Though fools at home condemn 'em' (III.iii.26–7). Gonzalo wonders about how his countrymen will react to his report: 'If in Naples/I should report this now, would they believe me/If I should say I saw such islanders?/(For certes these are people of the island)' (III.iii.27–34). The fantastic tales that Gonzalo heard as a boy seem to be true:

> When we were boys,
> Who would believe that there were mountaineers
> Dewlapped like bulls, whose throats had hanging at 'em
> Wallets of flesh? or that there were such men
> Whose heads stood in their breasts? which now we find
> Each putter-out of five for one will bring us
> Good warrant of.

> (III.iii.43–9)

But, once the Europeans let down their guard, the nymph transforms herself into a monstrous harpy. As Orgel points out, 'harpies had the faces and breasts of young women, the wings and bodies of birds, and talons for hands.'[23] Their leader was Celaeno, a witch, who controlled them. The words of the harpy resound with threats of violence:

> You are three men of sin, whom destiny –
> That hath to instrument this lower world
> And what is in't – the never-surfeited sea
> Hath caused to belch up you, and on this island,
> Where man doth not inhabit, you 'mongst men
> Being most unfit to live, I have made you mad;
> And even with such-like valor men hang and drown
> Their proper selves.

> (III.iii.53–60)

Indeed, the harpy reminds Alonso, Antonio, and Sebastian of their crimes against Prospero and Miranda (III.iii.69–72). The harpy's words have their intended effect, so much so that Gonzalo fears for the safety of his companions as he instructs Adrian to follow Alonso, Antonio, and Sebastian and 'hinder them from what this ecstasy/May now provoke them to' (III.iii.108–9). By presenting the Celaeno-like harpy, Ariel speaks for Prospero and creates a representation of Prospero, the 'witch,' behind the banquet.

The third female that Ariel presents is a non-threatening mother, the goddess Ceres: 'I presented Ceres,' he says (IV.i.167). But unlike the banquet, staged for male eyes and depicting a male nightmare, the masque of the goddesses is above all a male version of what a female fantasy about fertility, abundance, and 'hourly joys' ought to be. Juno, Iris, and Ceres bless Miranda's betrothal to Ferdinand:

> Honor, riches, marriage blessing,
> Long continuance, and increasing,
> Hourly joys be still upon you!

> (IV.i.106–7)

But also like the banquet, the masque contains a nightmare that enacts the fear of rape. As I have argued elsewhere,[24] the masque focuses on a subtext of a mother, Ceres, lamenting the fate of her daughter Proserpina:

> Tell me, heavenly bow [i.e. Iris],
> If Venus or her son, as thou dost know,
> Do now attend the queen [Juno]? Since they did plot
> The means that dusky Dis my daughter got,
> Her and her blind boy's scandalled company
> I have forsworn.

> (IV.i.86–91)

Ceres alludes to Proserpina, who was abducted and raped by 'dusky Dis' (Pluto), god of the underworld. Angry with Venus and Cupid, who conspired with Dis, Ceres suggests that perhaps the tragedy happened recently. Like Prospero, whose daughter was apparently almost raped by Caliban (I.ii.345–8), Ceres is concerned with her daughter's welfare; but unlike Miranda, Proserpina has already been violated. Even as she rejoices in Miranda's happiness, Ceres cannot forget her personal tragedy. She knows that both Cupid and Venus pose a real threat to Miranda. Within the masque lies the tragic story of a mother's suffering over her daughter's abduction. Strangely, Miranda's happiness intertwines with a demonic representation of Proserpina's rape.[25] The prospect of happiness gives way to an act of violence.

A sea-nymph who turns into a harpy and a mother whose daughter was raped by a creature from the underworld – all point to Prospero's own life. Apparently, Prospero fears for Miranda's safety. His own 'raptus' in secret studies bred an evil nature in his brother, who commits a political rape. Antonio has symbolically violated Prospero. In the masque we encounter vestiges of this rape, for Antonio posed the first threat to Miranda's honor and integrity. Undoubtedly, reminders of Antonio's acts of violence may explain the rapture with which Prospero pursues a happy resolution later in the play.

In the second triad, Miranda replaces the nymph; Claribel, Ceres; and Sycorax, the harpy. If Ceres represents the maternal instincts of a mother who lost a daughter to rape, Sycorax, Ceres's diabolical counterpart, could turn the nymph/Miranda into a harpy. As I will argue, Sycorax in many ways represents what Prospero could become but also what he must discard if he is to return to his European community. In fact, the play depicts this as a cross-cultural conflict between a European male and the African female. Judging from what Prospero says, however, one could conclude that he and Sycorax form inverted images of each other, although for both of them the island serves a similar purpose: as harbor for political exiles and cultural pariahs, whether they come from Milan or Algiers. Ironically, Prospero seems unaware of the many parallels between him and the witch and that, like him, she too was the victim of male aggression and was expelled from a male-dominated society. At first, however, their problems seem to be the opposite of each other.[26] Prospero was feminized through his withdrawal as a scholar; Sycorax was masculinized through her display of magical power. Curiously, two exiles representing unacceptable subcultures occupy the same space.

In order to distance himself from his African counterpart, Prospero fashions an ethnography of the island and of Algiers, piecing together accounts from two potentially contradictory sources: Ariel, Sycorax's slave, and Caliban, her son. Prospero recovers Sycorax's alien cultural system, wherein he discards his own former identity. He learns that Sycorax tamed and enslaved the autochthonous inhabitants (spirits) and bequeathed the island to her only son: 'This island's mine by Sycorax my mother' (I.ii.331). To nullify Caliban's claim of prior possession, Prospero also interprets Sycorax's Algerian past and thereby discredits both Sycorax and Caliban:

> This damned witch Sycorax,
> For mischiefs manifold, and sorceries terrible
> To enter human hearing, from Argier,
> Thou know'st, was banished.

> (I.ii.263–6)

He denigrates Sycorax's memory and refashions himself as an enlightened magician, hence her opposite. To bring about his return to Milanese society, Prospero forges a myth of a malevolent witch and a benevolent magician who has 'done nothing but in care of thee,/Of thee my dear one, thee my daughter' (I.ii.16–17).

Still, his manipulative powers become apparent, for example, in Ariel's discontent. Speaking for Ariel, Prospero notes that even Ariel found Sycorax's commands 'earthy and abhorred' (273); to punish Ariel for his disobedience, she took a 'cloven pine' 'within which rift/Imprisoned thou didst painfully remain/A dozen years' (I.ii.276–8). But when allowed to speak for himself, Ariel proves, in fact, 'moody,' rejects Prospero's commands, complains of 'more toil,' and demands his freedom. Apparently, Ariel deems service to Prospero no better than servitude to Sycorax. Only after Prospero threatens Ariel, does the spirit become 'correspondent to command.' Ariel rejects Prospero's control over his life, as he had Sycorax's.

Prospero demonizes every aspect of Sycorax's life, even her motherhood. Despite the lack of evidence, he suggests that Caliban was begotten 'by the devil himself/Upon thy wicked dam' (I.ii.319–20). Caliban, however, refers to Setebos as his mother's god, not as his father. To the royal party, Prospero describes Sycorax as 'a witch, and one so strong/That could control the moon, make flows and ebbs,/And deal in her command without her power' (V.i.269–71). One has to wonder precisely why. Perhaps he realizes that his and Sycorax's lives run parallel courses. Like Prospero, who could not stop a palace coup, Sycorax was powerless against the Algerians who disapproved of her actions. Prospero's popularity and the presence of an infant daughter apparently saved his life. Despite Sycorax's lack of public support, the Algerians spared her life because she was pregnant, as Prospero points out: 'This blue-eyed hag was hither brought with child/And here was left by th'sailors' (I.ii.269–70). As a witch, Sycorax was a pariah; as an expecting mother, she inspired pity in the Algerians, who decided to spare her life. Nonetheless, she was powerless to change her fate; in fact, she proved quite human: within a dozen years, she died (279), unable to return to her home country, unable to provide for her son. Caliban, like Miranda, stands to inherit a kingdom but not magical powers.[27]

Thus, by symbolic inversion, Sycorax becomes the foundation upon which Prospero erects a new identity, whereby he rejects his books and the image of himself that his secret studies and Antonio's scheming projected on his subjects' minds. Eventually, Prospero can emerge from his exile not as a vindictive witch who wants to destroy his enemies but rather as a noble and benevolent forgiver, who believes that 'The rarer action is/In virtue than in vengeance' (V.i.27–8). Tempted by evil powers, he can also forsake them and rid himself of the emblems of his and Sycorax's otherness; as he says, 'My charms I'll break' (V.i.31), promising to break and bury his staff and 'deeper than did ever plummet sound/I'll drown my book' (V.i.54–7). Paradoxically then, while Prospero depends on 'rough magic' and strange and uncanny coincidences to regain his duke-dom, he finds that he must abjure this same magic in order to be accepted.

In the epilogue, having forgiven his enemies, Prospero asks for the audience's forgiveness and prayer. His identity as a man of books still clearly poses a threat to him, if we are to judge from Sebastian's reaction to Prospero's story. 'The devil speaks in him' (V.i.130), says Sebastian as Prospero reveals himself as 'the wronged Duke of Milan.' A little later Alonso adds the comment that 'These are not natural events' (V.i.227). Prospero apparently dis-covers the extent to which forgiveness of one's enemies does not suffice to ensure one's political survival. Even though displays of magical power temporarily subdue his opponents, they do not erase prejudice, Antonio's ambition, or the crisis of succession in Milan.

Prospero's political mistakes and errors of judgment inevitably affect his daughter's political future. In some ways, one can read the action of *The Tempest* as his efforts to atone for the suffering that he has already caused. If at first he needs magic to regain the throne, he must also renounce it for the sake of his own reputation and for the sake of Miranda's political future. He must not do anything to compromise Miranda's future, as Alonso has done to his daughter Claribel.

A decade before Shakespeare wrote *The Tempest*, Naples saw an extraordinary event in its relations with the Barbary States.[28] In a letter dated 17/27 July 1601, Aurelianus Townshend wrote to Sir Robert Cecil: 'The latest news is of the Basha of Algiers, who in returning to Turkey was betrayed to the Neapolitans by his christian wife and is now in Naples.'[29] The said Bashaw may have been Daly-Hassen Bou Richa, who ruled Algiers from 1599 to 1603, or another unidentified Turkish officer.[30] This incident may have, in fact, suggested to Shakespeare the second female figure, which Prospero uses as an instrument of his return: Claribel, Alonso's daughter. In part, of course, Prospero depends on a fortunate coincidence: the King of Naples and Prospero's enemies coincidentally sail near the island and come under Prospero's spell. Prospero and Miranda's future thus depends on the marriage of Claribel to the King of Tunis. This marriage constitutes a political and dynastic puzzle, having apparently been arranged against Claribel's wishes, as Sebastian states to Alonso:

> Sir, you may thank yourself for this great loss,
> That would not bless our Europe with your daughter,
> But rather loose her to an African,
> Where she, at least, is banished from your eye
> Who hath cause to wet the grief on't.

(II.i.120–4)

Sebastian adds that several persons begged Alonso not to consent to this marriage, and even Claribel, 'the fair soul herself/Weighed, between loathness and obedience, at/Which end o'th'em should bow' (II.i.125–7). Not heeding these pleas, Alonso loses his daughter in Africa and his son temporarily at sea.

As they wander through the island and plot to kill Alonso, Sebastian and Antonio discuss Claribel's political fate. With Ferdinand presumably drowned, Antonio asks his co-conspirator: 'Who's the next heir of Naples?' (II.i.40). When Sebastian responds, 'Claribel,' Antonio describes her situation:

She that is Queen of Tunis; she that dwells
Ten leagues beyond man's life; she that from Naples
Can have no note, unless the sun were post –
The man i'th'moon's too slow – till new-born chins
Be rough and razorable; she that from whom
We all were sea-swallowed, though some cast again,
And, by that destiny, to perform an act
Where what's past is prologue, what to come,
In yours and my discharge.

(II.i.240–8)

Sebastian finally agrees that Tunis lies some distance from Naples:
"twixt which regions/There is some space' (II.i.250–1). Trapped in
an alien habitat in North Africa, Claribel cannot influence the events
in Naples. Indeed, Claribel's fate underscores what Miranda could
have become, if somehow she were trapped forever in an alien
world.

To forge a new European identity, Prospero above all depends on
Miranda. As he states, he has given her a European education and
courtly manners, raising her to assume her dynastic destiny: 'Have I,
thy schoolmaster, made thee more profit/Than other princess can,
that have more time/For vainer hours, and tutors not so careful'
(I.ii.172–4). By not teaching her witchcraft, he has also shielded her
from his magical practices. His actions suggest that he has indeed
raised Miranda to become Ferdinand's bride and future queen of
Naples. Later he 'introduces' Miranda and Ferdinand to each other.
When Ferdinand sees her for the first time, he associates her with the
sea-nymph that he has already encountered: 'Most sure, the god-
dess/On whom these airs attend' (I.ii.422–3). Falling in love with her
at first sight, Ferdinand offers to make her queen of Naples (450).
Prospero accomplishes his goal, 'They are both in either's pow'rs'
(I.ii.451), but he will make Ferdinand's life difficult, 'lest too light
winning/Make the prize light' (I.ii.452–3). Thus Prospero quickly
proceeds not only to bring Ferdinand and Miranda together but
also to celebrate their betrothal in Act IV, before Alonso or anyone
else can interfere. He is ensuring Miranda's dynastic position in the
kingdom of Alonso, whom Prospero had earlier described to Miranda
as 'an enemy/To me inveterate' (I.ii.121–2).

Even as he gives Miranda's hand to Ferdinand, Prospero remembers both present and past dangers. He warns Ferdinand not to

'break her virgin-knot before/All sanctimonious ceremonies may/ With full and holy rite be minist'red' (IV.i.15–17) and later not to 'give dalliance/Too much the rein: the strongest oaths are straw/To th'fire i'th'blood' (IV.i.51–3). If Ferdinand tries to violate Miranda, he will become a representation of Caliban, a 'demi-devil' (V.i.272–3), who, according to Prospero tried to rape Miranda: 'I have used thee/(Filth as thou art) with humane care, and lodged thee/In mine own cell till thou didst seek to violate/The honor of my child' (I.ii.345–8). Caliban, however, gloats on what he could have accomplished: 'I had peopled else/This isle with Calibans' (I.ii.349–50). This line seems to be a strange reply that suggests that Caliban can replicate himself, displace Prospero, and reconquer the island. He can also turn Miranda into Claribel, a European princess lost to an African king.[31]

Caliban instinctively recognizes Prospero's vulnerability in having a female heir who can become the mother to a conqueror's offspring. Caliban's boast that he can people the island with Calibans reminds Prospero of and underscores the threat of Antonio and Antonio's son. If Caliban has the power to produce male heirs, so does Antonio. We learn that, unlike Prospero, Antonio has a son. The only reference to Antonio's son occurs in the context of a comparison and rivalry between the two brothers:

FERDINAND: Yes, faith, and all his lords, the Duke of Milan
And his brave son being twain.
PROSPERO[*aside*]:   The Duke of Milan
And his more braver daughter could control thee,
If now 'twere fit to do't.

(I.ii.438–40)

This mysterious reference underscores the difference between the two brothers: one has a son; the other, a daughter. The dynastic implications of this difference are apparent. We do not know whether this was one of the reasons why Antonio decided to overthrow his brother; but we do know that later, believing that Ferdinand has drowned, he encourages Sebastian to bypass Claribel's claim to the Neapolitan throne. Each uncle is threatened by and desires to bypass his niece's claim to the throne. Antonio knows that a male heir perpetuates the male line; a female heir, even if she remains unmarried, as Queen Elizabeth did, creates dynastic problems that cannot be easily resolved. In a patriarchal society, a father/king with a female heir presides over the extinction of the male line and ironically becomes a substitute for the female Other until she herself is displaced by a husband. Such is the fate of Prospero and could be the fate of Alonso had Ferdinand died in the wreck. In the dynastic sense, the feminization of Prospero, which Caliban astutely perceives, had begun before he studied in secret. Antonio represented the continuation of the male line; Prospero, its extinction.

Prospero learns that in Italy, as in Algiers, the body politic relies on male primacy. This may explain the eagerness with which he displays his beautiful daughter for the young Neapolitan prince. Miranda's love, rather than magical power, must subdue Naples. A masculine Miranda with magical powers to control men like Antonio would be no more acceptable in Milan than Sycorax's displays of power were in Algiers. In an alien habitat, Prospero learns to accept Miranda's future husband's dominance and Neapolitan primacy, which at the beginning of the play he referred to as Milan's 'ignoble stooping' (I.ii.116). Through Miranda, Milan can forge a permanent alliance with Naples and thus preempt Antonio's dynastic ambitions. Clearly, Prospero realizes that, through Miranda's marriage to Ferdinand, Antonio will be forever deprived of his dynastic aspirations.

Like *The Tempest*, Ben Jonson's *The Masque of Queens*, presented at Whitehall on 2 February 1609, stages a fantasy of displacement and replacement. As part of this courtly entertainment, Jonson devised an antimasque of twelve witches, a 'spectacle of strangeness' that represented an overt attempt to subvert courtly order.[32] The hags fail, however, and are displaced and replaced by Perseus, '*expressing heroic and masculine virtue*,' who proudly presents his 'daughter, then, whose glorious house you see' (134–5). Prospero learns that his regime depends on a female heir, whom he has educated outside the realm of witchcraft and magic and who embodies the creole dream of reintegration into her culture. At the end of the play, we see him relinquishing not only his magical powers but also his dynastic control, as David Bergeron observes, 'thereby installing Miranda eventually as the true substitute, the genuine representation of himself.'[33] In this solution, Prospero projects female shadows which he meaningfully incorporates into his life: to settle a family squabble with his brother, he must achieve a political compromise with Naples. This political realignment requires a dynastic re-placement.

Thus the cross-cultural encounter in *The Tempest* becomes the foundation for a cultural re-encounter. A dynastic squabble between two brothers is intertwined with a cross-cultural conflict between the exiled duke of Milan and an African witch. Symbolic inversion permits Prospero to discover in Sycorax's plight a reflection of his own. In an alien habitat, he reconstructs the gender basis for the cross-cultural experience and for his brother's success in manipulating European politics. Through theatrical and magical devices, he projects female figures through whom he negotiates his cultural reintegration, but in the process he discovers his own permanent political displacement.

Conclusion

In his updating of Richard Eden's *The History of Trauayle* (1577), Richard Willis registers the ever-increasing fascination of his age with foreign lands and cultures, including 'newes of new founde landes, the sundry sorte of governement, the different manners & fashions of divers nations, the wonderfull workes of nature, the sightes of straunge trees, fruites, foule, and beastes, the infinite treasure of Pearle, Golde, Silver....'[1] Voyages of exploration open new trade opportunities, provide access to new commodities, and permit the Europeans to gaze at wondrous habitats, landscapes, and the world's great cultural diversity. Willis underscores neither the tension created when powerful European nations compete for commodities, commercial access, trade routes, and territory, nor the cross-cultural conflicts that the age of discoveries unleashed.

Shakespeare, on the other hand, vividly explores the dramatic potential of cross-cultural contact and of the appropriations that such interaction entails, although he does not ignore the wonder of the world's cultural and ethnic diversity. For Shakespeare, individuals gain shape from their cultural position. He brings to the stage members of cultural or ethnic minorities, representing alien communities. Some of these characters have a dual dimension as stereotypes that had long inhabited the European imagination and as individual human beings caught in the middle of fierce cultural and ideological wars. To varying degrees of resistance, they must confront another culture's prejudices and appropriation of their space, cultural heritage, and memory.

I have argued throughout this book that Shakespeare uses historical, pseudo-historical, mythological, and fictional figures in his representation of cross-cultural interaction: Amazons, Jews, French women, Moors, fictional Italians. Mythology offered a point of departure. In *A Midsummer Night's Dream*, Athenians have defeated the Amazons in battle and destroyed their way of life; yet the Amazons struggle to reconstruct their cultural perspective from the remnants and fragments of the cultural war. The Amazon

Hippolyta has been silenced and absorbed into a culture whose patriarchal values contradict everything her Amazon past stood for. Shakespeare dramatizes this cultural conquest as a stark repression of Hippolyta's memory. She struggles, however, to establish and maintain a perspective of her own. But her memory alone cannot compete with Athenian military expansionism. Titania's defiance of patriarchal control and references to her sisterhood partially recover an Amazon perspective, which, however, remains exiled in Fairyland. Shakespeare must have found this solution inadequate because years later he revisits it with his young collaborator, John Fletcher. In *The Two Noble Kinsmen*, the Amazons possess memory through which they attempt to reconstruct their former lives. In Greek male homoerotic desire, they find a metaphor for their own same-sex partnerships. Although Hippolyta argues that one cannot live in the past, her sister Emilia remembers her friend Flavina, resists marriage as long as she can, and struggles to restore her Amazonian heritage, of which only vestiges remain.

Shakespeare's Amazons of history, the Frenchwomen Joan of Arc and Margaret of Anjou, stand out for their extraordinary military abilities and strong performative presence. In some ways, Joan offers a model for Margaret to emulate; but whereas Joan wages war against the British on French soil, Margaret engages them in English territory. Both Frenchwomen attempt to establish through military means an alien perspective. These women become military leaders and prove themselves as capable as or more capable than men. To establish this perspective, they appropriate what their enemies construe as masculine qualities: male attire, military prowess, and bravery. The cross-cultural conflict turns into a gender conflict: the English characters appropriate and manipulate these women's images and their nation's reputation. Thereby, the English characters control and undermine the Frenchwomen's accomplishments, while simultaneously distancing and differentiating themselves from foreigners.

In an ironic twist, *The Merchant of Venice* depicts a European female who comes to embody her Italian culture, which she sets out to defend. This takes form as a love story between the rich heiress of Belmont and the young Venetian suitor. Portia, however, has to engage in a verbal battle of textual interpretation with foreigners who threaten to spoil her happiness. A great deal of racial and religious tension threatens to rip apart the cultural fabric of Italian life. The king of Morocco brings his memory and knowledge of

European cultural values and practices to bear upon his interpretation of the riddle of the caskets. If he finds the solution, he wins Portia's hand and fortune and gains a foothold in Venice. His half-remembered ethnographical knowledge, however, does not get him very far. It takes Bassanio, a cultural insider and the man Portia loves, to solve the riddle. Legal knowledge aids Portia when she confronts another alien, the Jew Shylock, who threatens Antonio, her husband's best friend. Her powers of textual interpretation defeat Shylock in the courtroom, ultimately disallowing the bond on a technicality. At this crucial moment, with Bellario's offstage help, Portia remembers and unearths a crucial decree in the legal archives of Venice. Her memory works, where everyone else's seems to fail. She remembers and invokes the decree against aliens, thereby decisively destroying Shylock. She successfully defeats him, dispossesses him of his fortune, and appropriates his heritage and identity through his forced conversion to Christianity.

Titus Andronicus depicts Aaron, a Moor who has no memory and no connection to a cultural community elsewhere. The color of his skin, however, associates him with a world elsewhere, preconditions the Romans' response to him, and invites prejudice about the nature of his character. With resentment and anger, Aaron desperately searches for an identity, not in a distant cultural community, but rather in the literary texts of his Roman enemies, where he finds his shadow. These texts, however, trap him into re-enacting acts of violence from Rome's literature. In contrast, Othello remembers, and in fact regales his Venetian hosts with stories of his foreign roots and experiences. Venetian prejudices about the nature of blackness and erroneous assumptions about his origins compete with his memory and undermine his accomplishments as a military leader and his love for Desdemona. Again the cross-cultural conflict finds expression through a love story, as a chasm opens in his relationship with Desdemona. Despite their sincere love for each other, Othello and Desdemona tragically fail to communicate their different cultural expectations of each other and therefore seem unable to understand and resist the forces of racism and prejudice that Iago employs to drive them apart.

In *Antony and Cleopatra* and *The Tempest*, Antony and Prospero, respectively, under different circumstances confront the weakening of the ties that bind them to their European cultural communities. Throughout the play, Antony constantly tries to remember who he is. After the death of his wife Fulvia, he in fact temporarily returns to

Rome, marries Octavia, renews his political ties to Octavius, and reestablishes his bonds with Rome. Memories of Egypt and love of Cleopatra compete with his desire for political and cultural reintegration into the life of Rome. He finds himself drawn to Egypt, his adopted land, and to Cleopatra, the woman he loves. To the end of his life, he is torn between rejection and reaffirmation of Roman values. Like Cleopatra, he battles Roman misconceptions about the Egyptians. Eventually, Rome's triumphal march of appropriation and assimilation cannot be stopped. Ironically, as part of his military role, Antony has entered an alien space, which his culture has set out to appropriate. But here he loses his heart, finds a culture he loves, and abandons his former cultural and political allegiances.

Prospero has every reason to reject, resent, and even hate anything European. After all, home was the site of betrayal, suspicion, rejection, misconceptions. Memories of home bring pain, not comfort. Under very different circumstances from Antony's, however, and to a different resolution, Prospero struggles to re-establish those ties. He refuses to become a misanthrope, a cultural pariah, and a permanent political exile. Although the island provided him shelter and the means of survival, he does not see it as place of escape from his troubles; rather, he distances himself from it. He does so by using strategies of cultural and ideological domination from his European cultural heritage. He appropriates the memories of Sycorax and Caliban, which he refashions to suit his own ends. Their story contains reminders of unsavory tactics, brutality, barbarism, exile. In distancing himself from his African double, Prospero fashions a new identity for himself as Sycorax's opposite. Through this cross-cultural negotiation, he rescues himself and Miranda from exile and brings about his dynastic reintegration into the political life of Europe.

Shakespeare associates individual memory with cultural identity. Cultural domination may entail erasure, suppression, or replacement of memory. Yet various markers signal and reinforce the cross-cultural experience, such as the color of one's skin, religious beliefs, bodies mutilated in the Amazonian fashion, cross-dressing, same-sex partnership and desire, and appropriation of the opposite sex's gender traits. Through symbolic inversion, Shakespeare reveals cross-cultural difference. Amazons become Greek wives, Frenchwomen turn into military leaders, a North African competes for a much sought-after rich Venetian heiress, a black general marries a Venetian Magnifico's daughter, a Roman general loses himself in the carnal and culinary pleasures of Egypt, the Duke of Milan becomes a scholar/magician on an island, formerly inhabited by an African witch. Opposites meet, intermingle, often exchange identity.

Through symbolic inversion, Shakespeare gives us glimpses of cultural diversity and the multiple ways of being human and living our lives. We encounter remnants of cultural systems that permit and encourage women warriors, same-sex partnerships and desire, racial and religious diversity, exotic flora and fauna and defining cultural practices in wondrous habitats, even exquisite artifacts, like Othello's strawberry-spotted napkin from a distant land. Shakespeare grapples with profound instability and social contradiction in the cross-cultural encounter, which exaggerates and exacerbates difference. One culture holds the mirror up to another, thus emerging in counterdistinction and often generating cross-cultural conflict. But in these cultural and ideological wars, radically different cultural systems compete with each other, exposing a Eurocentric perspective and the caricatures that cultures create of one another.

Notes

INTRODUCTION

1. Unless otherwise indicated, all quotations from Shakespeare will be from *The Complete Pelican Shakespeare*, edited by Alfred Harbage (New York and London: Penguin, 1969).

2. Named after Gerhardus Mercator (1512–94), Flemish geographer, mathematician, and cartographer. See Richard Hakluyt, *The Principal Navigations Voyages Traffiques & Discoveries of the English Nation* (Glasgow: James MacLehose and Sons; New York: Macmillan, 1904), 1: xii.

3. James Clifford, *The Predicament of Culture: Twentieth-Century Ethnography, Literature, and Art* (Cambridge, Mass.: Harvard University Press, 1988), p. 118.

4. James A. Boon, *Other Tribes, Other Scribes: Symbolic Anthropology in the Comparative Study of Cultures, Histories, Religions, and Texts* (Cambridge: Cambridge University Press, 1982), pp. 22, 26.

5. Boon, p. 26.

6. Erich Auerbach, *Mimesis: The Representation of Reality in Western Literature* (1953; rpt New York: Doubleday, 1957), p. 285.

7. Angus Fletcher, *Allegory: The Theory of a Symbolic Mode* (Ithaca, NY: Cornell University Press, 1964), pp. 35–6.

8. Stephen Greenblatt, *Marvelous Possessions: The Wonder of the New World* (Chicago: University of Chicago Press, 1991), p. 20.

9. Gomes Eannes de Azurara, *The Chronicle of the Discovery of Guinea*, translated by Charles Raymond Beazley (London: Hakluyt Society, 1896–7), 1: 81.

10. Azurara, 1: 85.

11. Lisa Jardine, *Worldly Goods: A New History of the Renaissance* (New York: Doubleday, 1996), p. 15.

12. Steven Mullaney, *The Place of the Stage: License, Play, and Power in Renaissance England* (Chicago: University of Chicago Press, 1988), p. 88. In *Fashioning Femininity and English Renaissance Drama* (Chicago: University of Chicago Press, 1991), Karen Newman cites Martin Frobisher's appropriation of Eskimo culture: 'In Frobisher's account, ethnography is domesticated: he constructs Eskimos' relations as an English marriage – domestic, naturalized, immanent. In doing so, he suppresses the Eskimos' strangeness not only for the Elizabethans but for modern readers of Renaissance texts as well, and thereby obscures the contingency of gender and sexuality' (pp. 98–9).

13. Wlad Godzich, Intro. to Michel de Certeau's *Heterologies: Discourse on the Other*, trans. Brian Massumi (Minneapolis: University of Minnesota Press, 1986), p. xiii.

14. Tzvetan Todorov, *The Conquest of America: The Question of the Other*, trans. Richard Howard (New York: Harper & Row, 1984) pp. 247–8. For other studies of the colonial experience, see, among others, Peter Hulme, *Colonial Encounters: Europe and the Native Caribbean, 1492–1797* (London and New York: Methuen, 1986); Mullaney, *Place of the Stage*; Francis Barker et al., eds, *Europe and Its Others*, Proceedings of the Essex Conference on the Sociology of Literature, 2 vols (Colchester: University of Essex, 1985).

15. See Margaret M. McGowan, 'Form and Themes in Henri II's Entry into Rouen,' *Renaissance Drama* NS 1 (1968): 199–251; *L'Entrée de Henri II à Rouen 1550: A Facsimile* with an Introduction by Margaret M. McGowan (New York and Amsterdam: Theatrvm Orbis Terrarvm Ltd, Johnson Reprint Corporation, 1970); Ferdinand Denis, *Une Fête Brésilienne Célébrée à Rouen en 1550* (Paris: J. Techener, Libraire, 1850; rpt Upper Saddle River, NJ: The Gregg Press, 1968); and Mullaney, *Place of the Stage*, pp. 65–9.

16. Richard Collinson, ed., *The Three Voyages of Martin Frobisher, in search of a passage to Cathaia and India by the North-West, A.D. 1576–8* (New York: Burt Franklin, 1963), p 74. See Hakluyt, 7: 301. Throughout this book, I attempt to retain the original Renaissance orthography of the texts from which I quote. However, I have silently regularized the i–js and u–vs. Also, for the convenience of the modern reader, I have made a few other minor changes, if I thought the odd spelling would impede intelligibility.

17. When Frobisher on his second voyage showed the picture to another captive, the prisoner was much amazed: '. . . beholding advisedly the same with silence a good while, as though he would streine courtesie whether should begin the speech (for he thought him no doubt a lively creature) [the captive] at length began to question with him, as with his companion, and finding him dumb and mute, seemed to suspect him, as one disdeinfull, and would with a little helpe have growen into choller at the matter, untill at last by feeling and handling, hee found him but a deceiving picture. And then with great noise and cryes, ceased not wondring, thinking that we could make men live or die at our pleasure.' See Hakluyt, 7: 301.

18. See Rachel Doggett, Monique Hulvey and Julie Ainsworth, eds, *New World of Wonders: European Images of the Americas 1492–1700* (Washington, DC: The Folger Shakespeare Library, 1992), p. 40.

19. Hakluyt, 11: 24. A Martin Cockeram of Plymouth was left in Brazil as a pledge for the safe return of the Brazilian cacique. When the Brazilian cacique died on the return voyage, Captain Hawkins feared that Cockeram would lose his life, but 'the Savages being fully perswaded of the honest dealing of our men with their prince, restored againe the said pledge, without any harme to him, or any man of the company: which pledge of theirs they brought home againe into England, with their ship fraighted, and furnished with

the commodities of the countrey' (24). Hakluyt reports that Sir John Hawkins, the son of William Hawkins, confirmed that the said Martin Cockeram became an officer of the town of Plymouth and 'was living within these fewe yeeres' (25).

20. The editor of the Pelican *Henry VIII*, F. David Hoeniger, suggests that the 'strange Indian' refers to a North American Indian for 'Virginia was much in the news in 1612–13,' but he does not identify any specific incident.

21. Richard Eden, *The History of Trauayle in the West and East Indies* (London, 1577), sig. A4r.

22. Marquis of Salisbury, *Calendar of the Manuscripts of the Marquis of Salisbury*, Hatfield House (London: HMSO, 1906), Part II: 569.

23. J. D. Rogers, 'Voyages and Exploration: Geography: Maps,' in *Shakespeare's England: An Account of the Life & Manners of His Age*, ed. C. T. Onions (1916; rpt Oxford: Clarendon Press, 1950), 1: 170.

24. Like Kim F. Hall, in *Things of Darkness: Economies of Race and Gender in Early Modern England* (Ithaca, NY and London: Cornell University Press, 1995), I believe that 'gender concerns are crucially embedded in discourses of race' (2); I do not, however, believe that modern English identity is synonymous with what she refers to as 'white male' culture.

25. Boon, p. ix.

26. Boon, p. ix.

27. Thomas Heywood, *An Apology for Actors*, in E. K. Chambers, *The Elizabethan Stage* (1923; rpt Oxford: Clarendon Press, 1961), 4: 251–2.

28. From time to time, however, Londoners expressed widespread hostility to alien merchants and artificers, as for example in the riots of Evil May-Day in 1517. See C. W. Chitty, 'Aliens in England in the Sixteenth Century,' *Race* 8 (1966): 131. See also G. K. Hunter, 'Elizabethans and Foreigners,' *Shakespeare Survey* 17 (1964): 37–52; and A. J. Hoenselaars, *Images of English and Foreigners in the Drama of Shakespeare and His Contemporaries: A Study of Stage Characters and National Identity in English Renaissance Drama, 1558–1642* (Rutherford, NJ: Fairleigh Dickinson University Press, 1992), especially chapter 2, 'Foreigners in England, 1558–1603.' For further information, consult the following Guildhall Library manuscripts: MSS 1588–1731, *London-Dutch Church Letters*; and MS 7428/11, Corporation of London, Court of Common Council, *An Act of Common Councell, prohibiting all Strangers borne, and Forrainers, to vse any Trades, or keepe any maner of shops in any sort within this Citty, Liberties and Freedome thereof* (London, 1606).

29. Gerald M. Berkowitz, 'Shakespeare in Edinburgh,' *Shakespeare Quarterly* 31 (1980): 163. In 'Bárbara Heliodora Cultua Shakespeare,' interview by 'Ségio de Carvalho, *O Estado de São Paulo*, 31 July 1997, Bárbara Heliodora, the renowned Brazilian critic, producer, and translator of Shakespeare, discusses Shakespeare's appeal to a Brazilian audience. She also discusses her book, *Falando de Shakespeare* (São Paulo: Editora Perspectiva, 1997).

30. James Kynge, 'Shakespeare in China,' *Plays and Players* (July 1986): 16.
31. Kynge, pp. 16–18.

1 'THE UTTERMOST PARTS OF THEIR MAPS': FRONTIERS OF GENDER

1. Plutarch, *The Lives of the Noble Grecians and Romans*, translated by Sir Thomas North (1579), eds Roland Baughman (New York: Heritage Press, 1941), 1: 5. Plutarch may be echoing Strabo's criticism of historians who confuse history and myth. Strabo seems particularly sensitive to the confusion regarding the Amazons: 'A peculiar thing has happened in the case of the account we have of the Amazons; for our accounts of other peoples keep a distinction between the mythical and the historical elements; for the things that are ancient and false and monstrous are called myths, but history wishes for the truth, whether ancient or recent, and contains no monstrous element, or else only rarely. But as regards the Amazons, the same stories are told now as in early times, though they are marvelous and beyond belief,' *The Geography of Strabo*, 8 vols, translated by Horace Leonard Jones (London: William Heinemann; New York: G. P. Putnam's Sons, 1928), 5: 235–7.
2. Plutarch, p. 5.
3. The proposed model resembles the gender system of the Igbo of Nigeria, a structure separate from biological sex, in which, as Ifi Amadiume has cogently described, 'Daughters could become sons and consequently male. Daughters and women in general could be husbands to wives and consequently males in relation to their wives.' See Ifi Amadiume, *Male Daughters, Female Husbands: Gender and Sex in an African Society* (London: Zed Books, 1987), p. 15.
4. The question of the authorship of *The Two Noble Kinsmen* is not essential to my argument for two reasons: Shakespeare's involvement in the composition of this play is undisputed; and the scenes I will primarily focus on are attributed to Shakespeare. See Eugene M. Waith, ed., Introduction to *The Two Noble Kinsmen* (Oxford and New York: Oxford University Press, 1989), pp. 4–23, especially p. 22. All quotations from this play will be from this edition.
5. Cited in Barbara A. Babcock, ed., Introduction to *The Reversible World: Symbolic Inversion in Art and Society* (Ithaca, NY: Cornell University Press, 1972), p. 13.
6. The woodcut, *Il Mondo alla Riversa*, is reprinted from David Kunzle's 'World Upside Down: The Iconography of a European Broadsheet Type,' in Babcock, pp. 44–7. Peter Stallybrass discusses the matter in 'The World Turned Upside Down: Inversion, Gender and the State,' in Valerie Wayne, ed., *The Matter of Difference: Materialist Feminist Criticism of Shakespeare* (Ithaca, NY: Cornell University Press, 1991), pp. 201–20.

7. Francis Bond, *Wood Carvings in English Churches* (Oxford: Oxford University Press, 1910), 1: 189. Bond writes that in Picardy on Easter Tuesday 'wives whipped their husbands. Another rich joke was to make the husband do the housework. At Ely, instead of the husband sitting idly while the wife does the work, it is the wife who does the looking on, while the husband, sitting among jugs and flagons, pounds corn in a mortar' (p. 190).

8. Babcock, p. 14. In *Centaurs and Amazons: Women and the Pre-History of the Great Chain of Being* (Ann Arbor: University of Michigan Press, 1982), Page duBois argues that this is precisely how the Greeks conceptualized their sexual, cultural, and species boundaries. See also Jeanne A. Roberts, *The Shakespearean Wild: Geography, Genus, and Gender* (Lincoln: University of Nebraska Press, 1991). In a study of the 'Rhetoric of Otherness' in Herodotus, François Hartog explores symbolic inversion in cross-cultural representations, 'whereby otherness is transcribed as antisameness' (*The Mirror of Herodotus: The Representation of the Other in the Writing of History*, trans. Janet Lloyd (Berkeley: University of California Press, 1988), p. 213). In symbolic inversion lies a structure of power. Writing in the context of European colonialism, Helen Carr suggests that 'the model of the power relationship between men and women' functions as the basis for the articulation of the relationship between European and non-European: 'here and in other colonized territories the difference man/woman provide[s] a fund of images and topoi by which the difference European/non-European could be politically accommodated.' See Helen Carr, 'Woman/Indian: "The American" and His Others,' *Europe and Its Others*, Proceedings of the Essex Conference on the Sociology of Literature, ed. Francis Barker et al. (Colchester: University of Essex, 1985), 2: 46.

9. Craig Felton and William B. Jordan, eds, *Jusepe de Ribera lo Spagnoletto 1591–1652* (Fort Worth, Tex.: Kimbell Art Museum, 1982), pp. 129–30. This painting is also known as 'La Mujer Barbuda' (The Bearded Woman). Juan Sánchez Cótan's painting, *The Bearded Woman of Peñaranda* (1590s, Museo del Prado, Madrid), offers an analogous example of a bearded lady (reproduced by Felton and Jordan, p. 131).

10. George T. Matthews, ed., *News and Rumor in Renaissance Europe (The Fugger Newsletters)* (New York: Capricorn books, 1959), pp. 247–8.

11. In *Curyosa, y oculta filosofia. Primera, y segunda parte de las maravillas de la Naturaleza, examinadas en várias questiones naturales* (Alcala, 1649), Fr. Ivan Eusébio of the Society of Jesus suggests that the power of the imagination is capable of bringing about a gender exchange (Chapter XVII).

12. Herodotus, *The Histories*, trans. Aubrey de Sélincourt (New York: Penguin Books, 1972), pp. 306–9; Plutarch, 1: 5–109; *Diodorus of Sicily*, 10 vols, trans. C. H. Oldfather (Cambridge, Mass.: Harvard University Press; London: William Heinemann, 1935), 2: 249–51; Strabo, 5: 233–43, 383–5, 405–25; Statius, *Thebaid*, trans. A. D. Melville (Oxford: Clarendon Press, 1992), pp. 320–30; Quintus Smyrnaeus, *The Fall of*

Troy, trans. Arthur S. Way (1913; rpt Cambridge, Mass.: Harvard University Press; London: William Heinemann, 1984).

13. See a fascinating discussion of Amazons in Gail Kern Paster's *The Body Embarrassed: Drama and the Disciplines of Shame in Early Modern England* (Ithaca, NY: Cornell University Press, 1993), pp. 234–9.
14. Paster, p. 236.
15. Herodotus, pp. 306–7.
16. Herodotus, p. 308.
17. Rudolf Wittkower, 'Marvels of the East: A Study in the History of Monsters,' *Journal of the Warburg and Courtauld Institutes* 5 (1942): 159–97; John Block Friedman, *The Monstrous Races in Medieval Art and Thought* (Cambridge, Mass.: Harvard University Press, 1981); Marie-Hélène Huet, 'Living Images: Monstrosity and Representation,' *Representations* 4 (1983): 73–87; and Karen Newman, ' "And wash the Ethiop white": Femininity and the Monstrous in *Othello*,' in *Shakespeare Reproduced: The Text in History and Ideology*, eds Jean E. Howard and Marion F. O'Connor (New York and London: Methuen, 1987), pp. 143–62.
18. *The Book of Duarte Barbosa: An Account of the Countries Bordering on the Indian Ocean and their Inhabitants, written by Duarte Barbosa, and Completed about the Year 1518 A.D.*, trans. by Mansel Longworth Dames (London: Hakluyt Society, 1918), 1: 12.
19. Samuel Purchas, *Hakluytus Posthumus or Purchas His Pilgrimes* (Glasgow: James MacLehose and Sons, 1905), 6: 507–8.
20. Christopher Columbus, *The Voyages of Christopher Columbus being the Journals of His First and Third, and the Letters Concerning his First and Last Voyages, to Which Is Added the Account of His Second Voyage Written by Andres Bernaldez*, trans. by Cecil Jane (London: Argonaut Press, 1930), p. 264.
21. Hakluyt, 10: 367.
22. Hakluyt, 10: 367–8.
23. Hakluyt, 10: 367–8.
24. The 1654 edition bears the title of *A View of the People of the Whole World* (London, 1654), p. 322.
25. John Bulwer, *Anthropometamorphosis: Man Transformed; or, the Artificial Changeling* (London, 1650), p. 239.
26. Judith Butler, *Bodies That Matter: On the Discursive Limits of 'Sex'* (New York and London: Routledge, 1993), p. 235. See Simon Shepherd, *Amazons and Warrior Women: Varieties of Feminism in Seventeenth-Century Drama* (Brighton, UK: Harvester Press, 1981), and Louis A. Montrose, *'A Midsummer Night's Dream* and the Shaping Fantasies of Elizabethan Culture: Gender, Power, Form,' in *Rewriting the Renaissance: The Discourses of Sexual Difference in Early Modern Europe*, eds Margaret W. Ferguson, Maureen Quilligan and Nancy J. Vickers (Chicago: University of Chicago Press, 1986), pp. 65–96.
27. Albert Feuillerat, *Documents Relating to the Revels At Court in the Time of King Edward VI and Queen Mary* (Louvain: A. Uystpruyst; Leipzig: O. Harrassowitz; London: David Nutt, 1914), p. 85.
28. Feuillerat, pp. 286–7.

29. Some have argued that Queen Elizabeth was represented as an Amazon. See Winfried Schleiner, '*Divina Virago*: Queen Elizabeth as an Amazon,' *Studies in Philology* 75 (1978): 163–80.

30. 'Ceremonial of the Baptism of Henry Prince of Scotland, 1594,' in John Nichols, *Progresses of Queen Elizabeth* (London: J. B. Nichols, 1823), 3: 356.

31. Ben Jonson, *The Complete Masques*, ed. Stephen Orgel (New Haven, Conn.: Yale University Press, 1969).

32. In *Amazons and Warrior Women*, Shepherd distinguishes the 'warrior woman' from the 'Amazon,' pp. 5–17.

33. Edmund Spenser, *The Faerie Queene*, ed Thomas P. Roche, Jr (New York: Penguin, 1979). All quotations are from this edition.

34. Page duBois, *Centaurs and Amazons: Women and the Pre-history of the Great Chain of Being* (Ann Arbor: University of Michigan Press, 1982), p. 34.

35. From tribal societies, anthropology has brought to light similar myths of upside-down worlds where females once ruled. Paradoxically, the myth often comes from patriarchal societies. See Joan Bamberger, 'The Myth of Matriarchy: Why Men Rule in Primitive Society,' *Woman, Culture, and Society*, eds Michelle Zimbalist Rosaldo and Louise Lamphere (Stanford, Calif.: Stanford University Press, 1974), pp. 265–9; and Carol R. Ember, 'A Cross-cultural Perspective on Sex Differences,' *Handbook of Cross-cultural Human Development* (New York: Garland, 1981), pp. 531–59. Thomas Gregor, who has lived among and studied the Mehinaku of Mato Grosso, Brazil, reports that the Mehinaku explain gender difference through a myth about the dangers of female dominance. The myth presents the tyranny of women and contains a reversal to justify the tyranny of men. The lesson does not escape the male audience: if the men do not defend their interests, the women will rise in order to control and tyrannize them. See Thomas Gregor, *Mehinaku: The Drama of Daily Life in a Brazilian Indian Village* (Chicago: University of Chicago Press, 1977), pp. 255 ff.; and Thomas Gregor, *Anxious Pleasures: The Sexual Lives of an Amazonian People* (Chicago: University of Chicago Press, 1985).

36. William Painter, *The Palace of Pleasure*, ed. Joseph Jacobs (London: David Nutt, 1890), 2: 159. Painter includes the following sources for his account of the Amazons: Strabo, Pliny, Quintus Curtius, Plutarch, Livy, Dionysius of Halicarnassus, Appian of Alexandria, Ovid, Horace, Sextus Propertius, Cicero, Valerius Maximus, Xenophon, Homer, Virgil, Matteo Bandello, Boccaccio, Giraldi Cinthio, and Belleforest.

37. Painter, 2: 161. In 2 *Iron Age* (1612), Penthesilea speaks of the rhythm of Amazon life: 'Then we forsake our Sun-burnt Continent, / And in a cooler clime, sport with our men, / And then returne' (Thomas Heywood, *The Second Part of the Iron Age*, in *The Dramatic Works of Thomas Heywood* (New York: Russell & Russell, 1964), p. 360). Likewise, Joannes Boemus writes that in Amazon society, 'the women onely did governe and exercise all publicke offices,' and that the Amazon custom was 'for a certaine space, to exercise them-selves in feates of armes, for preservation of theyr Virginity, and the time of

warre-fare once ended, then to couple themselves with men in marriage for cause of procreation' (Joannes Boemus, *The Manners, Lawes, and customes of All Nations* (London, 1611), pp. 52–3).

38. As indicated above, I borrow the term 'female husband' from Ifi Amadiume's study of the Igbo of Nigeria (p. 15).

39. Painter, 2: 162.

40. Hakluyt, 10: 367–8.

41. Stephen Batman, *Batman vppon Bartholome, His Booke De Proprietatibus Rerum* (London, 1582), sig. fol. 24r.

42. Batman, sig. fol. 214r.

43. Plutarch, 1: 38.

44. Plutarch, 1: 39.

45. M. Bowra, *Greek Lyric Poetry*, 2nd edn (Oxford: Oxford University Press, 1961), p. 89.

46. duBois, p. 58.

47. duBois, pp. 58; 71. In part based on the work of duBois, Jeanne Roberts formulates a model for this patriarchal center, dominated by what she terms white male 'Culture' and the surrounding 'Wilds,' associated with 'Amazons, Scythians, cannibals, and undomesticated animals.' Roberts suggests that patriarchy elicits repression near its center and transgression in the borderlands and wilds. See Roberts, p. 6.

48. As duBois writes, 'Centaurs and Amazons, and by extension animals and females, were linked with barbarians analogously, as the 'other' through which the subject of the *polis* culture, the male citizen, came to know himself' (p. 71). See also Henry J. Walker, *Theseus and Athens* (Oxford: Oxford University Press, 1995), who analyzes Theseus's place and role in mythology, literature, Athenian politics, and history.

49. Plutarch, 1: 6.

50. James L. Calderwood, '*A Midsummer Night's Dream*: Anamorphism and Theseus' Dream,' *Shakespeare Quarterly* 42 (1991): 427.

51. Calderwood, p. 427.

52. Theseus has a dual identity, neither side being flattering. According to Plutarch, he cruelly abandoned wives and often ravished other women. He had a male lover by the name of Pirithous. Plutarch criticizes Theseus's behavior and lack of honesty regarding women (Plutarch, 1: 113–14). In *A Midsummer Night's Dream*, Shakespeare avoids any reference to Pirithous and Theseus's bisexuality, and only in passing does he mention Theseus's reputation as a ravisher of women.

53. Clive Barnes, 'Review of *A Midsummer Night's Dream*,' reprinted in Lee A. Jacobus, *The Bedford Introduction to Drama*, 3rd edn (Boston: Bedford Books of St. Martin's Press, 1997), p. 476.

54. Richard Hillman, 'Shakespeare's Romantic Innocents and the Misappropriation of the Romance Past: the Case of *The Two Noble Kinsmen*,' *Shakespeare Survey* 43 (1990): 59–79, and Richard Abrams, 'Gender Confusion and Sexual Politics in *The Two Noble Kinsmen*,' in *Drama, Sex and Politics*, *Themes in Drama* 7 (1985): 69–75.

55. Hillman, p. 70n.

56. Abrams, p. 69.
57. Eve Kosofsky Sedgwick, *Between Men: English Literature and Male Homosocial Desire* (New York: Columbia University Press, 1985), p. 1. See also her *Epistemology of the Closet* (Berkeley: University of California Press, 1990), and Jonathan Goldberg, *Sodometries: Renaissance Texts, Modern Sexualities* (Stanford, Calif.: Stanford University Press, 1992).
58. Sedgwick, p. 2.
59. Sedgwick, p. 2.
60. Winfried Schleiner, '*Le feu caché*: Homosocial Bonds Between Women in a Renaissance Romance,' *Renaissance Quarterly* 45 (1992): 293–311. In addition to sources already cited, see Alan Bray, *Homosexuality in Renaissance England* (London: Gay Men's Press, 1982); Judith C. Brown, *Immodest Acts: The Life of a Lesbian Nun in Renaissance Italy* (Oxford: Oxford University Press, 1986); Michael Goodich, *The Unmentionable Vice: Homosexuality in the Later Medieval Period* (Santa Barbara, Calif.: Clio Press, 1979); John Boswell, *Christianity, Social Tolerance and Homosexuality: Gay People in Western Europe from the Beginning of the Christian Era to the Fourteenth Century* (Chicago: University of Chicago Press, 1980); Martin B. Duberman, Martha Vicinus, and George Chauncey, Jr, eds, *Hidden from History: Reclaiming the Gay and Lesbian Past* (New York: New American Library, 1989); and Michael Rocke, *Forbidden Friendships: Homosexuality and Male Culture in Renaissance Florence* (Oxford: Oxford University Press, 1996), especially pp. 19–44.
61. Geoffrey Chaucer, *Works*, ed. F. N. Robinson (1933; rpt Boston: Houghton Miffin; Cambridge, Mass.: Riverside Press, 1957). All quotations from Chaucer will be from this edition.
62. Waith suggests that this passage was derived from Ovid's description of the hunt for the Calydonian boar, which Atalanta, not Hippolyta helped to kill (p. 85n). Of particular interest here are Joseph Cady's essay, '"Masculine Love", Renaissance Writing, and the "New Invention" of Homosexuality,' *Journal of Homosexuality* 23.1–2 (1992): 9–40; and Charles R. Forker, '"Masculine Love", Renaissance Writing, and the "New Invention" of Homosexuality: An Addendum,' *Journal of Homosexuality* 31.3 (1996): 85–93.
63. Lois Potter, '*The Two Noble Kinsmen* Onstage: A Postscript,' *Shakespeare Quarterly* 48 (1997): 227.
64. Potter, p. 227.
65. Berkowitz, pp. 165–6. This production was later (21 November – 8 December 1979) presented at London's Young Vic Studio. See Tony Howard, 'Census of Renaissance Drama Productions,' *Research Opportunities in Renaissance Drama* 22 (1979): 75. For an overview of the stage history of this play, please consult G. Harold Metz, '*The Two Noble Kinsmen* on the Twentieth Century Stage,' *Theatre History Studies* 4 (1984): 63–9. See also 'Review of *Two Noble Kinsmen*,' *Cahiers Elisabethains* 30 (October 1986): 96–8; Giles Gordon, 'Two Kinsmen and a Swan,' *Plays and Players* (July 1986): 13–15; and John James,

'Well-drilled Pageantry,' *The Times Educational Supplement*, 12 June 1987: 33.
66. Quoted in David M. Bergeron, *Royal Family, Royal Lovers: King James of England and Scotland* (Columbia: University of Missouri Press, 1991), p. 178.
67. Bergeron, *Royal Family, Royal Lovers*, p. 178.
68. Bergeron, *Royal Family, Royal Lovers*, p. 178.
69. In 'The Jailer's Daughter and the Politics of Madwomen's Language,' *Shakespeare Quarterly* 46 (1995): 277–300, Douglas Bruster suggests that in the Jailer's Daughter's language of madness we find 'the richest picture of the arrangements of power in the play, of social relations in the early modern playhouse, and of transformations in the Jacobean culture that produced *The Two Noble Kinsmen*' (p. 277). In giving voice to certain cultural topics, the Jailer's Daughter is, according to Bruster, analogous to the play's 'unconscious' (p. 297).
70. Bruce R. Smith, *Homosexual Desire in Shakespeare's England: A Cultural Poetics* (Chicago: Chicago University Press, 1991), p. 72. Catherine Belsey argues: 'In a chivalric culture love endangers friendship when it becomes rivalry, as *The Knight's Tale* shows, but wives do not supplant friends: their role is quite different.' She adds that 'the new model of marriage in the sixteenth century, however, identified wives precisely as friends, and the texts of the period bring to light some of the uncertainties and anxieties which attend the process of definition' (p. 210). See Catherine Belsey, 'Love in Venice,' in *Shakespeare and Gender: A History*, eds Deborah Barker and Ivo Kamps (London and New York: Verso, 1995), pp. 196–213.

2 JOAN OF ARC, MARGARET OF ANJOU, AND THE INSTABILITY OF GENDER

1. For a discussion of England's frontiers and the concept of 'foreign' in the late Middle Ages, see Ralph A. Griffiths, 'Frontiers and Foreigners,' in *The Reign of King Henry VI: The Exercise of Royal Authority, 1422–1461* (Berkeley: University of California Press, 1981), pp. 154–77.
2. Edmund Spenser, 'A Letter of the Authors' to Sir Walter Raleigh, in *Edmund Spenser's Poetry*, ed. Hugh MacLean (New York: W. W. Norton, 1968), p. 3.
3. Michel de Certeau suggests that 'history' vacillates between two poles: 'On the one hand, it refers to a practice, hence to a reality; on the other, it is a closed discourse, a text that organizes and concludes a mode of intelligibility' (*The Writing of History*, trans. Tom Conley (New York: Columbia University Press, 1988), p. 21). For a discussion of the collapse of the real and the imaginary, see Sara Eaton, 'Defacing the Feminine in Renaissance Tragedy,' in Valerie Wayne, ed., *The Matter of Difference: Materialist Feminist Criticism of Shakespeare* (Ithaca, NY: Cornell University Press, 1991), pp. 181–98.

4. Graham Holderness, *Shakespeare's History* (Dublin: Gill & Macmillan; New York: St. Martin's Press, 1985), p. 16.
5. Holderness, *Shakespeare's History,* p. 16.
6. Natalie Zemon Davis, 'Women on Top: Symbolic Sexual Inversion and Political Disorder in Early Modern Europe,' in Barbara A. Babcock, ed., *The Reversible World: Symbolic Inversion in Art and Society* (Ithaca, NY and London: Cornell University Press, 1978), p. 174. Davis relies upon Marie Delcourt's *Hermaphrodite: Myths and Rites of the Bisexual Figure in Classical Antiquity* (London: Studio Books, 1956). In *The Allegory of Female Authority: Christine de Pizan's 'Cité des Dames'* (Ithaca, NY: Cornell University Press, 1991), Maureen Quilligan contends that in 'Ditié de Jehanne d'Arc' (July 1429), the only such poem written during Joan's lifetime, Christine de Pizan establishes a link between female authority and the female warrior (see pp. 1–2; 274–83). Quilligan offers a thought-provoking discussion of Christine's 'construction of a 'modern' authority for herself' and a self-conscious literary move to write works defending women from misogynistic attacks in works such as the *Roman de la rose* (pp. 2; 13). See also John Boswell, *Same-Sex Unions in Premodern Europe* (New York: Villard Books, 1994).
7. John Anson, 'The Female Transvestite in Early Monasticism: The Origin and Development of a Motif,' *Viator: Medieval and Renaissance Studies* 5 (1974): 5.
8. Anson, p. 7.
9. Anson, p. 8.
10. Jean Doresse, *The Secret Books of the Egyptian Gnostics* (New York: Viking Press, 1960), p. 370.
11. Anson, pp. 8–9.
12. Anson, p. 31.
13. See Vern L. Bullough, 'Transvestites in the Middle Ages,' *American Journal of Sociology* 79 (1974): 1381–94; *Cross Dressing, Sex, and Gender* (Philadelphia: University of Pennsylvania Press, 1993); *Sexual Practices and the Medieval Church* (Buffalo, NY: Prometheus Books, 1982); and Anson, pp. 1–32.
14. Bullough, 'Transvestites in the Middle Ages,' pp. 1384–6.
15. Bullough, 'Transvestites in the Middle Ages,' p. 1387.
16. Bullough, 'Transvestites in the Middle Ages,' p. 1387.
17. Bullough, 'Transvestites in the Middle Ages,' p. 1382.
18. See, for example, H. J. Warner, *The Albigensian Heresy* (1922; rpt New York: Russell & Russell, 1967), and Jacques Madaule, *The Albigensian Crusade: A Historical Essay,* trans. Barbara Wall (London: Burns & Oates, 1967).
19. W. P. Barrett, trans., *The Trial of Jeanne d'Arc* (London: George Routledge & Sons, 1931), p. 19. Joan's judges were Pierre Cauchon, Bishop of Beauvais and Jean Le Maistre, with the support of authorities from the University of Paris, including Beaupère, Midi, and Courcelles.
20. Barrett, p. 152.
21. Barrett, p. 152.
22. Barrett, p. 154.

23. Barrett, p. 156.
24. Barrett, p. 203.
25. Barrett, pp. 310–11.
26. Barrett, p. 318.
27. Barrett, p. 318.
28. Barrett, p. 318.
29. Reprinted in Barrett, pp. 342–3.
30. Barrett, p. 344.
31. Holinshed says that she was 18 years old. See Geoffrey Bullough, ed., *Narrative and Dramatic Sources of Shakespeare*, 8 vols (London: Routledge & Kegan Paul; New York: Columbia University Press, 1973). 3: 75.
32. Bullough, *Narrative and Dramatic Sources*, 3: 56.
33. Bullough, *Narrative and Dramatic Sources*, 3: 61.
34. Bullough, *Narrative and Dramatic Sources*, 3: 77.
35. Bullough, *Narrative and Dramatic Sources*, 3: 61.
36. Bullough, *Narrative and Dramatic Sources*, 3: 61.
37. Richard F. Hardin, 'Chronicles and Mythmaking in Shakespeare's Joan of Arc,' *Shakespeare Survey* 42 (1990): 25.
38. I am, of course, referring to the Amazons who appear in the Masque of Cupid and the Amazons in I.ii, and Alcibiades' whores, Phrynia and Timandra (IV.iii). See the contrast between the Amazons and Centaurs. Page duBois writes of the Centaurs: 'As liminal beings, half-horse, half-men, they tested the boundaries between man and beast, between nature and culture. In addition, they raised the question of male and female difference, since their bodies and their behavior indicated that they were an exclusively masculine species, doubly potent in possessing the sexual attributes of both human male and animal' (duBois, p. 32). See also Roberts, p. 128.
39. Phyllis Rackin, *Stages of History: Shakespeare's English Chronicles* (Ithaca, NY: Cornell University Press, 1990), p. 147.
40. Rackin, p. 148.
41. For a discussion of Joan's topical role as an Amazon and a witch, see Gabriele Bernard Jackson, 'Topical Ideology: Witches, Amazons, and Shakespeare's Joan of Arc,' *English Literary Renaissance* 18 (1988): 40–65; and David M. Bevington, 'The Domineering Female in *1 Henry VI*,' *Shakespeare Studies* 2 (1966): 51–8.
42. In *Puzzling Shakespeare: Local Reading and Its Discontents* (Berkeley: University of California Press, 1988), Leah S. Marcus discusses Joan's 'befuddling effect on English warriors and their accustomed roles' (p. 66).
43. When Leontes, in *The Winter's Tale*, wants to discredit and dismiss the outspoken Paulina, he calls her 'a mankind witch' (II.iii.67), a masculine woman who has defied his kingly authority.
44. Reginald Scot, *Discoverie of Witchcraft*, p. 8, cited in Wallace Notestein, *A History of Witchcraft in England from 1558 to 1718* (1911; rpt New York: Russell & Russell, 1965), p. 67.
45. Patricia-Ann Lee, 'Reflections of Power: Margaret of Anjou and the Dark Side of Queenship,' *Renaissance Quarterly* 39 (1986): 183–217.

46. Quoted in Lee, p. 199.
47. Bullough, *Narrative and Dramatic Sources*, 3: 102.
48. Gordon Kipling, 'The London Pageants for Margaret of Anjou: A Medieval Script Restored,' *Medieval English Theatre* 4 (1982): 5–27. Quotations from the pageants are from this edition. For a critical discussion of the pageants, see Gordon Kipling, ' "'Grace in this Lyf and Aftiwarde Glorie": Margaret of Anjou's Royal Entry into London,' *Research Opportunities in Renaissance Drama* 29 (1986–7): 77–84. See also Brian Crow, 'Lydgate's 1445 Pageant for Margaret of Anjou,' *English Literary Notes* 19 (1981): 170–4.
49. Kipling, 'Royal Entry,' p. 77.
50. Kipling, 'Royal Entry,' p. 78.
51. Kipling, 'Royal Entry,' p. 79.
52. Kipling, 'Royal Entry,' p. 82.
53. Kipling, 'Royal Entry,' p. 82.
54. For a compelling discussion of masculine/feminine inversion, namely Margaret's power and Henry VI's comic weakness, see Donald G. Watson, *Shakespeare's Early History Plays: Politics at Play on the Elizabethan Stage* (Athens: University of Georgia Press, 1990), pp. 52–5.
55. Bullough, *Narrative and Dramatic Sources*, 3: 101.
56. Bullough, *Narrative and Dramatic Sources*, 3: 101.
57. Bullough, *Narrative and Dramatic Sources*, 3: 102.
58. For a discussion of this episode, see my article, 'The Peasants' Revolt and the Writing of History in *2 Henry VI*,' in David M. Bergeron, ed., *Reading and Writing in Shakespeare* (Newark: University of Delaware Press, 1996), pp. 178–93.
59. Henry refuses to exercise his power as king. Margaret makes major decisions for him. Henry leaves Parliament in III.i., fully aware that 'these great lords and Margaret our queen / Do seek subversion of thy [Gloucester's] harmless life' (*2 Henry VI*, III.i.207–8). Henry swoons when Gloucester's death is announced (*2 Henry VI*, III.ii.32). He can neither fight nor flee the battlefield, as the Queen orders him to return to London (V.ii.80).
60. George Lyman Kittredge, *Witchcraft in Old and New England* (Cambridge, Mass.: Harvard University Press, 1929), p. 73.
61. Reginald Scot, *The Discoverie of Witchcraft*, ed. Revd Montague Summers (London: John Rodker Publisher, 1930): Bk. xii: ch. 16, p. 221. Scot cites a number of examples of image magic.
62. Joseph H. Marshburn, *Murder and Witchcraft in England, 1550–1640 as Recounted in Pamphlets, Ballads, Broadsides, & Plays* (Norman: Oklahoma University Press, 1971), p. 40. See also Frances E. Dolan, *Dangerous Familiars: Representations of Domestic Crime in England, 1550–1700* (Ithaca, NY: Cornell University Press, 1994).

3 TEXTUAL ENCODINGS IN *THE MERCHANT OF VENICE*

1. Michel de Certeau, *The Writing of History*, trans. Tom Conley (New York: Columbia University Press, 1988), p. 215.
2. Bergeron, *Royal Family, Royal Lovers*, p. 78.
3. Bergeron, *Royal Family, Royal Lovers*, p. 79. An example from the nineteenth century illustrates how archives can be searched to resuscitate a tradition or ceremony. After Dom Pedro, Crown Prince of Portugal, proclaimed Brazil's independence in 1822 and was proclaimed emperor, Brazilians searched the Portuguese archives to duplicate, in the New World, the coronation ceremonies used by the Portuguese kings. Particularly elaborate was the order of precedence used in the Portuguese court, which was carefully searched and adopted for the coronation of Dom Pedro. The archives were also searched for the state funeral of President Kennedy, which was carefully modeled on the funeral of President Lincoln. I have discussed these examples in 'The Peasants' Revolt and the Writing of History in *2 Henry VI*,' in *Reading and Writing in Shakespeare*, ed. David M. Bergeron (Newark: University of Delaware Press, 1996), pp. 178–93.
4. See my article, 'The Peasants' Revolt,' pp. 178–93.
5. In his book, *Shakespeare and the Jews* (New York: Columbia University Press, 1996), James Shapiro masterfully argues for the complexity of the issue of English and Jewish identities, and the extent to which Englishness and Jewishness both intertwine and separate (pp. 13–42).
6. See my review-essay, '*The Merchant of Venice*: Brazil and Cultural Icons,' *Shakespeare Quarterly* 45 (1994): 468–74.
7. E. K. Chambers, *The Elizabethan Stage* (1923; rpt Oxford: Clarendon Press, 1961), 3: 484.
8. John Gillies, *Shakespeare and the Geography of Difference* (Cambridge: Cambridge University Press, 1994), p. 123.
9. Cited by Gillies, p. 123.
10. Gillies, p. 125.
11. Gillies, p. 135.
12. Gillies, p. 136.
13. See Apollonius of Rhodes, *Jason and the Golden Fleece (The Argonautica)*, trans. Richard Hunter (Oxford: Oxford University Press, 1995), pp. xix–xxi.
14. Geoffrey Chaucer, *The Works*, ed. F. N. Robinson (1933; rpt Boston: Houghton Mifflin, 1957), pp. 506–7.
15. John Lydgate, *The Hystorye/Sege and Dystruccyon of Troye* (London, 1513), 1: sig. C4–C6. In the Folger Library copy of STC 5579, the illustration appears on sig. C4.
16. Robert Withington, *English Pageantry: An Historical Outline* (1918; rpt New York: Benjamin Bloom, 1963), 1: 176.
17. Withington, 1: 196.
18. Withington, 1: 186.

19.   David M. Bergeron, ed., *Pageants and Entertainments of Anthony Mun-
      day: A Critical Edition* (New York & London: Garland Publishing,
      1985), p. 77.
20.   See Bergeron, *English Civic Pageantry*, p. 195; and Bergeron, ed.,
      Pageants and Entertainments of Anthony Munday, pp. 139–42.
21.   Bergeron, *Pageants and Entertainments of Anthony Munday*, p. 140.
22.   David M. Bergeron, 'Politics and *The Tempest*,' lecture given at 'The
      Heart of America Shakespeare Festival' in Kansas City, Missouri, on 3
      July 1993.
23.   See *OED* definition.
24.   Robert Bassett, *Curiosities or the Cabinet of Nature, contayning Phy-
      losophicall Naturall and Morall Questions answered* (London: 1637), pp.
      11–12.
25.   It should be noted that the usage of 'casket' as 'coffin' is an Amer-
      icanism, the first recorded instance of which dates to 1849. In *Our Old
      Home* (1863), Hawthorne characterizes this usage as a 'vile modern
      phrase' (cf. *OED*).
26.   *Coffer*, however, signified both 'a box, a chest: esp. a strong box in
      which money or valuables are kept' and 'a coffin.' *Chest* meant both
      'a box, a coffer' and a coffin.
27.   Julian Litten, *The English Way of Death: The Common Funeral Since 1450*
      (London: Robert Hale, 1991), p. 92.
28.   From the Cotton MSS, British Library, cited by Litten, p. 40.
29.   Litten, p. 43.
30.   For a brief summary of the argument and the scholarly controversy
      over this issue, see *The Merchant of Venice*, edited by M. M. Mahood
      (Cambridge: Cambridge University Press, 1987), p. 115n; and John
      Russell Brown's comments in the Arden edition of the play (London:
      Methuen, 1955), p. 80.
31.   In 'The Theme of the Three Caskets,' reprinted in *Shakespeare: 'The
      Merchant of Venice': A Casebook*, edited by John Wilders (New York:
      Macmillan, 1969), pp. 59–68, Sigmund Freud examines the archetypal
      foundation for Bassanio's choice: how the goddess of love becomes
      intertwined with the goddess of death.
32.   David Cecil, *The Cecils of Hatfield House: An English Ruling Family*
      (Boston: Houghton Mifflin, 1973), p. 158. See also Olivia Bland, *The
      Royal Way of Death* (London: Constable, 1986); and Clare Gittings,
      Death, Burial and the Individual in Early Modern England (London:
      Croom Helm, 1984).
33.   See Kathleen Cohen, *Metamorphosis of a Death Symbol: The Transi Tomb
      in the Late Middle Ages and the Renaissance* (Berkeley: University of
      California Press, 1973). See Figure 5, tomb of Cardinal Lagrange (d.
      1402); Figure 10, illustration from *Disputacioun Betwyx the Body and
      Wormes* (1435–40); Figure 9, Fresco of the Three Quick and the Three
      Dead (end of fourteenth Century); and Figure 13, Tomb of Arch-
      bishop Henry Chichele (d. 1443), at Canterbury Cathedral.
34.   In the Appendix to Gasper Cantarini, *The Commonwealth and Gouern-
      ment of Venice*, trans. Lewis Lewkenor (London, 1599), sig. Cc2v.

35. Euripides, *Medea*, in *Medea and Other Plays*, trans. Philip Vellacott
     (London: Penguin; New York: Viking/Penguin, 1963), p. 33.
36. In '"Now by My Hood, a Gentle and No Jew"': Jessica, *The Merchant
     of Venice*, and the Discourse of Early Modern English Identity,' *PMLA*
     113. 1 (1998): 52–63, Mary Janell Metzger studies Jessica's 'ambivalent
     status,' and 'multiplicitous nature,' and 'the inherent incompatibility
     of the identities Shakespeare attempts to unite in Jessica' (p. 53).
37. Cantarini, sigs Cc2v and D1v.
38. Cantarini, sig. P2.
39. Shapiro, p. 7.
40. Bernard Glassman, in *Anti-Semitic Stereotypes without Jews: Images of
     the Jews in England 1290–1700* (Detroit, Mich.: Wayne State University
     Press, 1975), argues that 'As long as the Jews could supply the king
     with money in the form of fines, special taxes, and loans, they were
     allowed to maintain what amounted to a privileged place in society'
     (p. 15). See discussion of usury in Norman Jones, *God and the Money-
     lenders: Usury and Law in Early Modern England* (Cambridge: Basil
     Blackwell, 1989).
41. Glassman, p. 14. In England before the Restoration, usury was
     understood to mean the charging of any interest for the use of
     money. After the Restoration, it meant a higher interest rate than
     was allowed by law.
42. For detailed analyses, consult Scarlett Freund and Teofilo F. Ruiz, eds,
     *Jewish–Christian Encounters Over the Centuries: Symbiosis, Prejudice,
     Holocaust, Dialogue* (New York: Peter Lang, 1994); Richard H. Popkin
     and Gordon M. Weiner, eds, *Jewish Christians and Christian Jews: From
     the Renaissance to the Enlightenment* (Dordrecht and Boston: Kluwer
     Academic, 1994); B. Netanyahu, *The Origins of the Inquisition in Fif-
     teenth-Century Spain* (New York: Random House, 1995); and James
     Shapiro, *Shakespeare and the Jews* (New York: Columbia University
     Press, 1996).
43. Fynes Moryson, *Fynes Moryson's Itinerary*, ed. Charles Hughes (Lon-
     don: Sherratt & Hughes, 1903). Cf. chapter VI, 'A generall and brife
     discourse of the Jewes and Greekes,' pp. 487–95. Thomas Coryat,
     Coryat's Crudities (Glasgow: James MacLehose and Sons, 1905), 1:
     370–6.
44. Moryson, p. 487.
45. Coryat, 1: 373–4. Coryat adds, 'Whereas in Germany, Poland, and
     other places the Jewes that are converted (which doth often happen,
     as Emanuel Tremellius was converted in Germany) do enjoy their
     estates as they did before' (p. 374).
46. Coryat, 1: 372.
47. Coryat, 1: 372–3.
48. Coryat, 1: 370.
49. For a discussion of Elizabethan understanding of circumcision, 'an
     unmistakable sign,' anxieties about the Jewish ritual, and Christian
     attempts at 'uncircumcision,' see Shapiro, pp. 114–20. Shapiro also
     connects 'Shylock's cut,' his circumcision, to 'Antonio's flesh,' the
     word 'flesh' signifying penis (p. 127). Thus Shylock symbolically tries

to circumcise Antonio; and Antonio, in insisting that the Jew become a Christian, tries to 'uncircumcise' Shylock (p. 130). Shapiro concludes: 'Antonio and Shylock, who fiercely insist on how different they are from each other, to the last seek out ways of preserving that difference through symbolic acts that convert their adversary into their own kind' (p. 130).

50.   John Stow, *The Annales of England* (London, 1605), p. 137. See Shapiro, pp. 46–76.
51.   Glassman, *Anti-Semitic Stereotypes*, pp. 14–15.
52.   Glassman, p. 15.
53.   Stow, *Annales*, p. 251.
54.   *Holinshed Chronicles* (London, 1808), 2: 492.
55.   Stow, *Annales*, p. 1278.
56.   Cecil Roth, *A History of the Jews in England* (Oxford: Clarendon Press, 1949), pp. 143–4.
57.   George Carleton, *A Thankfvll Remembrance of Gods Mercie* (London, 1630), p. 164. This illustration is reproduced in the *Jewish Encyclopaedia* (New York, 1902), and in Alfred Rubens, *Anglo-Jewish Portraits* (London: Jewish Museum, 1935), with the following description: 'Lopes in academic costume, bearded and holding a book, is addressing a courtier (the Portuguese, Stephen Ferreira de Gama) with the question "Quid dabitis?" In the background a man is hanging from the gallows, above which appears the warning "Proditorum fines funis" ' (p. 66).
58.   Shapiro, p. 20.
59.   Andrewe Boorde, *The Fyrst Boke of the Introduction of Knowledge* (London, 1542).
60.   P. Boaistuau, *Certaine Secrete Wonders of Nature*, translated by Edward Fenton (London, 1569), fol. 141.
61.   For a detailed discussion of this and other incidents, see Shapiro, pp. 100–11.
62.   *Holinshed Chronicles*, 2: 437.
63.   Chaucer, *Works*, p. 162.
64.   Moryson, 495.
65.   Coryat, 1: 373.
66.   In *A Thousand Notable Things of Sundrie Sorts* (London, 1595), Thomas Lupton speaks of the power of the imagination whereby a Spanish woman, seeing the picture of an Ethiopian painted in her chamber, gives birth to a black boy. The Spanish lady was saved from being burned at the stake when the evidence from the Bible is summoned up: 'Bringing forth for the confirmation thereof, that place of the Bible, where Jacob put speckled rods before the Sheepe: by which imagination the Ewes brought forth speckled Lambes, which when hee [the Spanish woman's husband] had spoken, the Lady was delivered from burning' (Bk 6, p. 113).
67.   Gen. 31: 19–21. Quotation from *The New English Bible* (Oxford: Oxford University Press; Cambridge: Cambridge University Press, 1970).

68. Professor Gretchen Eick of Friends University, Wichita, Kansas, helped me see this point.
69. *The Merchant of Venice* also abounds with other references to writing and pen, especially in Act IV. One might argue that these function as a sounding board for the dominant theme I have been discussing, namely that the play is about the appropriation of texts. For a fascinating discussion of writing, authorship, the politics of print culture, and gender, see Wendy Wall, *The Imprint of Gender: Authorship and Publication in the English Renaissance* (Ithaca, NY and London: Cornell University Press, 1993). Wall does not discuss *The Merchant of Venice*.
70. Shapiro argues that Shakespeare's play 'reproduces the practice of translating anti-alien into anti-Jewish sentiment' (p. 189).

4 TEXTUAL INTERSECTIONS: *TITUS ANDRONICUS* AND *OTHELLO*

1. Barbosa's Portuguese title was 'Ministro e Secretário dos Negócios da Fazenda e Presidente do Tribunal do Tesouro Nacional.' The papers, books, and documents were to be gathered and sent to Rio de Janeiro, where they would be processed and immediately destroyed. See Américo Jacobina Lacombe, Eduardo Silva, and Francisco de Assis Barbosa, *Rui Barbosa e a queima dos arquivos* (Rio de Janeiro: Fundação Casa de Rui Barbosa, 1988). Barbosa's order is reprinted in his *Obras Completas* (Rio de Janeiro: Ministério da Educação e Saúde, 1942–88), 17: 338–40.
2. Certeau, *Writing of History*, p. 215.
3. Azurara, 1: 85.
4. Claude Lévi-Strauss, *Structural Anthropology*, trans. Claire Jacobson and Brooke Grundfest Schoepf (New York: Basic Books, 1976), p. 3. Lévi-Strauss is distinguishing ethnography from history.
5. Lévi-Strauss, p. 18.
6. Gustav Cross, Introduction to *Titus Andronicus*, in *The Complete Works*, ed. Alfred Harbage (New York: Penguin, 1969), p. 823.
7. E. K. Chambers, *The Elizabethan Stage* (1923; rpt Oxford: Clarendon Press, 1961), 4: 246.
8. For a fuller discussion of the stage history of the play, please consult Jonathan Bate, 'Introduction,' *Titus Andronicus*, The Arden Shakespeare, Third Series (London and New York: Routledge, 1995), pp. 37–69; and Alan Hughes, 'Introduction,' *Titus Andronicus*, The New Cambridge Shakespeare (Cambridge: Cambridge University Press, 1994), pp. 31–47.
9. Stanley Wells, 'Program Notes,' Royal Shakespeare Production of *Titus Andronicus*, directed by Deborah Warner, at the Pit, 1 July 1988.
10. See Intro. in *The Dramatic Works of George Peele* (New Haven, Conn.: Yale University Press, 1961), 2: 226–7.

11.   Eldred Jones, *Othello's Countrymen: The African in English Renaissance Drama* (London: Oxford University Press, 1965), p. 49.

12.   Other related religious movements include the Contestado uprising (1911–15); and the rebellion at Juazeiro (1872–1924), led by the priest Cícero Romão Batista.

13.   For a full discussion of these stage figures, please consult Jones, *Othello's Countrymen*; Jack D'Amico, *The Moor in English Renaissance Drama* (Tampa: University Presses of Florida, 1991); and David Dabydeen, *The Black Presence in English Literature* (Dover, NH and Manchester, UK: Manchester University Press, 1985). For the African presence in Europe in general, see Hans Werner Debrunner, *Presence and Prestige: Africans in Europe: A History of Africans in Europe before 1918* (Basel: Basler Africa Bibliographien, 1979).

14.   Jean Devisse and Michel Mollat, *Africans in the Christian Ordinance of the World: Fourteenth to the Sixteenth Century*, Tome 2 of Volume II, *From the Early Christian Era to the 'Age of Discovery'*, ed. Ladislas Bugner, trans. William Granger (Cambridge, Mass. and London: Harvard University Press, 1979), p. 7.

15.   Devisse and Mollat, pp. 7–8.

16.   See Terisio Pignatti, *Veronese* (Venice: Alfieri Edizioni D'Arte, 1976), 1: 186.

17.   See Pignatti, *Veronese*, 1: 136; and 2: Plates 455, 456, and 460 (detail).

18.   Emily C. Bartels, 'Making More of the Moor: Aaron, Othello, and Renaissance Refashionings of Race,' *Shakespeare Quarterly* 41 (1990): 443.

19.   The illustration is readily available in a number of sources. See, for example, the Arden edition of *Titus Andronicus*, ed. Jonathan Bate (London and New York: Routledge, 1995), p. 39.

20.   Cross, p. 824.

21.   See Plates VII and I in Pignatti, *Veronese*, 1: 33.

22.   Cleonice Berardinelli, ed., *Antologia do Teatro de Gil Vicente* (Rio de Janeiro: Grifo Edições, 1971), p. 347.

23.   This is a passage from Horace, *Odes*, 1.22.1–2.

24.   The passage appears in Lily's Latin grammar, *Brevissima Institutio*, which as Jonathan Bate points out in his Arden edition of the play, was 'the standard text-book in schools from 1540 onwards' (p. 220n).

25.   Bk I, 159–62 of John Milton's *Paradise Lost*, in *The Complete Poetry of John Milton*, ed. John T. Shawcross (New York: Doubleday Anchor, 1971).

26.   For a discussion of the wound motif in the Roman plays, see Coppélia Kahn, *Roman Shakespeare: Warriors, Wounds, and Women* (London and New York: Routledge, 1997).

27.   A number of critics have seen close parallels between Africanus and Othello. Most recently Emily Bartels argued that 'Leo Africanus's *A Geographical Historie of Africa* continues to be proffered as an important intertext for *Othello* because of parallels not only between the two texts but between Africanus and Othello. Both are Moors who have traveled extensively in Africa, who have been Christianized and embraced within European society, and who have become Europe's

own very eloquent authorities on Africa. Claims for a precise or intended correlation between Africanus and Othello, or even between the *Historie* and the play, however, seem speculative at best' ('Making More of the Moor,' pp. 435–6).

28. Leo Africanus, *The History and Description of Africa*, trans. John Pory, 3 vols (London, 1600); ed. Robert Brown (London: Hakluyt Society, 1894), 1: 190.

29. Stephen Greenblatt, *Renaissance Self-Fashioning: From More to Shakespeare* (Chicago: University of Chicago Press, 1980), p. 237. Greenblatt argues that 'Iago's attitude toward Othello is nonetheless colonial' (p. 233).

30. Louis O. Mink, 'Narrative Form as a Cognitive Instrument,' in *Historical Understanding*, eds Brian Fay, Eugene O. Golob, and Richard T. Vann (Ithaca, NY: Cornell University Press, 1987), p. 199. See also Hayden White, *Tropics of Discourse: Essays in Cultural Criticism* (1978; rpt Baltimore, Md. and London: Johns Hopkins University Press, 1992), esp. chapter 3, 'The Historical Text as Literary Artifact.'

31. Chambers, *Elizabethan Stage*, 4: 119. A total payment to 'John Hemynges one of his Ma*tes* players' for this performance: 'hallamas – in the Banquetting hos at Whitehall the Moor of Venis – perf*d*. by the K's players' (p. 171).

32. Bergeron, *English Civic Pageantry 1558–1642*, p. 77. See Plate No. 3.

33. Bergeron, *English Civic Pageantry*, p. 78.

34. King James, 'The Lepanto,' *The Poems of James VI. of Scotland*, ed. James Craigie (Edinburgh and London: William Blackwood & Sons, 1955), 1: 202 (ll. 9–11).

35. King James, *Poems*, 1: lix. For a succinct contemporary account of the battle, see George T. Matthews, ed., *News and Rumor in Renaissance Europe (The Fugger Newsletters)* (New York: Capricorn Books, 1959), pp. 39–42.

36. See Appendix A in King James, *Poems*, 1: 274–80.

37. See Richard Barnfield's sonnet, 'Against the Dispraysers of Poetrie,' in *The Complete Poems*, ed. George Klawitter (Selinsgrove, Pa.: Susquehanna University Press; London and Toronto: Associated University Presses, 1990).

38. Bullough, *Narrative and Dramatic Sources*, 7: 212. Bullough suggests that Shakespeare obtained materials about Italy from William Thomas's *History of Italy* (1549) and from Sir Lewis Lewkenor's *The Commonwealth and Government of Venice* (trans. in 1599).

39. In *Narrative and Dramatic Sources of Shakespeare*, Bullough writes that the scattering of the Turkish armada is reminiscent of events in English history (7: 213–14).

40. King James, *Poems*, 1: 198.

41. King James, *Poems*, 1: 200.

42. Bullough, *Narrative and Dramatic Sources*, 7: 242.

43. Cantarini, *Commonwealth and Government of Venice*, sig. S–S2v.

44. Charles Hughes, ed., *Shakespeare's Europe: Fynes Moryson's Itinerary* (London: Sherratt & Hughes, 1903), p. 139. Italics mine.

45. David McPherson, *Shakespeare, Jonson, and the Myth of Venice* (Newark: University of Delaware Press; London and Toronto: Associated University Press, 1990), p. 73.
46. Certeau, *Writing of History*, p. 211.
47. Boon, p. 26.
48. Bullough, *Narrative and Dramatic Sources*, 7: 245.
49. Bullough, *Narrative and Dramatic Sources*, 7: 245.
50. Debrunner, *Presence and Prestige*, p. 23. In *The French Encounter with Africans: White Response to Blacks 1530–1880* (Bloomington: Indiana University Press, 1980), William B. Cohen writes that Africans lived in France as early as the thirteenth century: 'A black woman from the Sudan, Ismeria, married a man of royal lineage, Robert d'Eppes. When she died, sometime in the mid-thirteenth century, she was enshrined as a black Madonna' (p. 4). Cohen continues: 'It is known that Francis I had among his mistresses a young black woman, and that Africans were brought to France in large numbers later in the sixteenth century. In 1571 a shipowner placed some blacks on sale in Bordeaux, but they were ordered released by the Parlement, on the grounds that slavery did not exist in France. Those blacks and others who had served as sailors lived in France for varying periods before returning to Africa' (p. 5).
51. Debrunner, *Presence and Prestige*, p. 23.
52. I believe that although there is strong opposition to the interracial marriage, Karen Newman in ' "And Wash an Ethiop White": Femininity and the Monstrous in *Othello*,' in *Shakespeare Reproduced: The Text in History and Ideology* (New York and London: Methuen, 1987) overstates her case when she writes: 'In *Othello*, the black Moor and the fair Desdemona are united in a marriage which all the other characters view as unthinkable' (p. 144). The Duke of Venice, upon hearing Othello's tale, remarks in public for all to hear, 'I think this tale would win my daughter too' (I.iii.171). Similarly, Cassio supports the relationship, having served as a messenger for the lovers. Even Iago suggests that Othello will 'prove to Desdemona / A most dear husband' (II.i.284–5).
53. Jones, *Othello's Countrymen*, p. 3.
54. William Cuningham, *The Cosmographical Glasse* (London, 1599), fol. 184. He adds that in Africa there are also 'innumerable multitude of venomous wormes, & wilde beastes, which are naturally enemies unto mankinde' (fol. 185).
55. Gomes Eanes de Azurara, *Crônica de Guynee* (Lisbon: 1506; rpt Lisbon: Empresa da Revista Diogo-Caão, 1937), p. 36.
56. In *Oeuvres Complètes*, 3 (Paris, 1873), p. 19, as quoted in William B. Cohen, *The French Encounter with Africans: White Response to Blacks 1530–1880* (Bloomington: Indiana University Press, 1980), p. 2.
57. Cuningham, *Cosmographical Glasse*, fol. 184. Most of these misconceptions come directly from Pliny's *Natural History*. See, for example, *A summarie of the antiquities, and wonders of the worlde, out of the sixtene first bookes of Plinie* (London, 1566); *The secrets and wonders of the world*

(London, 1585); and *The historie of the world*, trans. P. Holland (London, 1601).

58. Purchas, 9: 376.

59. Purchas, 9: 260.

60. Michael Neill, 'Changing Places in "Othello",' *Shakespeare Survey* 38 (1984): 115–31.

61. See Carol Thomas Neely, 'Circumscriptions and Unhousedness: *Othello* in the Borderlands,' in *Shakespeare and Gender: A History*, edited by Deborah Barker and Ivo Kamps (London and New York: Verso, 1995), pp. 302–15. She demonstrates that 'the categories of gender, race and sexuality are inseparable, unstable, disunited, and mutually constitutive' (p. 303). In 'Othello's Handkerchief: "The Recognizance and Pledge of Love," ' *English Literary Renaissance* 5 (1975): 360–74, Lynda B. Boose examines the two narratives of the handkerchief, relating the handkerchief to Othello and Desdemona's wedding-bed sheets,' the visual proof of their consummated marriage, the emblem of the symbolical act of generation so important to our understanding of the measure of this tragedy' (p. 363).

62. Bullough, *Narrative and Dramatic Sources*, 7: 246.

63. Iago, however, assumes that Othello's culture excludes women. With this in mind, we should not be surprised to hear Iago's fantastical homoerotic fantasy – a fantasy enacted by men, excluding women and simultaneously recognizing women's role in III.iii.419–26.

64. Neely's argument reinforces mine: 'From the perspective of white Venetian culture within which the now-Christian Othello resides, however, the marriage is transgressive because Othello's maleness gives him higher status, whereas Desdemona's cultural insiderness (in which skin colour becomes suddenly salient) gives her higher status, and because she elopes' ('*Othello* in the Borderlands,' p. 306).

5 HABITAT, RACE, AND CULTURE IN *ANTONY AND CLEOPATRA*

1. Chambers, *Elizabethan Stage*, 3: 488.

2. For a summary of the argument, see Bullough, *Narrative and Dramatic Sources*, 5: 215.

3. See John David Wortham, *The Genesis of British Egyptology 1549–1906* (Norman: University of Oklahoma Press, 1972), esp. pp. 3–23. An interesting first-hand account of Egypt is *The Travels of John Sanderson in the Levant 1584–1602*, ed. Sir William Foster (London: Hakluyt Society, 1931). Sanderson arrived in Cairo during an outbreak of the plague. He describes the incredible death toll: 'two hundred in a day at Cairo, but many died at Alexandria and at Rossetto. I mett, goinge to buriinge and one the beers at their dores, and in their yeards dead corps awashinge, everey morning in every street at least seven or eight' (p. 4). See Sanderson's description of Alexandria, Cairo, the Nile, the pyramids, mummies, crocodiles, and everyday life in Egypt

(*c.* 1587–8) (pp. 36–51). For a discussion of other Englishmen travelling abroad, see *Shakespeare's England: An Account of the Life & Manners of his Age* (1916; rpt Oxford: Clarendon Press, 1950), 1: 209–23.

4. See the *OED*.

5. Herodotus, *The Famous History of Herodotus*, trans. B. R. (London, 1584). All quotations, however, will be from the modern translation of *The Histories*, by Aubrey de Selincourt and A. R. Burn (London & New York: Penguin Books, 1972).

6. John Greaves, Professor of Astronomy at Oxford University, had to battle many such misconceptions. He made a research trip to Egypt in the early seventeenth century, and put together a study of the pyramids. He tried to dispel myths: for example, that the pyramids were built by the Jews during their captivity to serve as granaries and, therefore, were not pharaonic burial monuments. Greaves uses the Bible to prove that the Jews used bricks and could not, therefore, have built the pyramids, which are made out of stones. See *Pyramidographia: or a Description of the Pyramids of Aegypt* (London, 1646). For an overview of what 'Egypt' signified in the Renaissance, see Edward H. Sugen, *A Topographical Dictionary to the Works of Shakespeare and His Fellow Dramatists* (Manchester: Manchester University Press; London & New York: Longmans, Green & Co., 1925), pp. 166–9.

7. Hartog, *Mirror of Herodotus*, p. 15.

8. Hartog, p. 19.

9. Herodotus, *Herodotus: The Histories* (New York: Penguin Books, 1972), pp. 142–3.

10. Intro. to *Mandeville's Travels*, ed. Michael C. Seymour (Oxford: Clarendon Press, 1967), p. xx. Seymour writes: 'The chief source of *Mandeville's Travels* was a series of French translations of genuine itineraries, completed by Jean le Long, monk of St. Omer, 150 miles from Liège, and justly styled "the Hakluyt of the Middle Ages", in 1351. The major works in this huge compilation were the account of the Holy Land by William of Boldensele (1339), the description of the East by the Franciscan missionary Odoric of Pordenone (1330), and Haiton's *Fleurs des Histoires d'Orient* (before 1308); of which Jean le Long followed Nicholas Falcon's Latin translation. These travellers were factual and accurate observers and "Mandeville" copied large extracts from their writings (slightly distorted by scribes and translators) into his own book' (p. xiv). Other sources include the medieval encyclopedia of Vincent of Beauvais (*c.* 1250) (Seymour, p. xv). For a superb study of Mandeville, see Mary B. Campbell, *The Witness and the Other World: Exotic European Travel Writing, 400–1600* (Ithaca, NY: Cornell University Press, 1988), pp. 122–61.

11. Joannes Boemus, *The Fardle of Facions* (London, 1555), Sig. C8v. See chapter 5 of William Prat, *The Description of the Countrey of Aphrique* ([London,] 1554). Prat describes in great detail the presumed inversion of gender roles.

12. Joannes Boemus, *The Manners, Lawes, and Customes of All Nations* (London, 1611), pp. 18–19. Boemus derived this statement from Herodotus. See François Hartog, p. 213.

13. Henry Blount, *A Voyage into the Levant* (London, 1638), pp. 51–42.

14. See Robert Brown's introduction to Leo Africanus, *The History and Description of Africa*, 3 vols, trans. John Pory (London: Hakluyt Society, 1896), 1: i–cxi.

15. John Leo Africanus, *A Geographical Historie of Africa, written in Arabicke and Italian* (London, 1600), p. 30.

16. George Abbott, *A Briefe Description of the Whole World* (London, 1600), sig. E3.

17. Edward Topsell, *The Historie of Fovre-footed Beastes* (London, 1607) and *The Historie of Serpents* (London, 1608).

18. Thomas Andrewe, in *The Unmasking of a feminine Machiavell* (London, 1604), describes his 'feminine Machiavel' as someone who can 'weepe, but like the *Nile* bred *Crocadile*, / That on the pray she instantly devoures, / Dissembling teares in great abundant powers' (sig. C2 v).

19. Topsell, *Historie of Serpents*, sig. F5.

20. See Michael Lloyd, 'Cleopatra as Isis,' in *Shakespeare Survey* 12 (1959): 88–94. Lloyd points out the absence of Osiris: 'it must be concluded that Shakespeare deliberately denied to Antony that quality of devoted love which would have been associated with Osiris, and which he chose to keep as the peculiar attribute of Cleopatra-Isis' (p. 94). In *Suffocating Mothers: Fantasies of Maternal Origin in Shakespeare's Plays* (New York & London: Routledge, 1991), Janet Adelman argues that 'Egypt becomes the locus of the common mother's promiscuous generativity, indifferently producing figs and asps from its slime' (p. 175). She contrasts the abundance of Egypt with the 'scarcity' of Rome. She writes, 'But in *Antony and Cleopatra*, scarcity is the sign of the state from which the female has been excised: there are virtually no women in Rome, there is no natural abundance' (p. 176). She adds, 'The contest between Caesar and Cleopatra, Rome and Egypt, is in part a contest between male scarcity and female bounty as the defining site of Antony's heroic masculinity. Longing for that heroic masculinity is, I think, at the center of the play' (p. 177).

21. Peter Heylyn, Book 4 of *Cosmographie in four Bookes contayning the chorographie & Historie of the whole Worlde* (London, 1652), p. 5.

22. For a discussion of the myths surrounding the Nile, see Simon Schama, *Landscape and Memory* (New York: Alfred A. Knopf, 1995), pp. 256–63.

23. In *Hospitable Performances: Dramatic Genre and Cultural Practices in Early Modern England* (West Lafayette, IN: Purdue University Press, 1992), Daryl W. Palmer offers a most perceptive and intelligent study of hospitable practices in the Renaissance. He does not, however, discuss *Antony and Cleopatra*.

24. Palmer, *Hospitable Performances*, p. 3. In *The Antiquities of the Jews*, which appeared in an English translation by Thomas Lodge in

1602, Flavius Josephus makes this point. On progress into Judaea, Cleopatra became a guest of Herod the Great. Being addicted to the pleasures of the flesh, she tried unsuccessfully to seduce her host: 'she sought to allure and draw him to her lust' (Bullough, *Narrative and Dramatic Sources*, 5: 332). According to Josephus, Herod resisted her advances and even contemplated murdering her but, instead, was persuaded by his counsellors to feast and befriend her for fear of retaliation from Antony: 'so that contrariwise they induced him to offer *Cleopatra* many rich presents, and to conduct her onward on her way towards Aegypt' (Bullough, *Narrative and Dramatic Sources*, 5: 333). Herod, if only to appease Antony, felt compelled to become host to an unwanted and dangerous guest.

25. Chaucer, *Works*, p. 496. For a full discussion of the tradition surrounding Cleopatra and Mark Anthony, see Marilyn L. Williamson, *Infinite Variety: Antony and Cleopatra in Renaissance Drama and Earlier Tradition* (Mystic, Conn.: Lawrence Verry, Inc, 1974); and Mary Hamer, *Signs of Cleopatra: History, Politics, Representation* (London and New York: Routledge, 1993), especially the discussion of Cleopatra's ethnicity, p. 5.
26. Plutarch, *Lives*, 2: 1691, sections of which are reprinted by Bullough, *Narrative and Dramatic Sources*, 5: 275. Flavius Josephus, in *The Antiquities of the Jews*, does not describe Cleopatra's color, limiting himself to her character (Bullough, *Narrative and Dramatic Source*, 5: 332–3).
27. Bullough, *Narrative and Dramatic Sources*, 5: 328 (emphasis mine).
28. Bullough, *Narrative and Dramatic Sources*, 5: 342.
29. Bullough, *Narrative and Dramatic Sources*, 5: 370.
30. British Library Egerton MS 1500, Fol. 10v.
31. Abbott, *A Briefe Description*, sig. K3.
32. Donald Kenrick and Sian Bakewell, *On the Verge: The Gypsies of England* (London: Runnymede Trust, 1990), p. 18.
33. Bullough, *Narrative and Dramatic Sources*, 5: 436.
34. Bullough, *Narrative and Dramatic Sources*, 5: 411.
35. See Kenrick and Bakewell, pp. 1–18. The most complete study of the Gypsies is Angus Fraser, *The Gypsies*, 2nd edn (Oxford, UK and Cambridge, Mass.: Blackwell, 1995). For a study of surviving Gypsy customs, see Rena C. Gropper, *Gypsies in the City: Culture Patterns and Survival* (Princeton, NJ: Darwin Press, 1975), esp. pp. 174–83. Some recent estimates put the current Gypsy population of the British Isles at under 90,000. These are divided into four different groups: (1) the Romanies or Romany Chals, (2) the Kale of North Wales, (3) the Irish Travellers, and (4) more recent arrivals (Kenrick and Bakewell, pp. 1–18). See also George F. Black, *A Gypsy Bibliography* (Ann Arbor, Mich.: Gryphon Books, 1971); H. M. G. Grellmann, *Histoire des Bohémiens* (Paris, 1810); and John Hoyland, *A Historical Survey of the Customs, Habits, & Present State of the Gypsies* (London, 1816), especially chapter 5, 'The Gypsies in Great Britain,' pp. 75–90.
36. Kenrick and Bakewell, p. 13.
37. Kenrick and Bakewell, p. 9. See Dale B. J. Randall, *Jonson's Gypsies Unmasked: Background and Theme of 'The Gypsies Metamorphos'd'*

(Durham, NC: Duke University Press, 1975), pp. 47–66; and Fraser, *Gypsies*, esp. pp. 111–20.

38. Sir Anthony Fitzherbert, *The Newe boke of Iustices of the peas* (1538), sig. 98b.
39. Cf. Roger B. Merriman, *Life and Letters of Thomas Cromwell* (1902), cited in the *OED*:.
40. Cf. Thomas Nashe, *Works*, ed. McKerrow (1904–10), cited in the *OED*.
41. Cf. Edmund Spenser, *Works*, cited in the *OED*.
42. John Cowell, *The Interpreter: or Booke Containing the Signification of Words* (Cambridge, 1607), sig. Bb1 r&v.
43. Abbott, *A Briefe Description*, sig. K3.
44. Kenrick and Bakewell, p. 9.
45. Chambers, *Elizabethan Stage*, 4: 260.
46. Chambers, *Elizabethan Stage*, 4: 270
47. Kendrick and Bakewell, p. 9.
48. Apparently, some English subjects of Queen Elizabeth disguised themselves as gypsies. See Randall, p. 51.
49. Chambers, *Elizabethan Stage*, 4: 336–7.
50. Herodotus, p. 134.
51. Andrewe Boorde, *The First Boke of the Introduction of Knowledge* (London, 1548), sig. R2. See modern edition by F. J. Furnivall (London: Early English Text Society, 1870), p. 217.
52. Peter Heylyn, *Microcosmus: A Little Description of the Great World* (Oxford, 1625), p. 744.
53. Peter Heylyn, Book 4 of *Cosmographie in four Bookes contayning the chorographie & Historie of the whole Worlde* (London, 1652), p. 5.
54. See, for example, John Wilders, ed., *Antony and Cleopatra*, the Arden Shakespeare (London and New York: Routledge, 1995), p. 91n.
55. See the *OED*.
56. Chambers, *Elizabethan Stage*, 4: 337.

6 CULTURAL RE-ENCOUNTERS IN *THE TEMPEST*

1. Victor Turner, *The Ritual Process: Structure and Anti-Structure* (1969; rpt Ithaca, NY: Cornell University Press, 1977), p. 145. This chapter depends in part on the argument of my essay, '*The Tempest*, Comedy and the Space of the Other,' which was published in *Acting Funny: Comic Theory and Practice in Shakespeare*, ed. Frances Teague (Rutherford, NY: Fairleigh Dickinson University Press; London and Toronto: Associated University Presses, 1994), pp. 52–71. I have revised and refocused my essay. I am grateful to Julien Yoseloff, Associated University Presses and Harry Keyishian, Fairleigh Dickinson University Press, for granting permission to reprint my essay here.
2. Prospero raises, of course, the sea storm that causes the shipwreck of the Neapolitans, a power attributed to witches. In *Witchcraft and Religion: The Politics of Popular Belief* (Oxford and New York: Basil Blackwell, 1984), Christina Larner points out that during the trials for

treason by sorcery that took place in Scotland from November 1590 to May 1591, 'it was alleged that over 300 witches had gathered at various times to perform treason against the king. They were supposed to have raised storms while the King and his bride were at sea, to have attempted to effect his death by melting his effigy in wax, to have indulged in hitherto unheard of obscene rituals in the Kirk of North Berwick in the physical presence of their master, the Devil' (p. 9). James VI went to Denmark to fetch his bride in the Fall of 1589. 'When at last the Scottish party set sail in the spring of 1590 they had a very rough passage and one of the attendant ships was lost' (p. 10). In both Scotland and Denmark, witches were apprehended 'on charges of storm-raising against the King of Scotland' (p. 11).

3. Keith Thomas, *Religion and the Decline of Magic* (London: Weidenfeld & Nicholson, 1971), pp. 443. As Geoffrey Scarre points out in *Witchcraft and Magic in 16th and 17th Century Europe* (Atlantic Highlands, NJ: Humanities Press, 1987), even white witches from the lower classes 'ran some risk of being taken for black,' and those in higher status were less in danger; 'Some hard-line opponents of magic, such as Bodin or King James, thought that the more knowledgeable magicians were, the more they deserved punishment, for the more fully aware they should be of the iniquity of their activities. For such theorists, Shakespeare's Prospero would have been a more objectionable figure than the three weird sisters from *Macbeth*' (p. 31). In *Daemonology*, Elizabethan and Jacobean Quartos, ed. G. B. Harrison (1597; rpt New York: Barnes & Noble, 1966), King James argues that all magicians and witches 'ought to be put to death according to the Law of God'; no one, regardless of sex, age or rank, should be spared (p. 77).

4. In *The History of Witchcraft and Demonology* (New York: University Books, 1956), Montague Summers observes that Prospero's 'rough magic' is indeed a 'delicate situation to place before an Elizabethan audience' (p. 289).

5. E. E. Evans-Pritchard, *Social Anthropology* (1951), p. 102, as quoted by Macfarlane, p. 234. For a detailed anthropological study of witchcraft beliefs among the Azande, see E. E. Evans-Pritchard, *Witchcraft, Oracles and Magic Among the Azande* (1937; rpt Oxford: Oxford University Press, 1968).

6. Alan Macfarlane, *Witchcraft in Tudor and Stuart England: A Regional and Comparative Study* (1970; rpt New York: Harper & Row, 1971), p. 232.

7. Deborah Willis, 'Shakespeare's *Tempest* and the Discourse of Colonialism,' *SEL* 29 (1989): 280.

8. This passage presents obvious cruxes of interpretation, which modern editors of the play unfortunately ignore. In the Arden edition, Frank Kermode cites the proverb 'Trust is the mother of deceit,' which would support my reading, but he does not explain the meaning of 'beget of him.' Northrop Frye, in the Pelican edition, takes 'good parent' as an allusion to the proverb cited by Miranda: 'Good wombs have borne bad sons' (I.ii.120). Stephen Orgel, in the Oxford edition, apparently assumes that the passage poses no difficulties, and therefore, he offers no help.

9. Coppélia Kahn, 'The Absent Mother in *King Lear.*' In *Rewriting the Renaissance: The Discourse of Sexual Difference in Early Modern Europe*, eds Margaret W. Ferguson, Maureen Quilligan, and Nancy J. Vickers (Chicago: University of Chicago Press, 1986), pp. 33–49.
10. Kahn, p. 36.
11. Stephen Orgel, 'Prospero's Wife,' in *Rewriting the Renaissance*, pp. 50–64.
12. Bullough, *Narrative and Dramatic Sources*, 8: 237.
13. Bullough, 8: 276.
14. Bullough, 8: 278.
15. Bullough, 8: 282–3.
16. Bullough, 8: 281.
17. Bullough, 8: 280.
18. Bullough, 8: 278.
19. S. K. Heninger, Jr, *A Handbook of Renaissance Meteorology* (Durham, NC: Duke University Press, 1960), p. 39.
20. See L. T. Fitz, 'The Vocabulary of the Environment in *The Tempest*,' *Shakespeare Quarterly* 26 (1975): 42–7. Other significant discussions of the environment in the play include F. D. Hoeniger, 'Prospero's Storm and Miracle,' *Shakespeare Quarterly* 7 (1956): 33–8; and Douglas L. Peterson, *Time, Tide and Tempest* (San Marino: Huntington Library, 1973).
21. Bullough, 8: 276.
22. See Doggett et al., *New World of Wonders*, p. 37; and Stephen Greenblatt's Introduction to *The Tempest* in *The Norton Shakespeare*, edited by Stephen Greenblatt (London and New York: W. W. Norton, 1997), p. 3051.
23. In his introduction to his edition of *The Tempest* (Oxford and New York: Oxford University Press, 1987), Stephen Orgel writes: 'The episode is based on *Aeneid* iii. 225 ff.: Aeneas and his companions take shelter on the Strophades, the islands where the harpies live. The Trojans prepare a feast; but, as they are about to eat, the dreadful creatures swoop down on them, befouling and devouring the food. The sailors attempt to drive the harpies off, but find them invulnerable, and their leader, the witch Celaeno, sends Aeneas away with a dire prophecy' (p. 166n).
24. Geraldo U. de Sousa, 'Closure and the Antimasque of *The Tempest*,' *Journal of Dramatic Theory and Criticism*, 2 (1987): 41–51.
25. Sousa, 'Closure and the Antimasque of *The Tempest*,' 2 (1987): 47.
26. Sycorax apparently dared to affirm an identity outside the bounds of marriage and Algerian values. In fact, as Alan Macfarlane notes, 'Case histories show that women accused [of witchcraft] have usually shown unusual independence.' See chapter 18, 'The anthropological approach to the study of witchcraft (2): the sociology of accusations,' of Alan Macfarlane, *Witchcraft in Tudor and Stuart England*, pp. 226–39. In *Witchcraft and Religion: The Politics of Popular Belief*, Christina Larner observes that 'the stereotype witch is an independent adult woman who does not conform to the male idea of proper female behaviour. She is assertive; she does not require or give love (though she may

enchant); she does not nurture men or children, nor care for the weak. She has the power of words – to defend herself or to curse. In addition, she may have other, more mysterious powers which do not derive from the established order' (p. 84). See also Montague Summers' chapter on 'The Witch in Dramatic Literature,' pp. 276–313.

27. Left all alone, he had to fend for himself; therefore, he had to learn about the island's resources in order to survive. His knowledge is, in fact, remarkable. Having to survive on his own, Caliban apparently never acquired a native language as a child, and only later was he taught Italian by Miranda (I.ii.352–8). From her teachings, Caliban brags, 'I know how to curse' (363–4). Curiously, Miranda – like Prospero – assumes that Caliban's shortcomings derive not from the conditions of Caliban's upbringing but rather from the ethnic characteristics of his 'vile race' (358).

28. For a general discussion of European relations with Algiers, see John B. Wolf, *The Barbary Coast: Algiers Under the Turks 1500 to 1830* (New York and London: W. W. Norton, 1979), pp. 175–98.

29. Marquis of Salisbury, *Calendar of the Manuscripts of the Marquis of Salisbury,* Hatfield House (London: HMSO, 1906), Part 11: 289. The original letter written in Italian is reprinted in E. K. Chambers, ed., *Aurelian Townshend's Poems and Masks* (Oxford: Clarendon Press, 1912), pp. xiii–xliii.

30. See Mahfoud Kaddache, *L'Algérie durant la période Ottomane* (Algiers: Office de Publications Universitaires, 1991), p. 112. See also Mouloud Gaid, *L'Algérie sous les Turcs* (Algiers: Maison Tunisienne de L'Edition, 1974), p. 87. I have been unable to establish with certainty the identity of the said Pasha. My sources do not agree on the name of the Pasha. Gaid says that his name was Soliman.

31. Several American productions have emphasized the African dimension of Caliban's heritage. In 'Caliban and Ariel: A Study in Black and White in American Productions of *The Tempest* from 1945–1981,' Errol G. Hill discusses various productions in which black actors played Caliban and less frequently Ariel.

32. Jonson, *The Complete Masques*, p. 123.

33. Bergeron, *Shakespeare's Romances and the Royal Family* (Lawrence: University Press of Kansas, 1985), p. 194.

CONCLUSION

1. Richard Eden, *The History of Trauayle in the West and East Indies Newly set in order, augmented and finished by Richarde Willes* (London, 1577), fol. 11v.

Bibliography

PRIMARY SOURCES

Manuscripts

British Library
Additional MSS 16932; 20786
Cotton MS. Tiberius D.IX (*Voyages to East Africa to Suez and Red Sea*, fol. 1541 ff.)
Egerton 1500; 2579
Landsdowne 720
Sloane 1837 (*An Account of Africa, 1675*)

Guildhall Library
1588–1731. London-Dutch Church Letters.
7428/11. Corporation of London. Court of Common Council. *An Act of Common Councell, prohibiting all Strangers borne, and Forrainers, to vse any Trades, or keepe any maner of shops in any sort within this Citty, Liberties and Freedome thereof.* London, 1606.

Books

Abbott, George. *A Briefe Description of the whole worlde.* London, 1600.
Andrewe, Thomas. *The Unmasking of a feminine Machiavell.* London, 1604.
Armstrong, William A., ed. *Elizabethan History Plays.* London: Oxford University Press, 1965.
Azurara, Gomes Eannes de. *Crônica de Guynée. Cópia de 1506.* Edited by Fr Manuel Ruela Pombo. Reprint, Lisbon: Empresa da Revista Diogo-Caão, 1937; *The Chronicle of the Discovery of Guinea*, 2 vols. Translated by Charles Raymond Beazley. London: Hakluyt Society, 1896–7.
Barbosa, Duarte. *The Book of Duarte Barbosa: An Account of the Countries Bordering on the Indian Ocean and Their Inhabitants, Written by Duarte Barbosa, and Completed about the Year 1518 A.D.*, 2 vols. Translated by Mansel Longworth Dames. London: Hakluyt Society, 1918.
Barbosa, Rui. *Obras Completas.* Rio de Janeiro: Ministério da Educação e Saúde, 1942–88.
Barnfield, Richard. 'Against the Dispraysers of Poetrie.' In *The Complete Poems*, edited by George Klawitter. Selinsgrove, Pa.: Susquehanna University Press; London and Toronto: Associated University Presses, 1990.
Bassett, Robert. *Curiosities or the Cabinet of Nature, contayning Phylosophicall Naturall and Morall Questions answered. Translated out of Lattin French and Italian Authors.* London, 1637.
Batman, Stephen. *Batman vppon Bartholome, His Booke De Proprietatibus Rerum.* London, 1582.

Batman, Stephen. *The Golden Booke of the Leaden Godes.* London, 1577.

Bertelli, Pietro. *Diversarum Nationvm Habitvs.* Padua, 1594.

——. *Diversar. Nationvm Habitvs. Collectore Petro Bertello.* Padua, 1596.

Biddulph, William. *The Travels of Certaine Englishmen.* London, 1609.

Blount, Henry. *A Voyage into the Levant.* London, 1638.

Boaistuau, Pierre. *Theatrum mundi, the Theatre or rule of the World.* London, 1566.

Boemus, Joannes. *The Fardle of Facions.* London, 1555.

——. *The Manners, Lawes, and Cvstomes of All Nations.* London, 1611.

Boorde, Andrewe. *The First Boke of the Introduction of Knowledge.* Edited by F. J. Furnivall. London, 1870.

Brerewood, Edward. *Enqviries Tovching the Diversity of Langvages, and Religions through the cheife parts of the world.* London, 1614.

Breton, Nicholas. *Fantasticks: seruing for a Perpetvall Prognostication.* London, 1626.

Bulwer, John. *Anthropometamorphosis: man transform'd.* London, 1650, 1653, 1654.

——. *A View of the People of the Whole World.* London, 1654.

Cantarini, Gasper. *The Commonwealth of Gouernment of Venice.* Translated by Lewis Lewkenor. London, 1599.

Carleton, George. *A Thankfvll Remembrance of Gods Mercie.* London, 1627.

Chambers, E. K. *The Elizabethan Stage,* 4 vols 1923. Reprint, Oxford: Clarendon Press, 1961.

Chaucer, Geoffrey. *The Works of,* 2nd edn. Edited by F. N. Robinson. 1933. Reprint, Boston: Houghton Mifflin, 1957.

Collinson, Richard, ed. *The Three Voyages of Martin Frobisher, in search of a passage to Cathaia and India by the North-West, A.D. 1576–8.* New York: Burt Franklin, 1963.

Columbus, Christopher. *The Voyages of Christopher Columbus being the Journals of His First and Third, and the Letters Concerning his First and Last Voyages, to Which is Added the Account of His second Voyage Written by Andres Bernaldez.* Translated by Cecil Jane. London: Argonaut Press, 1930.

Coryat, Thomas. *Coryat's Crudities.* Glasgow: James MacLehose and Sons, 1905.

Cowell, John. *The Interpreter: or Booke Containing the Signification of Words.* Cambridge, 1607.

Cuningham, William. *The Cosmographical Glasse.* London, 1599.

Daniel, Samuel. *Daniel's The Tragedie of Cleopatra.* Edited by M. Lederer. London: David Nutt, 1911.

Denis, Ferdinand. *Une fête brésilienne célébrée à Rouen en 1550.* Paris, 1850; Reprint, Upper Saddle River, NJ: Gregg Press, 1968.

De Novo Mondo. A facsimile of a unique broadsheet containing an early account of the inhabitants of South America together with a short version of Heinrich Sprenger's Voyage to the Indies. Translated by M. E. Kronenberg. The Hague: Martinus Nijhoff, 1927.

Diodorus of Sicily. *Diodorus of Sicily,* 10 vols. Translated by C. H. Oldfather. Cambridge, Mass. Harvard University Press; London: William Heinemann, 1935.

Earle, John. *Micro-cosmographie or a Peece of the World discovered. In Essayes and characters*. London, 1628.

Eden, Richard. *The Decades of the newe Worlde or West India*, by Peter Martyr. London, 1555.

———. *The History of Trauayle in the West and East Indies, and other countryes*. London, 1577.

L'Entrée de Henri II à Rouen 1550: A Facsimile. With an Introduction by Margaret M. McGowan. New York and Amsterdam: Theatrvm Orbis Terrarvm Ltd, Johnson Reprint Corporation, 1970.

Euripides. *Medea*. In *Medea and Other Plays*. Translated by Philip Vellacott. London: Penguin; New York: Viking/Penguin, 1963.

Eusébio of the Society of Jesus, Fr Ivan. *Curyosa, y ocvlta filosofia. Primera, y segunda parte de las marauillas de la Naturaleza, examinadas en varías questiones naturales*. Alcala, 1649.

Fenton, Edward. *Certaine Secrete wonders of Nature, containing a description of sundry strange things, seming monstrous in our eyes and iudgement, because were are not priuie to the reasons of them*. London, 1569.

Feuillerat, Albert, ed. *Documents Relating to the Revels at Court in the Time of King Edward VI and Queen Mary*. Louvain: A. Uystpruyst; Leipzig: O. Harrassowitz; London: David Nutt, 1914.

Fitzherbert, Sir Anthony. *The Newe boke of Iustices of the peas*. London, 1538.

Foster, Sir William, ed. *The Travels of John Sanderson in the Levant 1584–1602*. London: Hakluyt Society, 1931.

Greaves, John. *Pyramidographia: or a Description of the Pyramids of Aegypt*. London, 1646.

Greenlee, William Brooks, ed. *The Voyage of Pedro Alvares Cabral to Brazil and India from Contemporary Documents and Narratives*. London: Hakluyt Society, 1938.

Grellmann, H. M. G. *Histoire des Bohémiens*. Paris, 1810.

Hakluyt, Richard. *The Principal Navigations Voyages Traffiques & Discoveries of the English Nation*, 12 vols. Glasgow: James MacLehose and Sons; New York: Macmillan, 1903–5.

Harbage, Alfred, ed. *The Complete Pelican Shakespeare*. New York and London: Penguin, 1969.

Hentzner, P. *Travels in England in the Reign of Elizabeth*. London, 1797.

Herodotus. *The Famous History of Herodotus*. Translated by B. R. London, 1584.

———. *The Histories*. Translated by Aubrey de Sélincourt and A. R. Burn. London and New York: Penguin, 1972.

Heylyn, Peter. *Cosmographie in foure Bookes contayning the chrographie & Historie of the whole Worlde, and all the Principall Kingdomes, Provinces, Seas, and Isles, thereof*. London, 1652.

———. *Microcosmus: A Little Description of the Great World*. Oxford: Printed by John Lichfield and William Turner, 1625.

Heywood, Thomas. *An Apology for Actors*. In *The Elizabethan Stage*, by E. K. Chambers, pp. 250–1. 1923. Reprint, Oxford: Clarendon Press, 1961.

———. *The Second Part of the Iron Age*, in *The Dramatic Works of Thomas Heywood*. New York: Russell & Russell, 1964.

Holland, Henry. *A Treatise Against Witchcraft*. Cambridge, 1590.

Hoyland, John. *A Historical Survey of the Customs, Habits, & Present State of the Gypsies.* London, 1816.

Jackson, G. A. *Algiers: Being a Complete Picture of the Barbary States.* London, 1817.

James I, King of England. *Daemonology.* Elizabethan and Jacobean Quartos. Edited by G. B. Harrison. 1597. Reprint, New York: Barnes & Noble, 1966.

James VI, King of Scotland. 'The Lepanto.' In *The Poems of James VI. of Scotland*, edited by James Craigie. Edinburgh and London: William Blackwood & Sons, 1955.

Jonson, Ben. *Every Man In His Humour.* In *Ben Jonson's Plays*, edited by Felix E. Schelling, pp. 1–58. 1910. Reprint, London: J. M. Dent; New York: E. P. Dutton, 1962.

——. *The Complete Masques.* Edited by Stephen Orgel. New Haven, Conn. Yale University Press, 1969.

Keeler, Mary Frear, ed. *Sir Francis Drake's West Indian Voyage 1585–86.* London: Hakluyt Society, 1981.

Leo, John, Africanus. *A Geographical Historie of Africa, written in Arabicke and Italian.* London, 1600.

——. *The History and Description of Africa and of the Notable Things Therein Contained*, 3 vols. Edited and with an introduction by Robert Brown. Translated by John Pory. 1600. Reprint, London: Hakluyt Society, 1896.

Léry, Jean de. *History of a Voyage to the Land of Brazil, Otherwise Called America.* Translated by Janet Whatley. Berkeley: University of California Press, 1990.

Lloyd, G. E. R., ed. *Hippocratic Writings.* Translated by J. Chadwick and W. N. Mann. 1950. Reprint, New York: Penguin, 1983.

Lupton, Thomas. *A Thousand Notable Things of Sundrie Sorts.* London, 1595.

Lydgate, John. *The Hystorye/Sege and Dystruccyon of Troye.* London, 1513.

Mandeville, Sir John. *Mandeville's Travels.* Edited by Michael C. Seymour. Oxford: Clarendon Press, 1967.

Marquis of Salisbury. *Calendar of the Manuscripts of the Marquis of Salisbury, Hatfield House.* Part II. London: HMSO, 1906.

Matthews, George T., ed. *News and Rumor in Renaissance Europe (The Fugger Newsletters).* New York: Capricorn Books, 1959.

Meierus, Albertus. *Certaine briefe and special Instructions for Gentlemen, merchants, students, souldiers, marriners, &c. Employed in seruices abrode, or anie way occasioned to conuerse in the Kingdomes, and gouernements of forren Princes.* London, 1589.

Milton, John. *Paradise Lost.* In *The Complete Poetry of John Milton*, edited by John T. Shawcross, pp. 249–517. New York: Doubleday Anchor, 1971.

Moryson, Fynes. *Shakespeare's Europe: Unpublished Chapters of Fynes Moryson's Itinerary.* Edited by Charles Hughes. London: Sherratt & Hughes, 1903.

Nash, Thomas. *Pierce Penilesse his Supplication to the Diuell: Describing the ouer-spreading of Vice, and the suppression of Vertue.* London, 1592.

New English Bible. Oxford: Oxford University Press; Cambridge: Cambridge University Press, 1970.

Nichols, John. *Progresses of Queen Elizabeth.* London: J. B. Nicols, 1823.

Nóbrega, Manuel da. *Cartas do Brasil.* Rio de Janeiro: Academia Brasileira, 1931.

Ortelius, Abraham. *The Theatre of the Whole World*. London, 1606.

The Oxford English Dictionary, 2nd edn. Prepared by J.A. Simpson and E.S.C. Weiner. Oxford: Clarendon Press; New York: Oxford University Press, 1989.

Page, William, ed. *Letters of Denization and Acts of Naturalization, 1509–1603*. Lymington: The Huguenot Society of London, 1893.

Painter, William. *The Palace of Pleasure*, 3 vols. Edited by Joseph Jacobs. London: David Nutt, 1890.

Parry, John H., and Robert G. Keith, eds. *New Iberian World*. 5 vols. New York: Times Books and Hector & Rose, 1984.

Peele, George. *The Battle of Alcazar*. In vol. 2 of *The Dramatic Works of George Peele*, edited by J. Yoklavich. New Haven, Conn.: Yale University Press, 1952.

Plinius Secundus, Caius. *A summarie of the antiquities, and wonders of the worlde, out of the sixtene first bookes of Plinie*. London, 1566.

———. *The secrets and wonders of the world*. London, 1585.

———. *The historie of the world*. Translated by Philemon Holland. London, 1601.

Plutarch. *The Lives of the Noble Grecians and Romans*, 2 vols. Translated by Sir Thomas North. Edited by Roland Baughman. New York: Heritage Press, 1941.

Prat, William. *The Description of the Countrey of Aphrique*. [London], 1554.

Purchas, Samuel. *Hakluytus Posthumus or Purchas His Pilgrimes Contayning a History of the World in Sea Voyages and Lande Travells by Englishmen and Others*, 20 vols. Glasgow: James MacLehose and Sons; New York: Macmillan, 1905.

Quinn, David B., and Alison M. Quinn, eds. *The English New England Voyages 1602–1608*. London: Hakluyt Society, 1983.

Quintus Smyrnaeus. *The Fall of Troy*. Translated by Arthur S. Way. 1913. Reprint, Cambridge, Mass.: Harvard University Press; London: William Heinemann, 1984.

Raleigh, Sir Walter. *The History of the World*. London, 1614.

Rye, William Brenchley. *England as Seen by Foreigners in the Days of Elizabeth and James the First*. London: John Russell Smith, 1865.

Sanderson, John. *The Travels of John Sanderson. Works Issued by the Hakluyt Society*, 2nd series, vol. 67. London: Hakluyt Society, 1931.

Scot, Reginald. *The Discoverie of Witchcraft*. Edited by Revd Montague Summers. [London:] John Rodker Publisher, 1930.

Shakespeare, William. *Antony and Cleopatra*, the Arden Shakespeare. Edited by John Wilders. London and New York: Routledge, 1995.

———. *The Complete Works*, the Pelican Shakespeare. Edited by Alfred Harbage. 1956. Reprint, New York: Penguin, 1969.

———. *Titus Andronicus*, the Arden Shakespeare. Edited by Jonathan Bate. London and New York: Routledge, 1995.

———. *Titus Andronicus*, the New Cambridge Shakespeare. Edited by Alan Hughes. Cambridge: Cambridge University Press, 1994.

Shakespeare, William, and John Fletcher. *The Two Noble Kinsmen*. Edited by Eugene Waith. Oxford and New York: Oxford University Press, 1989.

Sidney, Mary. Countess of Pembroke. *The Tragedie of Antonie Doone into English by the countesse of Pembroke*. London, 1595.

Sidney, Sir Philip. *The Defense of Poesy.* In *Poetry of the English Renaissance,* edited by J. William Hebel and Hoyt H. Hudson. 1929. Reprint, New York: Appleton-Century-Crofts, 1957.

Sousa, Gabriel Soares de. *Notícia do Brasil* (1587), 2 vols. Edited by Pirajá da Silva. São Paulo: Livraria Martins Editora, 1939.

Spenser, Edmund. '"A Letter of the Authors" to Sir Walter Raleigh.' In *Edmund Spenser's Poetry.* Edited by Hugh MacLean. New York: W. W. Norton, 1968.

———. *The Faerie Queene.* Edited by Thomas P. Roche, Jr. New York: Penguin, 1979.

Staden, Hans. *The True History of His Captivity.* Translated by Malcolm Letts. London: George Routledge & Sons, 1928.

Statius. *Thebaid.* Translated by A. D. Melville. Oxford: Clarendon Press, 1992.

Stow, John. *The Annales of England.* London, 1605.

———. *The Annales, or General Chronicle of England.* London, 1615.

Strabo. *The Geography of Strabo,* 8 vols. Translated by Horace Leonard Jones. London: William Heinemann; New York: G. P. Putnam's Sons, 1928.

Straet, Jan van der. *Nova reperta.* [Antwerp, *c.* 1600].

Topsell, Edward. *The Historie of Fovre-footed Beastes.* London, 1607.

———. *The Historie of Serpents.* London, 1608.

Vecellio, Cesare. *Habiti antichi, et moderni di tutto il mondo.* Venice, 1598.

SECONDARY SOURCES

Abrams, Richard. 'Gender Confusion and Sexual Politics in *The Two Noble Kinsmen.*' In *Drama, Sex and Politics, Themes in Drama* 7 (1985): 69–75.

Adelman, Janet. *Suffocating Mothers: Fantasies of Maternal Origin in Shakespeare's Plays.* New York & London: Routledge, 1991.

Amadiume, Ifi. *Male Daughters, Female Husbands: Gender and Sex in an African Society.* London: Zed Books, 1987.

Anson, John. 'The Female Transvestite in Early Monasticism: The Origin and Development of a Motif.' *Viator: Medieval and Renaissance Studies* 5 (1974): 1–32.

Apollonius of Rhodes. *Jason and the Golden Fleece (The Argonautica).* Translated by Richard Hunter. Oxford: Oxford University Press, 1995.

Auerbach, Erich. *Mimesis: The Representation of Reality in Western Literature.* 1953. Reprint, Garden City, NJ: Doubleday Anchor Books, 1957.

Babcock, Barbara, ed. *The Reversible World: Symbolic Inversion in Art and Society.* Ithaca, NY: Cornell University Press, 1972.

Bamberger, Joan. 'The Myth of Matriarchy: Why Men Rule in Primitive Society.' *Woman, Culture, and Society.* Edited by Michelle Zimbalist Rosaldo and Louise Lamphere. Stanford University Press, 1974, 263–80.

Barker, Deborah and Ivo Kamps, eds. *Shakespeare and Gender: A History.* London and New York: Verso, 1995.

Barker, Francis, et al., eds. *1642: Literature and Power in the Seventeenth Century: Proceedings of the Essex Conference on the Sociology of Literature, July 1980.* Colchester: University of Essex, 1981.

Barker, Francis and Peter Hulme. 'Nymphs and reapers heavily vanish: the discursive con-texts of *The Tempest.*' In *Alternative Shakespeares*, edited by John Drakakis, pp. 191–205. London and New York: Methuen, 1985.

Barker, Francis, et al., eds. *Europe and Its Others. Proceedings of the Essex Conference on the Sociology of Literature, July 1984*, 2 vols. Colchester: University of Essex, 1985.

Barnes, Clive. 'Review of *A Midsummer Night's Dream.*' Reprint, Lee A. Jacobus, *The Bedford Introduction to Drama*, 3rd edn. Boston: Bedford Books of St. Martin's Press, 1997.

Barrett, W. P., trans. *The Trial of Jeanne d'Arc*. London: George Routledge & Sons, 1931.

Bartels, Emily C. 'Making More of the Moor: Aaron, Othello, and Renaissance Refashionings of Race.' *Shakespeare Quarterly* 41 (1990): 443–54.

Bates, E. S. *Touring in 1600: A Study in the Development of Travel as a Means of Education*. Boston and New York: Houghton Mifflin Company, 1911.

Berardinelli, Cleonice, ed. *Antologia do Teatro de Gil Vicente*. Rio de Janeiro: Grifo Edições, 1971.

Bergeron, David M. *English Civic Pageantry 1558–1642*. London: Edward Arnold; Columbia: University of South Carolina Press, 1971.

——. ed. *Pageants and Entertainments of Anthony Munday: A Critical Edition*. New York and London: Garland, 1985.

——. 'Politics and *The Tempest.*' Lecture given at 'The Heart of America Shakespeare Festival' in Kansas City, Missouri, 3 July 1993.

——. *Royal Family, Royal Lovers: King James of England and Scotland*. Columbia and London: University of Missouri Press, 1991.

——. *Shakespeare's Romances and the Royal Family*. Lawrence: University Press of Kansas, 1985.

Berkowitz, Gerald M. 'Shakespeare in Edinburgh.' *Shakespeare Quarterly* 31 (1980): 163–8.

Bethell, Leslie, ed. *Colonial Brazil*. Cambridge: Cambridge University Press, 1987.

Bevington, David M. 'The Domineering Female in *1 Henry VI.*' *Shakespeare Studies* 2 (1966): 51–8.

Black, George F. *A Gypsy Bibliography*. Ann Arbor, Mich.: Gryphon Books, 1971.

Bland, Olivia. *The Royal Way of Death*. London: Constable, 1986.

Blickle, Peter. *The Revolution of 1525: The German Peasants' War from a New Perspective*. Translated by Thomas A. Brady, Jr. and H. C. Erik Midelford. Baltimore, Md.: Johns Hopkins University Press, 1981.

Bond, Francis. *Wood Carvings in English Churches*, 2 vols. Oxford: Oxford University Press, 1910.

Boon, James A. *Other Tribes, Other Scribes: Symbolic Anthropology in the Comparative Study of Cultures, Histories, Religions, and Texts*. Cambridge, UK and New York: Cambridge University Press, 1982.

Boose, Lynda E. 'Othello's Handkerchief: "The Recognizance and Pledge of Love."' *English Literary Renaissance* 5 (1975): 360–74.

Boswell, John. *Christianity, Social Tolerance and Homosexuality: Gay People in Western Europe from the Beginning of the Christian Era to the Fourteenth Century*. Chicago: University of Chicago Press, 1980.

Boswell, John. *Same-Sex Unions in Premodern Europe*. New York: Villard Books, 1994.

Bowra, M. *Greek Lyric Poetry*, 2nd edn. Oxford: Oxford University Press, 1961.

Bray, Alan. *Homosexuality in Renaissance England*. London: Gay Men's Press, 1982.

Briggs, Katherine M. *Pale Hecate's Team: An Examination of the Beliefs on Witchcraft and Magic among Shakespeare's Contemporaries and His Immediate Successors*. London: Routledge & Kegan Paul, 1962.

Brockbank, Philip. '*The Tempest*: Conventions of Art and Empire.' In *Later Shakespeare*, edited by J. R. Brown and B. Harris, pp. 183–201. London: Edward Arnold, 1966.

Brown, J. R., and B. Harris, eds, *Later Shakespeare*. London: Edward Arnold, 1966.

Brown, Judith C. *Immodest Acts: The Life of a Lesbian Nun in Renaissance Italy*. New York and Oxford: Oxford University Press, 1986.

Brown, Paul. '"This thing of darkness I acknowledge mine"': *The Tempest* and the discourse of Colonialism.' In *Political Shakespeare: New Essays in Cultural Materialism*. Edited by Jonathan Dollimore and Alan Sinfield, pp. 48–71. Ithaca, NY and London: Cornell University Press, 1985.

Bruster, Douglas. 'The Jailer's Daughter and the Politics of Madwomen's Language.' *Shakespeare Quarterly* 46 (1995): 277–300.

Bugner, Ladislas, ed. *The Image of the Black in Western Art*. Translated by William Granger Ryan. Cambridge, Mass. & London: Harvard University Press, 1979.

Bullough, Geoffrey, ed. *Narrative and Dramatic Sources of Shakespeare*, 8 vols. London: Routledge & Kegan Paul; New York: Columbia University Press, 1973.

Bullough, Vern L. *Cross Dressing, Sex, and Gender*. Philadelphia: University of Pennsylvania Press, 1993.

——. *Sexual Practices and the Medieval Church*. Buffalo, NY: Prometheus Books, 1982.

——. 'Transvestites in the Middle Ages.' *American Journal of Sociology* 79 (1974): 1381–94.

Bushman, Mary Ann. 'Representing Cleopatra.' In *In Another Country: Feminist Perspectives on Renaissance Drama*. Edited by Dorothea Kehler and Susan Baker, pp. 36–49. Metuchen, NJ: Scarecrow Press, 1991.

Butler, Judith. *Bodies That Matter: On the Discursive Limits of 'Sex'*. New York and London: Routledge, 1993.

Cady, Joseph. '"Masculine Love", Renaissance Writing, and the "New Invention" of Homosexuality.' *Journal of Homosexuality* 23.1–2 (1992): 9–40.

Calderwood, James L. '*A Midsummer Night's Dream*: Anamorphism and Theseus' Dream.' *Shakespeare Quarterly* 42 (1991): 409–30.

Campbell, Mary B. *The Witness and the Other World: Exotic European Travel Writings, 400–1600*. Ithaca, NY: Cornell University Press, 1988.

Carr, Helen. 'Woman/Indian: "The American" and His Others.' In *Europe and Its Others, Proceedings of the Essex Conference on the Sociology of Literature*, edited by Francis Barker et al., pp. 19–20. Colchester: University of Essex, 1985.

Cartelli, Thomas. 'Prospero in Africa: *The Tempest* as colonialist text and pretext.' In *Shakespeare Reproduced: The Text in History and Ideology*, edited by Jean Howard and Marion F. O'Connor, pp. 99–115. New York: Methuen, 1987.

Cawley, Robert Ralston. *The Voyagers and Elizabethan Drama*. Boston: D. C. Heath; London: Oxford University Press, 1938.

Cecil, David. *The Cecils of Hatfield House: An English Ruling Family*. Boston: Houghton Mifflin, 1973.

Certeau, Michel de. *Heterologies: Discourse on the Other*. Translated by Brian Massumi. Minneapolis: University of Minnesota Press, 1986.

——. *The Writing of History*. Translated by Tom Conley. New York: Columbia University Press, 1988.

Chambers, E. K. *Aurelian Townshend's Poems and Masks*. Oxford: Clarendon Press, 1912.

——. *The Elizabethan Stage*, 4 vols. 1923. Reprint, Oxford: Clarendon Press, 1961.

——. *William Shakespeare: A Study of Facts and Problems*, 2 vols. 1930. Reprint, Oxford: Clarendon Press, 1966.

Chiappelli, Aldo, ed. *First Images of America: The Impact of the New World on the Old*, 2 vols. Berkeley: University of California Press, 1976.

Chitty, C. W. 'Aliens in England in the Sixteenth Century.' *Race* 8. 2 (October 1966): 129–45.

Clifford, James. *The Predicament of Culture: Twentieth-Century Ethnography, Literature, and Art*. Cambridge, Mass. and London: Harvard University Press, 1988.

Clifford, James, and George E. Marcus, eds. *Writing Culture: The Poetics and Politics of Ethnography*. Berkeley, Los Angeles and London: University of California Press, 1986.

Cohen, Kathleen. *Metamorphosis of a Death Symbol: The Transi Tomb in the Late Middle Ages and the Renaissance*. Berkeley: University of California Press, 1973.

Cohen, William B. *The French Encounter with Africans: White Response to Blacks 1530–1880*. Bloomington: Indiana University Press, 1980.

Cross, Gustav. Introduction to *Titus Andronicus*, by William Shakespeare. In *The Complete Works*, edited by Alfred Harbage. New York: Penguin, 1969.

Crow, Brian. 'Lydgate's 1445 Pageant for Margaret of Anjou.' *ELN* 19 (1981): 170–4.

Dabydeen, David. *The Black Presence in English Literature*. Dover, NH and Manchester, UK: Manchester University Press, 1985.

D'Amico, Jack. *The Moor in English Renaissance Drama*. Tampa: University Presses of Florida, 1991.

Davis, Natalie Zemon. 'Women on Top: Symbolic Sexual Inversion and Political Disorder in Early Modern Europe.' In *The Reversible World: Symbolic Inversion in Art and Society*. Edited by Barbara A. Babcock, pp. 147–90. London: Cornell University Press, 1978.

Debrunner, Hans Werner. *Presence and Prestige: Africans in Europe: A History of Africans in Europe before 1918*. Basel: Basler Africa Bibliographien, 1979.

Delcourt, Marie. *Hermaphrodite: Myths and Rites of the Bisexual Figure in Classical Antiquity*. London: Studio Books, 1956.

Derrida, Jacques. *Writing and Difference*. Translated by Alan Bass. Chicago: Chicago University Press, 1978.

Devisse, Jean, and Michel Mollat. *Africans in the Christian Ordinance of the World: Fourteenth to the Sixteenth Century*, Tome 2 of Volume II, *From the Early Christian Era to the 'Age of Discovery'*, edited by Ladislas Bugner. Translated by William Granger. Cambridge, Mass. and London: Harvard University Press, 1979.

Dobson, R. B. *The Peasants' Revolt of 1381*, 2nd edn. London: Macmillan, 1983.

Doggett, Rachel, et al., eds. *New World of Wonders: European Images of the Americas 1492–1700*. Washington, DC: Folger Shakespeare Library, 1992.

Dolan, Frances E. *Dangerous Familiars: Representations of Domestic Crime in England, 1550–1700*. Ithaca, NY: Cornell University Press, 1994.

Dollimore, Jonathan, and Alan Sinfield, eds. *Political Shakespeare: New Essays in Cultural Materialism*. Ithaca, NY: Cornell University Press, 1985.

Doresse, Jean. *The Secret Books of the Egyptian Gnostics*. New York: Viking Press, 1960.

Drakakis, John, ed. *Alternative Shakespeares*. London and New York: Methuen, 1985.

Duberman, Martin B., Martha Vicinus, and George Chauncey, Jr, eds. *Hidden from History: Reclaiming the Gay and Lesbian Past*. New York: New American Library, 1989.

duBois, Page. *Centaurs and Amazons: Women and the Pre-History of the Great Chain of Being*. Ann Arbor: University of Michigan Press, 1982.

Eaton, Sara. 'Defacing the Feminine in Renaissance Tragedy.' In *The Matter of Difference: Materialist Feminist Criticism of Shakespeare*. Edited by Valerie Wayne, pp. 181–98. Ithaca, NY: Cornell University Press, 1991.

Ember, Carol R. 'A Cross-cultural Perspective on Sex Differences.' In *Handbook of Cross-cultural Human Development*, pp. 531–59. New York and London: Garland, 1981.

Engels, Frederick. *The Peasant War in Germany*. 1926. Reprint, New York: International Publishers, 1976.

Erlanger, Philippe. *Margaret of Anjou Queen of England*. London: Elek Books, 1970.

Erlich, Bruce. 'Shakespeare's Colonial Metaphor: On the Social Function of Theatre in *The Tempest*.' *Science and Society* 41 (1977): 43–65.

Evans-Pritchard, E. E. *Social Anthropology*. Glencoe, Ill.: Free Press, 1951.

——. *Witchcraft, Oracles and Magic Among the Azande*. 1937. Reprint, Oxford: Oxford University Press, 1968.

Fabian, Johannes. *Time and the Other: How Anthropology Makes its Object*. New York: Columbia University Press, 1983.

Felton, Craig, and William B. Jordan, eds. *Jusepe de Ribera lo Spagnoletto 1591–1652*, 129–31. Fort Worth, Tex.: Kimbell Art Museum, 1982.

Fitz, L. T. 'The Vocabulary of the Environment in *The Tempest*.' *Shakespeare Quarterly* 26 (1975): 42–7.

Fletcher, Angus. *Allegory: The Theory of a Symbolic Mode*. Ithaca, NY: Cornell University Press, 1964.

Fletcher-Jones, Pamela. *The Jews of Britain: A Thousand Years of History*. Moreton-in-Marsh, Glos.: The Windrush Press, 1990.

Forker, Charles R. ' "Masculine Love", Renaissance Writing, and the "New Invention" of Homosexuality: An Addendum.' *Journal of Homosexuality* 31.3 (1996): 85–93.

Fraser, Angus. *The Gypsies*, 2nd edn. Oxford, UK and Cambridge, Mass.: Blackwell, 1995.

Freedman, Barbara. *Staging the Gaze: Postmodernism, Psychoanalysis, and Shakespearean Comedy.* Ithaca, NY and London: Cornell University Press, 1991.

Freud, Sigmund. 'A Note upon the "Mystic Writing-Pad".' *SE* 19 (1925): 232.

Freund, Scarlett, and Teofilo F. Ruiz, eds. *Jewish-Christian Encounters Over the Centuries: Symbiosis, Prejudice, Holocaust, Dialogue.* New York: Peter Lang, 1994.

Frey, Charles. '*The Tempest* and the New World.' *Shakespeare Quarterly* 30 (1979): 29–41.

Friedman, John Block. *The Monstrous Races in Medieval Art and Thought.* Cambridge, Mass. Harvard University Press, 1981.

Fryde, E. B. *The Great Revolt of 1381.* London: Historical Association, 1981.

Gaid, Mouloud. *L'Algérie sous les Turcs.* Algiers: Maison Tunisienne de L'Edition, 1974.

Garber, Marjorie, ed. *Cannibals, Witches, and Divorce: Estranging the Renaissance.* Baltimore, Md. and London: Johns Hopkins University Press, 1987.

Gates, Henry Louis, Jr, ed. *'Race,' Writing, and Difference.* Chicago and London: University of Chicago Press, 1986.

Geertz, Clifford. *The Interpretation of Cultures: Selected Essays.* New York: Basic Books, 1973.

———. *Local Knowledge: Further Essays in Interpretive Anthropology.* New York: Basic Books, 1983.

Gillies, John. *Shakespeare and the Geography of Difference.* Cambridge: Cambridge University Press, 1994.

Gittings, Clare. *Death, Burial and the Individual in Early Modern England.* London: Croom Helm, 1984.

Glassman, Bernard. *Anti-Semitic Stereotypes without Jews: Images of the Jews in England 1290–1700.* Detroit, Mich.: Wayne State University Press, 1975.

Glotfelty, Cheryll and Harold Fromm, eds. *The Ecocriticism Reader: Landmarks in Literary Ecology.* Athens, Ga. and London: University of Georgia Press, 1996.

Godzich, Wlad. Introduction to *Heterologies: Discourse on the Other,* by Michel de Certeau. Translated by Brian Massumi. Minneapolis: University of Minnesota Press, 1986.

Goldberg, Jonathan. *Sodometries: Renaissance Texts, Modern Sexualities.* Stanford, Calif. Stanford University Press, 1992.

Goodich, Michael. *The Unmentionable Vice: Homosexuality in the Later Medieval Period.* Santa Barbara, Calif.: Clio Press, 1979.

Gordon, Giles. 'Two Kinsmen and a Swan.' *Plays and Players* (July 1986): 13–15.

Greenblatt, Stephen. *Learning to Curse: Essays in Early Modern Culture.* New York and London: Routledge, 1990.

———. *Marvelous Possessions: The Wonder of the New World.* Chicago: University of Chicago Press, 1991.

Greenblatt, Stephen. *Renaissance Self-Fashioning: From More to Shakespeare.* Chicago: University of Chicago Press, 1980.

Gregor, Thomas. *Anxious Pleasures: The Sexual Lives of an Amazonian People.* Chicago: Chicago University Press, 1985.

Gregor, Thomas. *Mehinaku: The Drama of Daily Life in a Brazilian Indian Village.* Chicago: University of Chicago Press, 1977.

Griffiths, Ralph A. 'Frontiers and Foreigners.' In *The Reign of King Henry VI: The Exercise of Royal Authority, 1422–1461*, pp. 154–77. Berkeley and Los Angeles: University of California Press, 1981.

Griffiths, Trevor R. ' '"This Island's Mine": Caliban and Colonialism.' *Yearbook of English Studies* 13 (1983): 159–80.

Gropper, Rena C. *Gypsies in the City: Culture Patterns and Survival.* Princeton, NY: Darwin Press, 1975.

Hall, Kim F. *Things of Darkness: Economies of Race and Gender in Early Modern England.* Ithaca, NY and London: Cornell University Press, 1995.

Hamer, Mary. *Signs of Cleopatra: History, Politics, Representation.* London and New York: Routledge, 1993.

Hardin, Richard F. 'Chronicles and Mythmaking in Shakespeare's Joan of Arc.' *Shakespeare Survey* 42 (1990): 25–35.

Hartmann, Heidi. 'The Unhappy Marriage of Marxism and Feminism: Towards a More Progressive Union.' In *Women and Revolution: The Discussion of the Unhappy Marriage of Marxism and Feminism*, by Lydia Sargent, pp. 1–41. Boston: South End Press, 1981.

Hartog, François. *The Mirror of Herodotus: The Representation of the Other in the Writing of History.* Translated by Janet Lloyd. Berkeley and London: University of California Press, 1988.

Harvey, I. M. W. *Jack Cade's Rebellion of 1450.* Oxford: Clarendon Press, 1991.

Haswell, Jock. *The Ardent Queen: Margaret of Anjou and the Lancastrian Heritage.* London: Peter Davies, 1976.

Heliodora, Bárbara. 'Bárbara Heliodora Cultua Shakespeare.' Interview by Sérgio de Carvalho. *O Estado de São Paulo*, 31 July 1997: Section 2.

———. *Falando de Shakespeare.* São Paulo: Editora Perspectiva, 1997.

Heller, Thomas C., et al., eds. *Reconstructing Individualism: Autonomy, Individuality, and the Self in Western Thought.* Stanford, Calif: Stanford University Press, 1986.

Heninger Jr, S. K. *A Handbook of Renaissance Meteorology.* Durham, NC: Duke University Press, 1960.

Herzfeld, Michael. *Anthropology through the Looking-Glass: Critical Ethnography in the Margins of Europe.* Cambridge and New York: Cambridge University Press, 1987.

Hill, Errol G. 'Caliban and Ariel: A Study in Black and White in American Productions of *The Tempest* from 1945–1981.' *Theatre History Studies* 4 (1984): 63–9.

Hillman, Richard. 'Shakespeare's Romantic Innocents and the Misappropriation of the Romantic Past: the Case of *The Two Noble Kinsmen*.' *Shakespeare Survey* 43 (1990): 59–79.

Hoeniger, F. D., ed. *Henry VIII*. In *The Complete Pelican Shakespeare*, edited by Alfred Harbage, pp. 780–817. New York and London: Penguin, 1969.

———. 'Prospero's Storm and Miracle.' *Shakespeare Quarterly* 7 (1956): 33–8.

Hoenselaars, A. J. *Images of English and Foreigners in the Drama of Shakespeare and His Contemporaries: A Study of Stage Characters and National Identity in English Renaissance Drama, 1558–1642*. Rutherford, NJ: Fairleigh Dickinson University Press; London and Toronto: Associated University Presses, 1992.

Holderness, Graham. *Shakespeare's History*. Dublin: Gill & Macmillan; New York: St. Martin's Press, 1985.

Holmes, Ronald. *Witchcraft in British History*. London: Frederick Muller, 1974.

Howard, Jean E., and Marion F. O'Connor, eds, *Shakespeare Reproduced: The Text in History and Ideology*. New York and London: Methuen, 1987.

Huet, Marie-Hélène. 'Living Images: Monstrosity and Representation.' *Representations* 4 (1983): 73–87.

Hulme, Peter. *Colonial Encounters: Europe and the Native Caribbean, 1492–1797*. New York and London: Methuen, 1986.

——. 'Hurricanes in the Caribbees: The Constitution of the Discourse of English Colonialism.' In *1642: Literature and Power in the Seventeenth Century. Proceedings of the Essex Conference on Sociology of Literature, July 1980*. Edited by Francis Barker et al., pp. 55–83. Colchester: University of Essex, 1981.

Hunter, G. K. 'Elizabethans and Foreigners.' *Shakespeare Survey* 17 (1964): 37–52.

Impey, Oliver and Arthur MacGregor, eds. *The Origins of Museums: The Cabinet of Curiosities in Sixteenth- and Seventeenth-Century Europe*. Oxford: Clarendon Press, 1985.

Jackson, Gabriele Bernard. 'Topical Ideology: Witches, Amazons, and Shakespeare's Joan of Arc.' *English Literary Renaissance* 18 (1988): 40–65.

James, John. 'Well-drilled Pageantry.' *The Times Educational Supplement*, 12 June 1987: 33.

Jardine, Lisa. *Worldly Goods: A New History of the Renaissance*. London and New York: Doubleday, 1996.

Jones, Eldred. *Othello's Countrymen: The African in English Renaissance Drama*. London: Oxford University Press, 1965.

Jones, Norman. *God and the Moneylenders: Usury and Law in Early Modern England*. Cambridge: Basil Blackwell, 1989.

Kaddache, Mahfoud. *L'Algérie durant la période Ottomane*. Algiers: Office de Publications Universitaires, 1991.

Kahn, Coppélia. 'The Absent Mother in *King Lear*.' In *Rewriting the Renaissance: The Discourse of Sexual Difference in Early Modern Europe*, pp. 33–49. Edited by Margaret Ferguson, Maureen Quilligan, and Nancy J. Vickers. Chicago: University of Chicago Press, 1986.

——. *Roman Shakespeare: Warriors, Wounds, and Women*. London and New York: Routledge, 1997.

Kamps, Ivo, ed. *Materialist Shakespeare*. London and New York: Verso, 1995.

Kenrick, Donald, and Sian Bakewell. *On the Verge: The Gypsies of England*. London: Runnymede Trust, 1990.

Kipling, Gordon. ' "Grace in this Lyf and Aftiwarde Glorie" ': Margaret of Anjou's Royal Entry into London.' *Research Opportunities in Renaissance Drama* 29 (1986–7): 77–84.

Kipling, Gordon. 'The London Pageants for Margaret of Anjou: A Medieval Script Restored.' *Medieval English Theatre* 4 (1982): 5–27.

Kittredge, George Lyman. *Witchcraft in Old and New England.* Cambridge, Mass.: Harvard University Press, 1929.

Kunzle, David. 'World Upside Down: The Iconography of a European Broadsheet Type.' In *The Reversible World: Symbolic Inversion in Art and Society.* Edited by Barbara Babcock, pp. 39–94. Ithaca, NY: Cornell University Press, 1972.

Kynge, James. 'Shakespeare in China.' *Plays and Players* (July 1986): 16–18.

Lacombe, Américo Jacobina, Eduardo Silva, and Francisco de Assis Barbosa. *Rui Barbosa e a queima dos arquivos.* Rio de Janeiro: Fundação Casa de Rui Barbosa, 1988.

Larner, Christina. *Witchcraft and Religion: The Politics of Popular Belief.* Oxford, UK and New York: Basil Blackwell, 1984.

Lee, Patricia-Ann. 'Reflections of Power: Margaret of Anjou and the Dark Side of Queenship.' *Renaissance Quarterly* 39 (1986): 183–217.

Lévinas, Emmanuel. *Time and the Other [and Additional Essays].* Translated by Richard A. Cohen. Pittsburgh, Pa.: Duquesne University Press, 1987.

Lévi-Strauss, Claude. *Structural Anthropology.* Translated by Claire Jacobson and Brooke Grundfest Schoepf. New York: Basic Books, 1976.

Litten, Julian. *The English Way of Death: The Common Funeral Since 1450.* London: Robert Hale, 1991.

Lloyd, Michael. 'Cleopatra as Isis.' *Shakespeare Survey* 12 (1959): 88–94.

Macfarlane, Alan. *Witchcraft in Tudor and Stuart England: A Regional and Comparative Study.* London: Routledge & Kegan Paul, 1970; New York: Harper & Row, 1971.

McGowan, Margaret M. 'Form and Themes in Henri II's Entry into Rouen.' *Renaissance Drama*, NS, 1 (1968): 199–251.

McGrane, Bernard. *Beyond Anthropology: Society and the Other.* New York: Columbia University Press, 1989.

McGuire, Philip C. *Shakespeare: The Jacobean Plays.* London: Macmillan; New York: St. Martin's Press, 1994.

MacLean, Ian. *The Renaissance Notion of Woman: A Study in the Fortunes of Scholasticism and Medical Science in European Intellectual Life.* Cambridge: Cambridge University Press, 1989.

McPherson, David C. *Shakespeare, Jonson, and the Myth of Venice.* Newark: University of Delaware Press; London and Toronto: Associated University Press, 1990.

Madaule, Jacques. *The Albigensian Crusade: An Historical Essay.* Translated by Barbara Wall. London: Burns & Oates; New York: Fordham University Press, 1967.

Marcus, George E., and Michael M. J. Fischer. *Anthropology as Cultural Critique: An Experimental Moment in the Human Sciences.* Chicago and London: University of Chicago Press, 1986.

Marcus, Leah S. *Puzzling Shakespeare: Local Reading and Its Discontents.* Berkeley: University of California Press, 1988.

Marshburn, Joseph H. *Murder and Witchcraft in England, 1550–1640 as Recounted in Pamphlets, Ballads, Broadsides, and Plays.* Norman: University of Oklahoma Press, 1971.

Manguin, Jean-Marie. Review of *The Two Noble Kinsmen*. *Cahiers Elisabethains* 30 (October 1986): 96–8.

Metz, G. Harold. '*The Two Noble Kinsmen* on the Twentieth Century Stage.' *Theatre History Studies* 4 (1984): 63–9.

Metzger, Mary Janell. '"Now by My Hood, a Gentle and No Jew"': Jessica, *The Merchant of Venice*, and the Discourse of Early Modern Identity.' *PMLA* 113.1 (1998): 52–63.

Mink, Louis O. 'Narrative Form as a Cognitive Instrument.' In *Historical Understanding*. Edited by Brian Fay, Eugene O. Golob, and Richard T. Vann, pp. 129–49. Ithaca, NY: Cornell University Press, 1987.

Montrose, Louis A. '*A Midsummer Night's Dream* and the Shaping Fantasies of Elizabethan Culture: Gender, Power, Form.' In *Rewriting the Renaissance: The Discourses of Sexual Difference in Early Modern Europe*. Edited by Margaret W. Ferguson, Maureen Quilligan, and Nancy J. Vickers, pp. 65–96. Chicago: University of Chicago Press, 1986.

Mullaney, Steven. *The Place of the Stage: License, Play, and Power in Renaissance England*. Chicago and London: University of Chicago Press, 1988.

Neely, Carol Thomas. 'Circumscriptions and Unhousedness: Othello in the Borderlands,' in *Shakespeare and Gender: A History*, eds Deborah Barker and Ivo Kamps, pp. 302–15, London and New York: Verso, 1995.

Neill, Michael. 'Changing Places in "Othello".' *Shakespeare Survey* 38 (1984): 115–131.

Netanyahu, B. *The Origins of the Inquisition in Fifteenth-Century Spain*. New York: Random House, 1995.

Newman, Karen. '"And wash the Ethiop white": Femininity and the Monstrous in *Othello*.' In *Shakespeare Reproduced: The Text in History and Ideology*. Edited by Jean E. Howard and Marion F. O'Connor, pp. 143–62. New York and London: Methuen, 1987.

——. *Fashioning Femininity and English Renaissance Drama*. Chicago and London: University of Chicago Press, 1991.

Notestein, Wallace. *A History of Witchcraft in England from 1558 to 1718*. 1911. Reprint, New York: Russell & Russell, 1965.

Onions, C. T., ed. *Shakespeare's England: An Account of the Life & Manners of His Age*, 2 vols. 1916. Reprint, Oxford: Clarendon Press, 1950.

Orgel, Stephen. Introduction to *The Tempest*. Oxford Shakespeare. Oxford: Oxford University Press, 1987.

——. 'Prospero's Wife.' In *Rewriting the Renaissance: The Discourses of Sexual Difference in Early Modern Europe*. Edited by Margaret W. Ferguson, Maureen Quilligan, and Nancy J. Vickers, pp. 50–64. Chicago: University of Chicago Press, 1986.

——. 'Shakespeare and the Cannibals.' In *Cannibals, Witches, and Divorce: Estranging the Renaissance*, edited by Marjorie Garber, pp. 40–66. Baltimore. Md. and London: Johns Hopkins University Press, 1987.

Ortner, Sherry B. 'Gender and Sexuality in Hierarchical Societies: The Case of Polynesia and Some Comparative Implications.' In *Sexual Meanings: The Cultural Construction of Gender and Sexuality*, pp. 359–409. 1981. Reprint, Cambridge, London, and New York: Cambridge University Press, 1984.

Palmer, Daryl W. *Hospitable Performances: Dramatic Genre and Cultural Practice in Early Modern England.* West Lafayette, IN: Purdue University Press, 1992.

Paster, Gail Kern. *The Body Embarrassed: Drama and the Disciplines of Shame in Early Modern England.* Ithaca, NY: Cornell University Press, 1993.

Patterson, Annabel. *Shakespeare and the Popular Voice.* Oxford: Basil Blackwell, 1989.

Peterson, Douglas L. *Time, Tide, and Tempest.* San Marino: Huntington Library, 1973.

Pignatti, Terisio. *Veronese.* Venice: Alfieri Edizioni D'Arte, 1976.

Popkin, Richard H., and Gordon M. Weiner, eds. *Jewish Christians and Christian Jews: From the Renaissance to the Enlightenment.* Dordrecht and Boston: Kluwer Academic, 1994.

Potter, Louis. 'The Two Noble Kinsmen Onstage: A Postscript.' *Shakespeare Quarterly* 48 (1997): 225–7.

Quilligan, Maureen. *The Allegory of Female Authority: Christine de Pizan's 'Cité des Dames'.* Ithaca, NY: Cornell University Press, 1991.

Rackin, Phyllis. *Stages of History: Shakespeare's English Chronicles.* Ithaca, NY: Cornell University Press, 1990.

Randall, Dale B. J., *Jonson's Gypsies Unmasked: Background and Theme of 'The Gypsies Metamorphos'd'*, pp. 47–66. Durham, NC: Duke University Press, 1975.

Ravenstein, E. G., ed. *The Strange Adventures of Andrew Battell of Leigh, in Angola and the Adjoining Regions.* London: Hakluyt Society, 1901.

Roberts, Jeanne Addison. *The Shakespearean Wild: Geography, Genus, and Gender.* Lincoln: University of Nebraska Press, 1991.

Rogers, J. D. 'Voyages and Exploration: Geography: Maps.' In *Shakespeare's England: An Account of the Life & Manners of His Age,* edited by C. T. Onions, p. 170. 1916. Reprint, Oxford: Clarendon Press, 1950.

Rosaldo, Michelle Zimbalist, and Louise Lamphere, eds. *Woman, Culture, and Society.* Stanford, Calif.: Stanford University Press, 1974.

Ross, Michael. *Forbidden Friendships: Homosexuality and Male Culture in Renaissance Florence.* Oxford: Oxford University Press, 1996.

Roth, Cecil. *A History of the Jews in England,* 2nd edn. Oxford: Clarendon Press, 1949.

Rubens, Alfred. *Anglo-Jewish Portraits.* London: Jewish Museum, 1935.

——. *A Jewish Iconography.* London: Jewish Museum, 1954.

Said, Edward W. *Orientalism.* New York: Pantheon Books, 1978.

——. 'Orientalism Reconsidered.' In *Europe and Its Others. Proceedings of the Essex Conference on the Sociology of Literature July 1984.* 2 vols. Edited by Francis Barker et al. Colchester: University of Essex, 1985.

Scaglione, Aldo. 'A Note on Montaigne's "Des Cannibales" and the Humanist Tradition.' In *First Images of America: The Impact of the New World on the Old.* edited by Fredi Chaipelli, p. 63. Berkeley: University of California Press, 1976.

Scarre, Geoffrey. *Witchcraft and Magic in 16th and 17th Century Europe.* Atlantic Highlands, NJ: Humanities Press International, 1987.

Schama, Simon. *Landscape and Memory.* New York: Alfred A. Knopf, 1995.

Schleiner, Winfried. '*Divina Virago*: Queen Elizabeth as an Amazon.' *Studies in Philology* 75 (1978): 163–80.

——. '*Le feu caché*: Homosocial Bonds Between Women in a Renaissance Romance.' *Renaissance Quarterly* 45 (1992): 293–311.

Sedgwick, Eve Kosofsky. *Between Men: English Literature and Male Homosocial Desire*. New York: Columbia University Press, 1985.

——. *Epistemology of the Closet*. Berkeley and Los Angeles: University of California Press, 1990.

Shapiro, James. *Shakespeare and the Jews*. New York: Columbia University Press, 1996.

Shepherd, Simon. *Amazons and Warrior Women: Varieties of Feminism in Seventeenth-Century Drama*. Brighton, Sussex: Harvester Press, 1981.

Skura, Meredith Anne. 'Discourse and the Individual: The Case of Colonialism in *The Tempest*.' *Shakespeare Quarterly* 40 (1989): 42–69.

Smith, Bruce R. *Homosexual Desire in Shakespeare's England: A Cultural Poetics*. Chicago and London: University of Chicago Press, 1991.

Society for the Psychological Study of Social Issues. 'The Function of Male Initiation Ceremonies at Puberty.' *Readings in Social Psychology*, 3rd edn. pp. 359–70. New York: Henry Holt, 1958.

Sorlien, Robert Parker. *The Diary of John Manningham of the Middle Temple 1602–1603*. Hanover, NH: University Press of New England, 1976.

Sousa, Geraldo U. de. 'Closure and the Antimasque of *The Tempest*.' *Journal of Dramatic Theory and Criticism* 2 (1987): 41–51.

——. '*The Merchant of Venice*: Brazil and Cultural Icons.' *Shakespeare Quarterly* 45 (1994): 468–74.

——. 'The Peasants' Revolt and the Writing of History in *2 Henry VI*.' In *Reading and Writing in Shakespeare*. Edited by David M. Bergeron, pp. 178–93. Newark: University of Delaware Press, 1996.

——. '*The Tempest*, Comedy and the Space of the Other.' In *Acting Funny: Comic Theory and Practice in Shakespeare*. Edited by Frances Teague, pp. 52–71. Rutherford, NJ: Fairleigh Dickinson University Press; London and Toronto: Associated University Presses, 1994.

Stallybrass, Peter. 'The World Turned Upside Down: Inversion, Gender and The State.' *The Matter of Difference: Materialist Feminist Criticism of Shakespeare*. Edited by Valerie Wayne, pp. 201–20. Ithaca, NY: Cornell University Press, 1991.

Stone, Lawrence. *Family, Sex, and Marriage in England 1500–1800*. New York: Harper Colophon Books, 1979.

Sugen, Edward H. *A Topographical Dictionary to the Works of Shakespeare and His Fellow Dramatists*. Manchester: Manchester University Press; London and New York: Longmans, Green & Co., 1925.

Summers, Montague. *The History of Witchcraft and Demonology*. New York: University Books, 1956.

Thomas, Keith. *Religion and the Decline of Magic*. London: Weidenfeld and Nicholson, 1971.

Todorov, Tzvetan. *The Conquest of America: The Question of the Other*. Translated by Richard Howard. New York: Harper & Row, 1984.

Turner, Victor. *The Ritual Process: Structure and Anti-Structure*. 1969. Reprint, Ithaca, NY: Cornell University Press, 1977.

Vaughan, Alden T. 'Shakespeare's Indian: The Americanization of Caliban.' *Shakespeare Quarterly* 39 (1988): 137–53.

Walker, Henry J. *Theseus and Athens.* Oxford: Oxford University Press, 1995.

Wall, Cheryl A., ed. *Changing Our Own Words: Essays on Criticism, Theory, And Writing by Black Women.* New Brunswick, NY and London: Rutgers University Press, 1989.

Wall, Wendy. *The Imprint of Gender: Authorship and Publication in the English Renaissance.* Ithaca, NY and London: Cornell University Press, 1993.

Warner, H. J. *The Albigensian Heresy.* 1922. Reprint, New York: Russell & Russell, 1967.

Watson, Donald G. *Shakespeare's Early History Plays: Politics at Play on the Elizabethan Stage.* Athens: University of Georgia Press, 1990.

Wells, Stanley. 'Programme Notes' for Royal Shakespeare Company's production of *Titus Andronicus* at the Pit, 1 July 1988. Directed by Deborah Warner.

White, Hayden. *Tropics of Discourse: Essays in Cultural Criticism.* 1978. Reprint, Baltimore Md. and London: Johns Hopkins University Press, 1992.

Whiting, W. M., et al. 'The Function of Male Initiation Ceremonies at Puberty.' In *Readings in Social Psychology,* 3rd edn, pp. 359–70. New York: Henry Holt, 1958.

Williamson, Claude C. H. *Readings on the Character of Hamlet 1661–1947.* London: George Allen & Unwin, 1950.

Williamson, Marilyn L. *Infinite Variety: Antony and Cleopatra in Renaissance Drama and Earlier Tradition.* Mystic, Conn.: Lawrence Verry, 1974.

Willis, Deborah. 'Shakespeare's *The Tempest* and the Discourse of Colonialism.' *SEL* 29 (1989): 277–89.

Winkler, John J. *The Anthropology of Sex and Gender in Ancient Greece.* New York: Routledge, 1990.

——. *The Constraints of Desire: The Anthropology of Sex and Gender in Ancient Greece.* New York and London: Routledge, 1990.

Withington, Robert. *English Pageantry: An Historical Outline.* 1918. Reprint, New York: Benjamin Bloom, 1963.

Wittkower, Rudolf. 'Marvels of the East: A Study in the History of Monsters.' *Journal of the Warburg and Courtauld Institutes* 5 (1942): 159–97.

Wolf, John B. *The Barbary Coast: Algiers Under the Turks 1500 to 1830.* New York and London: W. W. Norton, 1979.

Wortham, John David. *The Genesis of British Egyptology 1549–1906.* Norman: University of Oklahoma Press, 1971.

Index